The Body in Psychotherapy

To Sandnes and Shannon

The Body in Psychotherapy

Edward W.L. Smith

McFarland & Company, Inc., Publishers
Jefferson, North Carolina, and London

Acknowledgments

I thank all of the patients, trainees, and supervisees who have in their various ways guided my thinking by their feedback. This book is what I have come to with your help.

Thanks go to E. Mark Stern, editor, *Voices*, for permission to use portions of "Seven Decision Points," by Edward W.L. Smith, from vol. 15, no. 3 (1979), pp. 45–50.
Also, thanks to *Journal of Contemporary Psychotherapy* for permission to use portions of "Altered States of Consciousness in Gestalt Therapy," by Edward W.L. Smith, from vol. 7, no. 1 (1975), pp. 35–40, ©1975 by Human Sciences Press, Inc., New York.

The present work is a reprint of the library bound edition of The Body in Psychotherapy, *first published in 1985.*

Library of Congress Cataloguing-in-Publication Data

Smith, Edward W.L., 1940–
    The body in psychotherapy
        p.   cm.
    Includes bibliographical references and index.

    ISBN 0-7864-0966-5 (softcover : 50# alkaline paper) ∞

    1. Mind and body therapies.   I. Title.
[DNLM: 1. Body Image.   2. Psychophysiology.
3. Psychotherapy—methods. WM 420 S646b]
RC489.M53S65   2003
616.89'14   84-43201

British Library cataloguing data are available

Front cover: Detail of *Study for "The Libyan Sibyl,"* Michelangelo, 1511. © 2000 Art Today

Manufactured in the United States of America

McFarland & Company, Inc., Publishers
    Box 611, Jefferson, North Carolina 28640
    www.mcfarlandpub.com

Table of Contents

List of Figures

Preface

"... psyche depends on body and body depends on psyche."
— Jung (*The Practice of Psychotherapy*, p. 4)

Jung wrote this circa 1935. A major trend in psychotherapy just during the past fifteen years or so has been the bringing of the body into psychotherapy. Even so, body-oriented psychotherapy is clearly still a minority position, and as is the frequent burden of minorities, it finds itself often the target for calumnious misunderstanding.

Interest in body-oriented psychotherapy is clearly present; the major professional psychotherapy organizations for the past several years have offered workshop and seminar programs in body-oriented work. The professional journals have, too, reflected this interest. For example, *Voices* (the journal of the American Academy of Psychotherapists) has devoted two entire issues to this theme. The summer 1976 issue was titled "Psychotherapy and the Body." The fall 1980 issue was titled "The Body Confronts the Mind of Psychotherapy." There are scattered articles on this theme in almost every issue of most of the psychotherapy journals.

What has not been published previously is a book which integrates the major material on the body in psychotherapy. The many books which do exist are focused on a particular approach—bioenergetics, Gestalt therapy, psychomotor, radix, Reichian orgonomy, and so forth. All of these approaches are of value, and not one of them is a complete system having a total perspective on psychopathology, growth, and learning. When these several valuable approaches are integrated, one has a body of concepts, theories, and methods which serve far better in describing and facilitating the process of human growth from undeveloped or diminished states to states of being more approximate to that which is possible and desirable.

The task which I have undertaken in this book is to integrate in a meaningful way those body-oriented approaches to psychotherapy which I know. My training in psychotherapy has included training in bioenergetics, Gestalt therapy, and psychomotor therapy. Additionally, I have had exposure to Malcolm Brown's work, radix, and Reichian orgonomy. As adjuncts to this training in body-oriented psychotherapy, I have had varying degrees of experiential exposure to aikido, Alexander technique, Feldenkrais technique, sensory-awareness training, t'ai ch'i chuan, and yoga. I am also certified in applied kinesiology. Finally, one of my greatest passions, weightlifting, is an activity I have been variously involved in for many years. From this background comes my personal and professional interest in the body aspect of the person, or more broadly, my organismic view of the person.

I enjoy integrating material from various sources. Integration seems natural to me, something I tend toward without necessarily any intention. So in the writing of this book, I have drawn upon bits and pieces gleaned from my various degrees of exposure to many people including John Bellis, Malcolm Brown, Charles Brooks and Charlotte Selver, Joen Fagan, Moshe Feldenkrais, Vivian Guze, Stanley Keleman, Alexander Lowen, Laura Perls, Al Pesso, John Pierrakos, Erv and Mariam Polster, Eva Reich, Virginia Satir, Irma Shepherd, Jim Simkin, and Barry Stevens. In addition to these people, I have been influenced by my patient-hood and friendships with several people who are identified with experiential psychotherapy (a position developed at the early Atlanta Psychiatric Clinic), especially Earl Brown, Rives Chalmers, Dick Felder, and John Warkentin. The impact of these experiential therapists on my thinking has led me to the position of seeing all psychotherapy, including the use of body-focused techniques, as primarily an inter*personal* event, involving the person of the therapist and the person of the patient. So, when asked to state briefly what I do as a psychotherapist I say that I do a body-oriented Gestalt therapy, integrating aspects of Reichian, neo-Reichian, and other body-focused growth methods in the context of the therapist-patient relationship.

I take Gestalt therapy as my basic theoretical and procedural umbrella. Many other things fit comfortably for me under that umbrella. In a 1978 *Voices* article I described the Gestalt umbrella as follows (*Voices*, 1978, 14, 3, 44–47):

> My own view is that the Gestalt approach involves a philosophical position, a theory of personality, and a therapeutic style. The philosophical position is basically existential, with emphasis on personal responsibility, choice, and the I-Thou relationship. In addition, there is the Taoist-Zen flavor of "slowing down" and "getting in harmony with nature." This is a valuing of awareness and experience of "what is," with the knowing that paradoxically I only change as I accept and experience more fully who I am. The goal is the realization of my true nature, and this does not come through thinking, but through allowing

my natural experiential process to flow. The personality theory of the Gestalt approach is a holistic one, viewing the person as flowing through homeostatic need cycles (or contact/withdrawal cycles), with the all-encompassing need being self-actualization. The therapeutic style is phenomenological, focusing in facilitation of the patient's awareness in the here-and-now. Techniques are created which enhance the patient's experience and allow a psychodramatic living out of his process as defined by the "wisdom of his organism." (... I have ... written at length about these ideas in "The Roots of Gestalt Therapy," 1976).

I consider this blend of existential and Zen philosophy, this organismic personality theory, and this phenomenological experiential style of working to be the necessary and sufficient conditions to define the Gestalt approach. I don't define the Gestalt approach by techniques. The Gestalt approach is given life by the "person" of the particular therapist. Therefore, there are many styles of Gestalt therapy, each reflecting the "person" of that therapist/artist. With an appreciation of this, I have no wish to "cult-ivate" Gestalt therapy.

It is the exquisite focus on organism-in-environment *process* which appeals most to me about the Gestalt approach. To this I add the awesome power of the Reichian and neo–Reichian procedures for assessing and facilitating that process. My friend Jim Dublin has pointed out a subtle difference in saying that although both Gestalt and bioenergetics are organismic in focus, Gestalt is from-the-head-down (a mind-body therapy) and bioenergetics is from-the-body-up.

From my interest in this integration this book grew. For the past fifteen years, I have been learning, evolving and teaching this position. Most of what is in *The Body in Psychotherapy* I have now taught in workshops and seminars. The form in which it appears herein has benefited from the questions and comments offered by supervisees and trainees. And now, I offer it to you in printed form.

Edward W.L. Smith, Ph.D.
Atlanta, Georgia
Spring, 1985

Part I
Historical and Theoretical Perspective

Part I of the *The Body in Psychotherapy* is concerned with the historical roots of body work and an organismic perspective on personality functioning, psychopathology, and psychotherapy. In Chapter 1 the tradition of focusing on the body in psychotherapy is traced from Freud to present-day positions. The roots of a body focus are clearly stated in Freud's writing, but it was Reich who delineated a body-oriented psychotherapy and who is largely responsible for the tradition of the body in psychotherapy. Through his clinical work and research Reich provided a solid base for movement beyond the limitations of Freudian analysis. Several of Reich's students carried on the tradition with great creativity and innovation both in theory and technique. The tradition, as I see it, includes Kaiser's work, Perl's Gestalt therapy, Baker's medical orgonomy, Lowen and Pierrakos' bioenergetics, Brown's organismic psychotherapy and Kelley's radix work. I have reviewed each of these therapies. I have also included another position, Pesso's psychomotor therapy, even though it does not have direct ancestry in Reich, because it is a powerful system with a clearly holistic focus.

Chapters 2, 3, and 4 are explorations of the organismic perspective on natural personality functioning, disturbed personality functioning, and treatment of disturbed functioning, respectively. The basic model is the contact/withdrawal cycle, introduced in Chapter 2. This model is offered as a way of understanding natural personality dynamics. Chapter 3 extends the discussion into the realm of disturbances in the natural rhythms of contact and withdrawal. Then, in Chapter 4 the theory of restoration of natural contact/withdrawal cycles is presented.

The position taken in Part I is a holistic one. So, to aid in the understanding of the following chapters, I want to give some background on the holistic doctrine.

Holism, although a word in vogue for several years now in humanistic psychology circles, is not widely understood even among professionals. Dualistic thinking, the separation of "mind" and "body," has deep roots in our philosophy, and was embossed in bold relief by Descartes with his distinction of "res cogitans" and "res extensa." From this philosophical heritage came the dualistic sciences we know today. Consider the often-asked question about an ache or pain, "Is it physical or mental?"

Preholistic views are basically of three types. First is mechanistic materialism, the view that psychic manifestations are totally reducible to physical causes. This is the position of reductionistic psychiatry, seeing all behavior as only the manifestation of a biochemical event. This view is popular among those whom Williams James called the "tough-minded." These are the "hard-nosed scientists" today.

Second is metaphysical idealism, wherein it is believed that spirit creates matter. Essentially the opposite of the first position, metaphysical idealism sees every psychic manifestation as having only psychic causes. And, somatic illness is of psychic origin. Espousers of this view would tend toward James's "tender-minded." Today this view is often assumed by those who enjoy "pop psychology" and "pop-spiritualism."

The third view is psychophysical parallelism. This view is that the psychic and the somatic processes are parallel and have reciprocal effects on one another. In other words, mind affects body and body affects mind. It is this view which is usually taken when the term holistic is used.

All of these three ways of thinking maintain a dualistic understanding of the person. The alternative to such dualism is the holistic or organismic view. This holistic or organismic position is explored in the following chapters.

1. The Tradition of the Body in Psychotherapy

The mind-body dichotomy has been so entrenched in Western thought that to consider the "mind" to be the bailiwick of the *psycho*therapist and the "body" the bailiwick of the *physici*an seems perfectly logical to most Western people. Given this Western bias, let us see how a body orientation evolved in psychotherapy.

A convenient point of departure in the historical tracing of the body in psychotherapy is Freud. Interestingly, Freud (1960, p. 17) stated in 1923 that the ego is "first and foremost a body-ego." This was a statement of recognition that the experience of ego develops as experience of body. Or, as Freud (1960, p. 16) wrote:

> the ego is ultimately derived from bodily sensations, chiefly from those springing from the surface of the body. It may thus be regarded as a mental projection of the surface of the body.

The important developmental implication of Freud's statements is that lack of certain body sensations will limit ego development. That is, to the extent that the child does not have certain body experiences, that child will not develop ego in that realm, but would be as if he or she had holes in his or her personality. For example, if the child does not receive enough experience in being supported against gravity by the parenting figures, then the ego would develop with a deficiency in the self-support function. Holding, rocking, picking up and laying down the child would be experiences which would give the body sensations of support and would provide, therefore, early ego growth in the realm of support. The person who did not have benefit of enough of these support experiences would be expected then to be deficient in self-support later in life. The ensuing lack of self-support might manifest on the body-ego plane as the experience of being "weak in the knees" or having weak legs, ankles, or feet.

There is a profound therapeutic implication to all of this — if the

3

person has an ego deficiency because of inadequate ego-forming body experiences, then analysis and insight into the problem will be inadequate to bring about change. For change to come about means to provide body experiences which are ego-developing. Psychotherapy, in such situations, would need to provide the opportunity for the patient to have an adequate amount of the experiences which were inadquately present in the previous learning history. Put simply, ego growth and development come about through experiential learning, not from analyzing.

What I see in this is Freud's laying the groundwork for a psychotherapy which would include a focus on the body. The developmental and therapeutic implications of Freud's view of the ego as a body-ego provide a theoretical rationale for body work in psychotherapy.

Returning to Freud, as early as 1899 in a letter to Fleiss, he implied the expansion of the therapeutic technique into the body arena. "From time to time I visualize a second part of the method of treatment — provoking patients' feelings as well as their ideas, as if that were quite indispensable" (Lowen, 1971, p. xi). Here is the recognition of the need for more than cognitive work in psychotherapy; more than remembering, analyzing, and producing intellectual insight. The second part of treatment to which Freud referred, the provocation of affect, implies work with the body. Although talking can be provative of feeling, the most direct access to affect involves manipulation of body experience.

Some further indications of Freud's attention to body are his discussions of hysteria and obsessions. In hysteria Freud saw the conversion of psychic energy into motor behavior, whereas in the dynamic of obsessiveness he saw thought being substituted for action. Also, in *Jokes and Their Relation to the Unconscious* (1960) Freud wrote of the activity of laughter as a motor discharge of psychic tensions which had been built up in the "foreplay" of the joke. An elegant, detailed analysis of the body-language of posture is found in Freud's (1914) discussion of Michelangelo's sculpture of Moses. In all of this material mentioned, Freud demonstrated his keen awareness of the body.

Freud did not follow through, however, on the groundwork which he did for a body focus in psychotherapy. The implications were clear, but the majority of the psychoanalysts continued to view ego defenses only from the mental perspective and to develop therapeutic techniques which did not focus on the body plane. In this context, the exceptions are very notable.

While maintaining a basic allegiance to Freud, Ferenczi experimented with modifications of the traditional psychoanalytic technique. What Ferenczi was responding to was a lack of therapeutic impact of the traditional technique on certain psychological problems which seemed to have their genesis in pre-oedipal events. To deal with these pre-oedipal problems he developed what he termed "activity techniques." These "activity techniques" are based on Ferenczi's careful attention to muscular activity and bodily expressions in his patients. Some examples of his technical innovations include prohibiting the patient from urinating immediately before or after a therapy session, fidgeting during a session, and self-stroking or plucking at one's body. Ferenczi also used relaxation exercises to overcome inhibitions and resistance to free association. The importance of the "activity techniques" is summarized by Ferenczi in the following quote from 1919:

> The fact that the expression of emotion or motor actions forced from the patients evoke secondarily memories from the unconscious rests partly on the reciprocity of affect and idea emphasized by Freud.... The awakening of a memory can – as in catharsis – bring an emotional reaction with it, but an activity exacted from the patient, or an emotion set at freedom, can equally well expose the repressed ideas associated with such processes [Lowen, 1971, p. 10-11].

Ferenczi distinguished his approach from the traditional in the following way. The

> purely passive association technique [which] starts from whichever psychic superficies is present and works back to the preconscious cathexes of unconscious material might be described as "analysis from above," to distinguish it from the "active" method which I should like to call "analysis from below" [Lowen, 1971, p. 11-12].

It seems clear from the above that Ferenczi's innovations were technical ones, methodological improvements on the traditional psychoanalytic approach. The theoretical position is basically orthodox.

The next developments, introduced by Ferenczi's student Wilhelm Reich, brought about a true body focus. With Reich, the body became primary.

Central to Reich's (1949) position, and perhaps his most important theoretical contribution, was the concept of the "muscular armor." Reich suggested that the neurotic solution of the infantile instinctual conflict (the chronic conflict between instinctual demands on the one hand and the counterdemands of the social world) is brought about through a generalized alteration in functioning which ultimately crystalizes into a neurotic "character" (Shapiro, 1965). This "character" is, then, essentially a narcissistic protective mechanism, originally formed for protection against punishment of the child's instinctual expression by the parents or other agents of the social order. It is retained for protection against instinctual "dangers" from within. Character is an organismic phenomenon, manifesting on the physical plane as chronic muscular rigidities. These chronic muscular rigidities, or muscular armor, serve to negate or block impulses to action which are inconsistent with the neurotic character. In time, the muscular armor serves to bind free-floating anxiety. With this concept of muscular armoring, Reich introduced the notion of defenses as total organismic functions. That is, the character defenses are manifest in the physical structure of the body.

In addition to the theoretical contribution of the muscular armor, Reich (1949) broke with the classical psychoanalytic position by introducing techniques of intensive body contact with the patient. These body contacts were both diagnostic and therapeutic. First, by feeling the patient's body, Reich could assess the muscular armoring, locating the focal points of bound energy. Second, release of the energy sometimes could be facilitated by exerting pressure on these points of tension in the patient's body. In doing this, Reich set a precedent for the therapist to have direct physical contact with the patient as an integral part of psychotherapy.

Reich assumed a procedural position which implied body involvement in psychotherapy. Reich's (1949) rule of therapy was that remembrances must be accompanied by appropriate affect. This discovery of the necessity of the appropriate feelings concomitant with the thoughts in order for a therapeutic effect to occur was not original with Reich, for Freud had spoken of this finding. Freud said, with an apt metaphor, that a neurosis cannot be hanged in effigy. But Reich took an extreme position on this point, putting heavy emphasis on the elicitation of powerful feelings and dealing with them in the therapy session. Often, then, feelings would be elicited through body contact techniques.

Even more dramatic than these theoretical and technical contributions was Reich's (1949) elaboration of Freud's concept of the libido. Reich moved to a position of seeing libido as a measurable physical energy which he referred to as "bioelectrical energy" and later as "orgone" energy. This was a further step in introducing a unitary concept of mind and body. The connection is the orgone, as a physical substance, being impeded or blocked in its flow by the tensing of the muscles, that is, by the muscular armor. Reich reported that when he dissolved a muscular tension one of three biological excitations would regularly occur: anxiety, anger or sexual excitation. The solution to neurosis, then, involves the economy of the orgone. Orgone energy is produced and expended in homeostatic cycles. The muscular armor, corresponding to a psychological character structure, interferes with the homeostasis. This is the neurotic mechanism of binding energy. Reich (1942) saw the orgasm as the essential biological equilibrating mechanism by which excess orgone is drained away, thus leading to a collapse of the neurotic structure. Reich reported that full orgastic potency is absent in neurosis. Thus, the attainment of orgastic potency was for Reich the necessary and sufficient condition to designate the cure of a neurosis.

With Reich's work the body was undeniably a part of psychotherapy. However, Reich's work was slow to be accepted. As Reich moved away from conducting psychotherapy and in the direction of research in "orgonomy" or "life energy" in the 1940's, he entered into realms which were increasingly controversial, resulting in a severe limitation in his respectability with the professional community (Mann and Hoffman, 1980; Raknes, 1971).

But, before entering this second period of his professional career, Reich was therapist, supervisor, or trainer to several people who were to make their own mark on the evolving art of psychotherapy, with attention to the body. Two of these people, Helmuth Kaiser and Fritz Perls, studied with him around 1933. Although their work is decidedly influenced by Reich's, neither of them emphasized body work as much as some of Reich's later students, Elsworth Baker, Charles Kelley, Alexander Lowen, and John Pierrakos. These later therapists were associated with Reich later and for a longer period of time than were Kaiser and Perls. And their work shows a strong emphasis on body work.

Kaiser was certainly not a body therapist, but he did attend to body manifestations in a focused manner. His point of departure from psychoanalysis was Reich's notion that the "how" of the patient's communication is more important than the "what." Regarding the "how" or stylistic component of communication as the elucidator of the patient's resistances, following Reich, Kaiser shifted his emphasis from "psychoanalysis" to "resistance analysis," later changing the name to "defense analysis" (Fierman, 1965). His style of working, with the emphasis on the analytic dissolution of defenses, led to strongly abreactive experiences. For this, he was criticized by some of the psychoanalytic establishment.

Central to Kaiser's position (Fierman, 1965) was his coming to see that much of the patient's behavior could be understood as an attempt to merge with the therapist, creating an "illusion of fusion." His central thesis was that the neurotic communicates in a way such as to give himself the feeling that he is not responsible for his words and actions. To elaborate on this, whenever one values something not valued by others, wants something not wanted by others, or makes a decision which is not supported by authority, the fact of his basic aloneness is emphasized, sometimes poignantly. Everyone creates some degree of the illusion of fusion to ease the harshness of the existential fact of aloneness. This illusion is lived out through belonging to teams, clubs, religious groups, or various organizations. But, to the extent that one's aloneness is intolerable and one tries to make the illusion real, he is, according to Kaiser, neurotic. The neurotic's technique is duplicitous communication. He communicates in an inauthentic manner which denies his own responsibility and thus his aloneness. Kaiser saw the therapeutic task to be the establishment of nonduplicitous communication with the patient. For Kaiser, then, the good therapist is one who is sensitive to duplicity in others, who is himself relatively free from duplicity, and who has the desire to engage in straightforward communication with relatively noncommunicative persons.

Kaiser's position can be summarized as follows (Fierman, 1965). The *universal psychopathology* is the attempt to create in reality the illusion that one is not alone, but is fused with others, i.e., the "illusion of fusion." The *universal symptom* is the failure to be congruent within or between channels of communication, i.e., "duplicitous communication." The *universal treatment* is nonduplicitous communication. These three points constitute the "universal triad" of Kaiser's theory.

Where the body is of concern is as a channel, or perhaps several channels of communication. In assessing duplicitous communication, the therapist would attend to posture, gesture, breathing, voice quality, changes in skin color (blushing, blanching), stomach rumblings, eye contact, body complaints (psychosomatic manifestations) and so forth, as well as the verbal channel. So, in this respect, the therapist following Kaiser's approach to therapy would be body-focused. The body focus is also shown in Kaiser's basic rule of thumb for conducting therapy: never withdraw in the patient-therapist encounter, either physically ("bodily") or psychologically.

Out of his contempt for dogma and mechanical techniques in therapy, Kaiser was very cautious in describing actual working procedures (Fierman, 1965). This attitude follows directly from Reich's (1949) emphatic declaration that for any given patient at any given point in treatment there is only one technique, and that technique could be derived only from the patient's particular circumstances. Reich opposed the use of any "ready-made schema" in therapy.

The other person in Reich's seminar of about 1933 who went on to contribute to a body focus in psychotherapy was Fritz Perls. Along with his wife, Laura, and with input from several colleagues over the years, Perls developed the approach which he first called concentration therapy, but which became well-known as Gestalt therapy. There are several sources on which Perls drew heavily — psychoanalysis, Reichian character analysis, existential philosophy, Gestalt psychology, and Eastern religion (Smith, 1976). In addition, Laura brought with her a background in movement and training with Elsa Gindler in body awareness. Perls' genius was not in the combining of these various elements into a new eclecticism, but in his creating a new system which in its essence goes beyond the constituent elements. Of the several people whom Reich influenced strongly, and who went on to develop their own body-oriented approaches, Perls made the greatest departure from Reich.

In terms of Reich's influences, there are several (Smith, 1975). Perls found in Reich the rule of therapy that remembrances must be accompanied by the appropriate affect (Reich, 1949). Reich based this rule on the discovery that for a therapeutic effect to occur requires that the appropriate feelings be experienced in conjunction with the thoughts. Reich took an extreme position on this point, putting far more emphasis on the elicitation of powerful feelings and dealing with them in therapy sessions than had the orthodox psychoanalysts. Perls showed his strong support of this position by distinguishing between the awareness-enhancing experience of psychodramatically returning to the past incident and the emotionally avoidant, purely cognitive "mind-fucking" (Perls, 1973). He went so far as to declare that dealing with anything which is not experienced (felt) in the here-and-now is a waste of time therapeutically (Perls, 1969a).

Another influence is evident in Perls' including much of Reich's holistic orientation in his system, even stating that the deepest split, long ingrained in our culture is the mind-body dichotomy. Thus, Perls (1969b) advised that in therapy one attend to the patient's non-verbal communications: voice quality, posture, gestures, psychosomatic language. Perls also encouraged enhanced body awareness and bodily involvement to facilitate organismic completion of emotions, even suggesting exercises to those ends (Perls, Hefferline and Goodman, 1951).

Similar to Reich's concept of body armor, Perls spoke of "retro-flection" as one of the major means of limiting one's awareness of self-functioning. Retroflection refers to the process of negating or blocking an impulse to action through opposing musculoskeletal tension. So, body armor amounts to a chronic state of retroflection.

Another of Reich's concepts, which seems likely to have influenced the development of Perls' view, is the notion of the "phase of the break-down of secondary narcissism." In terms of Reich's (1949) theory, the lasting frustration of primary natural needs leads to a chronic contraction of the armor. This conflict between inhibited primary impulses and the inhibiting character armor leads to the formation of a secondary narcissism (as contrasted to the primary narcissism of the infant which results from his cathecting his own body parts as part-objects of love). That is, as investment of libido in the outside is made more difficult or is withdrawn, the energy builds up within, intensifying a secondary narcissism. Reich spoke of the loosening and dissolution of the characterological protective mechanisms as bringing about a temporary condition of complete helplessness, an aspect of successful treatment which he termed the "phase of the breakdown of secondary narcissism." During the phase the patient moves into a position of strong, freed energy with a concomitant lack of "safe" neurotic controls. It is because of these two factors that this phase of treatment is stormy, often including strong feelings of negative transference.

Perls seems to have included the essence of Reich's dynamic formulation of the phase of breakdown of secondary narcissism in his five layer model of the neurosis. Perls (1969b; Levitsky and Perls, 1970) was consistent in his conceptual presentation of the layers of neurosis, but was not consistent in numbering of the layers. Disregarding, then, the arbitrary numbering, the layers emerge as follows: Neurosis is characterized by a cliché layer, or layer of tokens of meaning. Below that is the layer Perls named the Eric Berne or Sigmund Freud layer of playing games, playing roles, behaving "as if." Beneath this phony layer is the impasse, characterized by the phobic attitude. The phobic attitude results in avoidance, and in turn, the feeling of being stuck, lost, empty, confused. Beneath the impasse or phobic layer is the death layer or the implosive layer. At this layer the person is paralyzed by opposing forces; he is trying to pull himself in, hold himself safely together. The implosive layer may unfold into the final layer of explosion.

The explosive layer is characterized by the person's authentic experiencing and expressing of his emotions. The explosion may be into grief, if a loss had not been assimilated, orgasm, if a sexual block had been present, anger, or joy. There are striking parallels between Reich's "phase of breakdown of secondary narcissism" and Perls' progression through "impasse, implosion and explosion." In both cases the essence is the dissolution of organismic (holistic) core defenses in order to emerge, after a "walk through hell," with an authentic (organismically appropriate) behavior. The impasse was defined by Perls (1969b) in terms which sound very much like Reich's concept, saying that the impasse is the position where environmental support or obsolete inner support is no longer adequate and authentic self-support has not yet been achieved. Staying with the experience of the impasse, enduring the hell of confusion and helplessness, leads to organismic growth. In his later work Perls (1973) referred to such staying with one's confusion as a "withdrawal into the fertile void." If one stays with his techniques of interruption, and his confusion to the utmost, he may experience something like a hypnogogic hallucination or miniature schizophrenic experience leading to a "blinding flash of insight." This phase of therapy is not for the novice or the squeamish, as Reich warned therapists, and this warning is equally applicable in Perls' system.

In several additional ways Perls seems to have been influenced by

Reich (Smith, 1975), but since these are not directly relevant to the evolution of a body focus in psychotherapy, I will not explore them here.

Perls took some interesting departures from Reich. Although sometimes included in Gestalt therapy, body contact is not emphasized or formalized into a treatment mode as it is in Reich's work or later outgrowths from Reich's work. Perls differed from Reich's view that emotions are disturbers of the peace and to be gotten rid of. Rather than something undesirable, Perls viewed emotions as natural elements in the organism's homeostatic cycles. Emotions arise naturally and are the movers toward action in the service of getting needs met.

An important difference between Reich and Perls is in their views of what is blocked in the neurotic, and released through effective therapy. I discussed above the parallel between Reich's "phase of breakdown of secondary narcissism" and Perls' "impasse phenomenon." The important difference is that for Reich it is the release of previously blocked energy through orgasm that is of prime importance. It is this sexual release which is the criterion of cure. Perls saw the neurotic as blocked in emotional expression, and saw the cure as being reflected in the patient's ability to express fully all of the basic contact emotions. The release may be into orgasm, if it was sexual expression that was blocked. The explosive release could also be into crying the grief for a lost object, laughing a joy, or striking out at an object of rage. So that love, hate, joy, grief are, for Perls, all basic contact emotions which may have their expression blocked. Effective therapy would lead to the full organismic expression of any of these which had been blocked.

Perhaps Perls most significant input in the evolution of body-oriented psychotherapy is his holistic/*organismic* view of the person, flavored with existential and Eastern philosophy. Reich had moved to a holistic position, but one which still was based in psychoanalytic bias. The holistic/*organismic* view of Perls (Smith, 1976) contains these premises: (1) The normal personality is characterized by unity, integration, consistency, and coherence. Pathology is characterized by the converse. (2) Analysis of the person begins with the whole and proceeds by a differentiation of that whole into its aspects. (3) The individual is unified and motivated by a sovereign drive, self-actualization or self-realization. (4) The influence of the inherent potentialities is emphasized, while the influence of external forces is minimized. (5) The vocabulary and principles of Gestalt psychology are used (e.g., "learning is discovery," and Perls' "basic law of organismic regulation" which is that the figure-ground formation which is strongest at a given time will temporarily take over the control of the total organism). (See Emerson and Smith, 1974.)

The existential flavor in Perls is in his emphasis on personal responsibility and choice. The basic message is that one must take personal responsibility for one's own existence. Perls sometimes wrote "responsi-bility" as "response-ability," meaning that the basic given in life is the ability to personally respond. This is the essence of self-support. Perls drew on Buber's "I-Thou" relationship as the model for the therapist-patient relationship. This precludes the "doing to" the patient or any manipulation which bespeaks the defining of the therapy relationship in terms of an "I-It." Perls saw the Gestalt approach as existential in that it did not deal with what "should be," or what "could be," but rather with "what is." The implicit injunctions are: (1) Live now (concern with the present as opposed to the past or future). (2) Live here (concern with what is present as opposed to what is absent). (3) Stop imagining (experience what is real). (4) Stop unnecessary thinking (hear, see, smell, touch, taste). (5) Express directly (rather than explain, judge, manipulate). (6) Be aware of the unpleasant as well as the pleasant. (7) Reject all "shoulds." (8) Take full responsibility for one's actions, feelings, and thoughts. (9) Surrender to being as one really is (Naranjo, 1970). The value under-lying these injunctions is that one is better off being aware of what is. For Perls, then, psychotherapy means facilitating the patient to be aware of that which he tried to avoid. And, where there is awareness, organismic expression follows.

In terms of the Eastern flavor, Perls infused into Gestalt therapy some of the essence of what is Taoist and Zen. The Gestalt approach is to experience fully. This means a "slowing down" and "getting in touch with." Through this process of experiencing, oftentimes a primary undif-ferentiated feeling is discovered and progressively differentiated into its poles. This is allowed by the finding of one's natural rhythm of organismic experience, getting in touch with one's true nature. The eastern symbolization of this process is the wu gi, or circle of nonbegin-ning, and the tai gi, or yin yang circle of progressive differentiation into opposites and integration of all possible opposites (Perls, 1969a). Paradox is common in Zen and in Gestalt. Powerful in its therapeutic implications is the paradox of change, nicely explicated by Beisser (1970, p. 77): "... change occurs when one becomes what he is, not when he tries to become what he is not." Perls (1973), showing the Taoist-Zen regard for true nature, stated that man transcends himself only through his true nature. What I must do to grow is to know my nature and allow that nature to un-fold and be. I cannot be other than that which it is my nature to be.

In Taoism is found a principle for growth which is to create a void so that nature can develop there. Perls, Hefferline, and Goodman (1951) use this principle in discouraging the compelling of one's self and instead encourage that one clear the path of growth of whatever obstacles in-cluding one's self, are in the way. Perls was fond of saying, "Don't push the river."

Another paradox of Gestalt therapy is Perls' (1973) view that sometimes the therapist must be cruel in order to be kind. Perls' view, like that of the Zen master, is based on the belief that growth is born of frustration and that the "helpful" teacher who offers second-hand information is an impediment to growth through discovery and personal experience.

Perls (1973) emphasized the importance of letting go of ambition and artificial goals. The realization of one's true nature is the goal. As biological creatures we are ensconced in the process of nature, while as social creatures we live "as if" existences in which reality, fantasy, and pretending get confused. This "as if" existence is known in Eastern thought as "Maya." Zen and Gestalt therapy, each with its own methods, seek to lift the veil of Maya and bring its followers into the enlightenment of immediate contact with reality. Borrowing an Eastern term, Perls (1973) described this immediate, and sometimes dramatic recontacting of reality as a "mini-satori." And, again with Zen flavor, Perls (1969a) stated that through satori one realizes that "good" and "bad" are not facts of nature, but only judgmental reactions to nature.

The Eastern sages speak of making oneself empty so that one can be filled. Perls' version of this was to implore people to lose their minds and come to their senses. So in both Zen and Gestalt therapy excessive thought is seen as an impediment to seeing, hearing, tasting, smelling, and touching nature. So, for immediate contact with nature, thought must be suspended. Much of the methodology of Zen and of Gestalt therapy is in the service of suspension of thought.

A final Eastern principle found in the Gestalt approach is that there is no set method. Each person must find his own specific path of growth.

And so, with Perls, the evolution of body-oriented psychotherapy took a distinctive turn away from the psychoanalytic view of personality functioning and brought to bear the philosophies of existentialism and of the East.

Some of those who studied with Reich a few years after Kaiser and Perls developed their own distinctive positions, but stayed closer to the Reichian work than either Kaiser or Perls did. Others of those later students such as Ola Raknes and Elsworth Baker remained orthodox Reichians while further developing and expounding Reich's theories and techniques.

The major contribution of Raknes and Baker has been their continuation of Reich's work and their teaching the pure Reichian theory and practice which they term Orgonomy. Raknes presents a very readable introduction to orgonomy, or Reich's science of life energy in his book *Wilhelm Reich and Orgonomy* (Raknes, 1971). The focus of this book, first published in 1970, is on the liberation of sexual energy, the functional identity of mind and body, the four-beat orgasm formula (tension ►charge ►discharge ►relaxation), and the relevance of life energy to religion, education, medicine, psychology, and biophysics.

Baker, who seldom deviates from Reich's views, was appointed training therapist for medical orgonomy by Reich around 1949. Baker continues in this function, training only M.D.'s, most of whom are psychiatrists. This is a flavor of the work which he teaches: therapy is one-to-one (no group work), usually with one fifty-minute session per week. The therapist is seen as a physician who is working to cure an illness (neurosis, armor, etc.). A standard position for working is with the patient lying on her/his back on a couch, knees bent, with the orgonomist seated at the side. Much of the work is nonverbal, involving breathing and body movements expressive of emotions, and sometimes direct body manipulation (pinching or prodding tense muscles) by the orgonomist. The work to loosen the body armor is always systematic, progressing from the head to the bottom of the body. This direct body work is combined with character analysis à la Reich. Disturbed sexual functioning is seen as the universal symptom and the criterion for cure is, of course, the establishment of orgastic potency (Kelley, 1978).

In 1968, Baker and his colleagues founded a professional organization, the American College of Orgonomy, with a journal now of ten or so volumes, *The American Journal of Orgonomy*. Baker (1967) has also published a very systematic presentation of Reich's work, *Man in the Trap*.

The most widely known position to evolve from Reich's work, and to be clearly identified as a body psychotherapy is bioenergetics, founded by Alexander Lowen and John Pierrakos. These two M.D.'s broke away from Reich and Baker in 1952 and established the Institute for Bioenergetic Analysis in 1954 (Lowen, 1974). Bioenergetics is firmly rooted in Reich's concepts of life energy and muscular armor, but differs considerably in procedure from Reich. First, a brief sketch of the bioenergetic position, and then I will delineate several specific points on which Bioenergetics and Reichian work differ.

Bioenergetics is defined by Lowen (1974, p. 263) as "the study of personality in terms of the body." This study of personality is based on the propositions that each person is her/his body and that the body is an energy system. This viewpoint is strikingly different from most theories of personality found in contemporary psychology, with their focus either on the pragmatics of behavior or an ethereal concept of the person. The implications of the Bioenergetic position for personality assessment and psychotherapy are several. The personality is seen as the way an individual is in the world, body-wise. The way the person moves and the way he/she holds the body are diagnostic of character styles. This notion of "character" types is found in its early development in Freud and was extended by Abraham. Reich systematized his own further elaborations in *Character Analysis* (1949). Lowen (1971) continued this line of development by presenting an extended and much more systematic organization of character types and their relationships (first published in 1958 and given most recent version in Lowen, 1975).

Lowen (1974) presents five basic holding patterns:

(1) *Holding Together* in response to a fear of falling apart or fragmenting, which defines the *Schizoid Character*;

(2) *Holding On* out of fear of rejection or being left, which defines the *Oral Character*;

(3) *Holding Up* against fear of falling down (failure or dominance by others), which defines the *Psychopathic Character*;

(4) *Holding In* out of fear of letting go and exploding into a release of feeling, which defines the *Masochistic Character*;

(5) *Holding Back* in response to the fear of falling forward and being swept away to feelings of love and surrender, which defines the *Rigid Character*.

Lowen points out that rarely will a person show only one holding pattern. Rather, there are five patterns of being in the world which represent five syndromes which are in evidence in some combination of strengths in each personality. These patterns or character types can be read directly from the physical structure of the body and the body's manner of motility. For this reason, bioenergetics relies heavily on "reading the body" as a means of assessing personality. That is, the bioenergetic therapist would view the patient's body (usually in a bathing suit) standing and moving in order to diagnose character via the body structure.

Lowen (1974) sees the general procedure of psychotherapy as helping the patient to become aware of unconscious conflicts and fears which limit and control his responsiveness and helping the patient to realize that those fears and conflicts are of the past, so are no longer valid in the present. This position is, of course, basically psychoanalytic. Lowen goes on to point out that while theoretically an insight into the origin and development of the previously unconscious conflict and fear would be curative, this rarely is the case. "Insight" therapy often fails because the insight is only at the idea level and therefore lacks the strong emotional charge necessary for change. For this reason, the bioenergetic procedure is to: (1) get in touch with the tensions in the body; (2) release the tensions, thereby freeing the emotions previously blocked by the muscular armor; (3) provide analytic interpretations of the memories and emotions which emerge from the unconscious as the body work proceeds, as well as interpreting dreams and the developing transference situation. Lowen tends to begin with body work and to add the analytic work as the therapy develops.

A frequently used procedure for facilitating step (1) is the "stress posture." Lowen and Pierrakos developed a number of these positions as ways of magnifying body tensions, thus making it easier for the patient to bring the tensions into consciousness. These stress postures are described and illustrated fully in a manual of bioenergetic exercises (Lowen and Lowen, 1977).

Moving to step (2), the release of tension, requires an increase in energy level. This is done by increasing the effectiveness of breathing. Lowen (1974, p. 272) has gone so far as to state that "The inhibition of breathing is the key to all personality problems." Various exercises (Lowen et al., 1977) might be used to increase the respiration including the use of the "breathing stool." This breathing stool is essentially a well-padded bar stool, over which the patient can lean back providing a gravitational pull to expand the rib cage.

If, as is often the case, the increase in energy level alone is not adequate for a spontaneous emotional release, two general options are available. The first is for the therapist to apply pressure skillfully to the spastic muscles. This takes the form of deep massage. The second option is to introduce an expressive exercise (Lowen et al., 1977). An example is having the energized patient hit a mattress with the fists to release reported or suspected anger. To dissolve the muscular armor requires many releasing experiences, so Lowen (1974) uses bioenergetic exercise classes and exercises to be done at home as adjuncts to the therapy sessions.

Consistent with Reich, Lowen regards orgastic potency as the criterion of cure, since full orgastic potency is only possible when the muscular armor has been dissolved (neurotic conflicts and fears resolved). Only in the absence of spastic muscles can the life energy stream throughout the body.

There are several specific ways in which bioenergetics differs from Reich's position. These differences constitute the special contributions of Lowen and Pierrakos to the use of the body in psychotherapy.

Bioenergetics places more emphasis on analysis than does Reichian work. Although Reich began as a classical analysis, his psychotherapeutic work can be divided conveniently into an earlier and a later period (Reich, 1949). It is the work of the later period which is distinctly "Reichian" (orgonomy) and which is predominantly body work.

The variety of techniques used in working with the body is greater in bioenergetics. In developing bioenergetics, Lowen and Pierrakos had the benefit of being exposed to the "human potentials movement" with all of the techniques which were being tried. Meetings of groups such as the Association for Humanistic Psychology offered a veritable circus of growth systems and procedures ranging from the fairly traditional to the highly exotic. But much earlier, even before he met Reich, Lowen had studied Emile Jacques-Dalcroze's "eurythmics," Edmund Jacobson's "progressive relaxation," and hatha yoga (Lowen, 1975). The influence of these can be seen in the bioenergetics exercises and postures. Lowen and Lowen (1977) describe no fewer than 102 of these.

Although the bioenergetics therapy work is predominantly one-to-one, as is orgonomy work, group work is used for training, and exercise and massage groups are used as adjuncts to therapy. This feature makes bioenergetics a less "private" system than Reichian therapy.

There is a difference between the two systems in how the body is used as an analytic focus. In Reichian work character is analyzed from resistances in therapy. The resistance manifests in "characterological" behaviors and in muscle tensions. In bioenergetics, character would be "read" from the overall body structure and from body movement. So bioenergetics takes a somatic approach to character. For example, a bioenergetics therapist might view a patient's body and interpret to the patient an "oral body." A Reichian with the same patient would interpret an "oral defense" as manifested by a particular muscle tension. This difference is subtle, and yet gives the two approaches a different flavor. Reich focused on specific muscle tensions; Lowen focused on the total body configuration of which these specific tensions are components.

One of the theoretical differences is in the energy concept. The "bioenergy" of bioenergetics is much less carefully and thoroughly defined than is Reich's "orgone." Lowen speaks of bioenergy at times as if it were synonymous with metabolic energy. In contrast, Reich (1949; Raknes, 1971) writes at great length about orgone, relating it to cosmic phenomena. "Energy" is just not as profound in bioenergetics. Reich's understanding of orgone has led to a lengthy, scholarly volume by Mann, *Orgone, Reich, and Eros* (1973).

Consistent with this difference in their regard of "energy," Reichian work and bioenergetics emphasize a somewhat different focus of working with the body's energy. Bioenergetics focuses on the processing of energy through the voluntary muscles. The focus here is on "expressive energy," the energy of movement of the musculo-skeletal system. The Reichian approach would include work with "expressive energy," but would emphasize the "vegetative energy." The expressive work would be in the service of releasing muscular blocks for the purpose of freeing the normal flow of vegetative energy through the body.

Reich (1949) reports having discovered a natural pathway of flow of the vegetative energy (orgone) in the body. The body is segmented, according to him, into seven segments and a block in vegetative energy flow may be at any one or combination of the segments. The segments consist of horizontal bands around the body in the following locations:

eyes, mouth, throat, chest, diaphragm, abdomen, and pelvis. Reich's claim is that blocks in these segments must be released, in order, from the ocular segment downward through the oral, the throat, the chest or thoracic segment, the diaphragmatic, the abdominal, and last of all the pelvic segment. This order is standard in Reichian work for the release of segmental blocks and the return to normal orgonic streaming in the body. Bioenergetic work does not follow this order. Usually, bioenergetic work begins with the legs and feet which, in Reichian theory, are extensions of the pelvic segment (just as the arms and hands are regarded as extensions of the thoracic segment). Lowen refers to this work with the legs and feet as "grounding" and sees it as basic to successive body work. The body must be well grounded (literally in strong supportive contact with the ground) through the legs and feet in order for the organism to be able to hold a strong energy charge (be highly alive) and discharge strongly (energetically express emotion). Once the person is adequately grounded, the bioenergetic therapist would move to work on any blocked body area without regard for the order which Reich proposed.

A final difference between Reich and bioenergetics is in the style and focus of writing. In my opinion, Reich's works are profound, complex, and written for the sophisticated reader. I see the bioenergetics writing of Lowen as less profound and complex, in places fraught with oversimplification, but much more easily read than Reich. The exception is Lowen's 1958 book *Physical Dynamics of Character Structure* which was republished in 1971 as *The Language of the Body*. This earlier book is a complex work and remains, in my opinion, the essential source in bioenergetics. I believe Reich is to be studied. The audience is the professional. Lowen is to be read. The audience is the professional and the educated lay person. Lowen has performed an extremely valuable service by popularizing the essential messages of the Reichian tradition. Lowen has done more than any other single person to promote the knowledge of the body in psychotherapy to a wide professional and non-professional audience.

In the 1960's Charles Kelley originated the term "neo–Reichian" to describe the work which he and his students were doing. This was an accurate term, in that Kelley's work was firmly rooted in Reich's discoveries and included Kelley's extensions of both theory and technique. As the term "neo–Reichian" began to be used by other practitioners who saw their own approach as having Reichian influence, Kelley began referring to his work as "radix" and renamed his Interscience Research Institute of Connecticut (established in 1960) the Radix Institute, in 1974.

Kelley (1974, p. VII) says of the Radix Institute, "We work with the origins of feeling and expression in the body, with the processes of pulsation, charge, counterpulsation, armor, blocking, release and discharge." The question is: What is it that pulsates and charges; is blocked or discharged? Kelley's answer is that "It is really a substratum from which energy and feeling are created and which forms the connecting link between the two" (p. vii). The term he chose for that substratum is "radix," defined as source, root, or primary cause. So, "The radix flow through the body produces feeling and movement. It is the radix that pulsates and charges the body, the radix flow that is blocked by the armor, the radix that is discharged in emotional release" (p. vii).

Radix work has integrated ideas and procedures from Nathanial Branden, Gestalt therapy, transactional analysis, and Harvey Jackin's reevaluation counseling. In his earlier development of radix, Kelley was influenced by D.H. Lawrence, Synanon, bioenergetics, Ayn Rand, and T.A. Ribot, in addition to Reich, of course (Kelley, 1974). The influences of these various sources are evident, even though radix's roots in Reich are unmistakable.

Compared to previously presented positions, radix is less analytical than bioenergetics or medical orgone therapy. That is, the radix work involves less interpretation of meaning and less verbal interchange between the persons involved. The *content* of the person's emotional issues (i.e., the origin of the person's block, the history of its development, the target of the unexpressed feeling) is not the focus. Rather, the focus is on the *process*, the how of the person's emotional blocking.

As much as half of all of the radix work is done in groups. This heavy emphasis on the group context and the group techniques is a clear departure from Reich, medical orgone therapy and bioenergetics.

The radix view repudiates the medical or therapeutic model of viewing emotional blocks. So, there are not patients, therapists, and cure. Instead, feelings are opened to expression through educational, personal growth processes led by a teacher. In some of the group sessions, the students work with each other under the teacher's supervision. One ramification of this view and approach to emotional expression work is that the growth process and the "professional" are demystified (Kelley, 1978).

Another important difference between radix and bioenergetics, and to a lesser degree even medical orgone therapy, is the strong focus of radix on the vegetative processes. This focus gives much of radix work a softer, less dramatic quality than the bioenergetics work which focuses on strong expression of feelings via the voluntary muscles.

The characterology used by Kelley is different from the Reich-Lowen system and is based on whether the student is blocking fear, anger, or pain, primarily. This system is not based on the notion of fixation or stoppage of development at a psychosexual stage, as is the Freud-Reich-Lowen system.

Kelley has come to prefer concentrated work in residential workshops to the traditional once a week therapy sessions. This choice is based on Kelley's experimenting with various schedules. His experience has been that emotional release is cumulative in its effect and the more frequent sessions of a concentrated residential program often allow greater personal growth than would be allowed by the same number of sessions spread out in a once or twice per week schedule. The residential program, which includes individual work daily and two or three group sessions daily, provides important growth-supporting features. First, the environment is a protected one, away from the pressures of the usual work and home situations. Second, there is the support from the other participants, all sharing in the growth experience. Third, by the frequent repeating of work on a significant defense, the person does not have sufficient time between sessions to re-establish the defense in a major way. The unusualness of the radix environment often has a powerful impact on the students. Since re-entry to one's life situation and integration of the new learning into that life situation can be difficult, periodic radix sessions are often used as a follow-up to the concentrated program. Such sessions might be scheduled for every other week.

Kelley's academic background was in the experimental psychology of vision. In keeping with this background, the first radix groups in the late 1960's were myopic persons and included vision improvement as a goal. This early radix work involved a synthesis of Reichian methods and the methods of vision improvement developed by William H. Bates (1976), an ophthalmologist. Although improvement of vision per se is not the primary objective of radix work today, there is an emphasis on visual awareness, eye contact, seeing and being seen, and visualization techniques. This emphasis is one of the hallmarks of radix work.

Among the body psychotherapies, radix is unique in its explicit dual objectives. As Kelley (1974, p. xi) has stated, "The objective of the program is an opening of the capacity for deep spontaneous emotion, together with a growth in the ability to live purposively, i.e., to choose appropriate goals and to pursue them effectively." This dual objective is reflected in the title of Kelley's 1974 book, *Education in Feeling and Purpose*. Kelley credits Ayn Rand with helping him to understand the role of purpose in human life. Purpose, Kelley explains, requires the capacity to feel and also the capacity to think, conceptualize, plan. It is this purpose or "self-direction" which gives man control of his life and which lends his life significance. The learning of purpose is the learning to focus and direct one's energy in the service of one's life. Kelley is careful to distinguish this purpose from compulsive goal-seeking, which he sees as "an abortion of purpose that must be unlearned, for it blocks both feeling and purpose" (Kelley, 1974, p. 44). Kelley (1974) describes several exercises which are designed for the teaching of purpose in the radix program.

Firmly rooted in Reichian theory and practice, radix is a creative integration of several positions which, on the surface, seem to have little relationship. Kelley has established a clearly distinctive approach to personal growth.

Continuing in the basically Reichian tradition, Malcolm Brown developed a style of work which he termed direct body-contact psychotherapy and which he more recently has come to call organismic psychotherapy. His work is not widely known for at least two reasons. First, to date he has not published the major part of his theoretical and technical work. This material is in unpublished manuscript form and not readily available. His most recent manuscript, *The Healing Touch: An Introduction to Organismic Psychotherapy* has been available only to people who enroll in Brown's training program. Second, Brown has spent the past several years in Europe and has come to the United States only for occasional training workshops with a few carefully selected therapists. Although born in the United States, and having practiced in Berkeley, California, for several years, Brown obtained his Ph.D. from the University of London and has spent half of his adult life living in Europe. He and his wife/coworker Katherine Ennis Brown currently reside in Northern Italy. The Browns have been together since 1974. Interestingly, Katherine's background before meeting Malcolm was in directing a Gestalt-oriented day care center for children and practicing therapeutic massage which was rooted in sensory awareness.

Brown moved from an existential-Rogerian style of therapy to a body-oriented therapy through the influence of Alexander Lowen, Simeon Tropp, Ola Raknes, and Gerde Boyesen. His position is neither orthodox Reichian nor orthodox bioenergetics, but clearly his own.

Organismic psychotherapy focuses on the awakening of the "core longitudinal energy currents and universal psychic tendencies in such a way that the Agape-Eros, Logos, Hara, and Spiritual-Phallic Warrior capacities of the embodied soul can become integrated into the self-structure of the mature adult" (quoted from Brown in a postgraduate training workshop brochure for 1981–1982). Brown sees the use of the various energy mobilizations and energy redistribution techniques as steps toward "soul-building." This is the case in that not only is each region of the body a locus for chronic character-muscular tensions, but each region is also the mediator of universal instinctual psychic tendencies. As the muscular tensions are dissolved, primary unsatisfied feeling needs are uncovered. Their satisfaction constitutes healing and growth.

Important to the therapy process is the interaction of a man-woman treatment team. This embodiment of the yin-yang interaction provides a healing power which encourages a regression to the emotionally fixated past. This regression involves a dissolution of the idealized self-image. The goal of organismic psychotherapy is the discovery of the "ultimate instinctual psychodynamic polarities within the organism-and-soul." In earlier stages of therapy the "ultimate instinctual psychodynamic polarities" present themselves as rapidly alternating opposite reactions. Later, the form is "balanced soul-powers," usually in the form of archetypes.

In terms of technique, Brown uses both hard and soft body interventions, seeing both as valuable and necessary at different times. The hard interventions include heavy pressure on muscles in the form of deep massage. Bioenergetics stress postures are also used. The soft interventions consist of light hand pressure to various parts of the patient's body.

Concerning such light pressure to the upper abdomen, Brown says, "The bioenergetically healthy response to this initial direct body-contact position usually takes the form of a progressive surrender of the body to the therapist's touch.... It can be regarded as the most primitive reaction of a vegetative nervous system which is relatively intact and fully functioning" (from an undated, unpublished manuscript, *An Introduction to Direct Body-Contact Psychotherapy*, p. 1). This progressive surrender involves a deepening and slowing of breathing and a progressive relaxation of the metabolism. This is a mobilization of energy charge and blood flow which accounts for a gradual "thawing out" or softening of the periphery of the body. It is rare that a person is so bioenergetically healthy that this effect radiates to include the entire organism just from this touch to the upper abdominal region. Therefore, successive touches are made to various designated body regions. This soft touch is used to uncover energy blockages, indicated by hardening responses rather than softening and by shifts away from deeper slower breathing.

When a blockage is discovered, the therapist must decide whether continued soft contact, hard contact, or withdrawal of contact is called for in the dissolution of the armoring. Skillful use of this direct contact facilitates the patient's going "into their ailing, painful bodily parts and vital organism sphere of experiences with the full illumination of their own consciousness" (Brown, *An Introduction to Direct Body-Contact Psychotherapy*, p. 3). The return to these painful parts time and time again, session after session, can lead to a transition from the immediate experience of the localized pain or tension to the exploration of the significance of that bodily pain or tension from either a here-and-now psychodynamic perspective or an historical-etiological perspective. The spontaneity of this process is highly emphasized by Brown, and he cautions against the therapist's overprogramming the patient's emotional response by telling the patient to behave in a certain manner, such as shouting a certain repetitive statement or simulating the performed expression of a therapist-specified emotion.

In addition to the "blood synergic" (i.e., mobilization of energy charge and blood flow throughout the capillaries) contact already discussed, Brown employs some additional contact methods (e.g., the Bulow-Hansen dynamic relaxation technique which involves systematic application of "shock-impulse" to specified body parts in sequence and heavy pressure movement touching). Brown also employs bioenergetics exercises and some body positions developed by Raknes. Near the end of treatment Brown includes exercises in vocal tone production.

A point of departure of Brown from Reich and Lowen is their libidinally-oriented charge-discharge model of metabolic energy regulation. In lieu of this model, Brown follows Kurt Goldstein's holistic principle of equalization: Every stimulus excitation has a natural tendency to distribute itself throughout all of the neural substratum. This distribution is regulated by a pattern of figure-ground stimulation which requires time to develop and time to dissolve. So, Brown's view is that following every temporary rise in energy charge, there will be not a discharge of excess energy, but a diminishing and diffusism of the energy until an optimally relaxed equilibrium pervades the total organism. In fact, the *release* of pent-up tension is symptomatic of organismic malfunctioning. Brown proceeds to state that the Reich-Lowen misunderstanding of energy regulation led to the technical error of unduly focusing on the voluntary muscles along the peripheral regions of the body. Brown sees the Reich-Lowen techniques as mistakenly interpreting the cathartic release of transient surface energy, brought about by a forced discharge in the form of willfully controlled athletic-like movements of the voluntary muscles, as being the therapeutic task. Brown's view is that energy mobilization techniques are for the purpose of strengthening the spontaneous self-regulation of the visceral organ network as mediated by the autonomic nervous system.

To lend theoretical support to Brown's contention, I quote from *An Introduction to Direct Body-Contact Psychotherapy*:

> the involuntary musculature throughout the deeper and more central region .. is more intimately bound up with the vegetative or autonomic nervous system, and it is the autonomic nervous system, as distinct from the central nervous system, that is the primary neural mediator of the entire inner feeling and metabolic energy flow. ... The fundamental physiological mechanism responsible for the mediating of passively negative feelings of guilt and depression, bodily sensations of pain and negative emotional outburst of rage, anxiety and fear is what is called an adrenergic patterning of metabolic excitation, whereas the fundamental physiological mechanism which is responsible for mediating positive feelings, including bodily sensations of pleasure, self-fulfilling emotional expressions of love, aggressive self-assertion, and a

sense of joyous well-being, is termed a cholinergic patterning of metabolic excitation. The former is bound up with the sympathetic division of the autonomic nervous system, whereas the latter is bound up with its complementary antagonist, the parasympathetic division of the autonomic nervous system. The term adrenergic refers specifically to the secretion of adrenalin from the adrenal glands in the abdominal cavity and the term cholinergic refers specifically to the secretion of cholinestrase, a grandular chemical which is an antidote to adrenalin [p. 19].

Relating Brown's body work to the above rationale, the task is to strengthen the cholinergic patterning of metabolic excitation and simultaneously to neutralize excessive chronic adrenergic patterning. He sees a loosening of both central and peripher muscular hypertensions as necessary for holistic, spontaneous self-regulation of energy flow.

There are two goals clearly stated by Brown. The first is the stimulation and mobilization of the involuntary feeling centers. The second is the development of spontaneous channels of interaction between those centers and the rational consciousness of the "mind-brain." So, positive personality change does not come about just from releasing chronic tensions and loosening metabolic blockages. In addition, there must be an expansion of spiritual awareness which is the realization of one's uniqueness as a distinct person and multi-dimensional being, what Brown terms the "core self."

A final, and important characteristic of Brown's work is his emphasizing the need to give emotional support and reassurance to the patient concerning the unusual sensations which will be experienced from the direct body contact methods. This emotional support must be strong enough to allow the patient's continuation of the therapeutic process.

In another unpublished manuscript, entitled *My Twelve-Hour Workshops in Direct Body-Contacting*, Brown describes in great detail a wide variety of techniques for working in a group context. These varied techniques include group chanting, and the use of accommodator figures in psychodramatic scenes similar to some aspects of Pesso's Psychomotor work. This is in addition to various procedures for direct body contact, which remains the cornerstone of Brown's work.

So far in this historical-theoretical view of a body orientation in psychotherapy, there has been a linear, branching development. The development flows clearly from Freud to Ferenczi to Reich and on to the early branching from Reich and the later branching from Reich. Then there are those therapists who continue from one of the branches. As I evaluate the contributions to body-oriented psychotherapy, I note another position which, interestingly, is not of this tradition. That position is psychomotor therapy.

Psychomotor therapy was developed by Albert and Diane Pesso, starting in the early 1960's. Neither of this husband and wife team had formal training in psychotherapy. Their background was in dance, and later, in choreography. The Pessos began using movement techniques for therapeutic purposes at the Boston Veterans Administration Hospital, and this evolved into a four-year research project beginning in 1964 (Pesso, 1969). Since that time the Pessos have been very active in teaching psychomotor therapy (now sometimes termed Pesso System Psychomotor, or P.S.P.) both in the United States and in Europe, and in continually developing their theory and techniques.

The outstanding characteristic of psychomotor work is making energy interactive. To understand this process of why and how to make energy interactive requires delving into a fairly complex theoretical system. The starting point is a developmental model. The Pessos' idea is that there are four basic human needs: nurturance, support, protection, and limits. These are necessary conditions for the growth and development of the self. The conditions are provided first by the womb, then by the parents after the child is born, and then by the ego. If, however, there has been a womb dysfunction or parent dysfunction (i.e., if the womb or the parents did not provide ample experience of one or more of the four basic needs) there will be a corresponding ego dysfunction. One perspective on psychopathology, then is that psychopathology is an ego dysfunction in which the ego fails to provide adequate nurturance, support, protection, and limits for the self to "be" and "become." The therapeutic task is to provide experiences which compensate for the earlier inadequacies in experienced nurturance, support, protection, and limits. And since these experiences are interactive ones, the task is one of interaction. This is the why of making energy interactive.

These therapeutic interactions take place in the context of a "symbolic regression." This means that the patient is treated as if regressed while the adult aspects of the patient are present for consultation with the therapist. In other words, the patient flows in and out of the regressed state during a therapy session, at times talking with the therapist adult to adult about what is needed next and at times being in the child position to receive without having to ask. (Pesso has suggested that some patients have such extreme ego deficits that they cannot work with symbolic regression and must work from a position of literal regression which is offered in some residential treatment programs [personal communication, 1976].)

Pesso (1973) makes a nice bridge from the why to the how of making energy interactive in the therapy session: "All this could be done in fantasy, but it is important to include concrete sensory and motoric input to the fantasy to make it a more believable and educational experience" (p. 16).

In conducting a therapy session, the psychomotor approach is first to identify the energy in the patient. Energy, synonymous with emotion, feeling, tension, is the "unborn self." It is *being* in the process of *becoming* that which is not concrete and real yet. There is a natural Gestalt consisting of:

Energy ► Action ► Interaction ► Symbol

Energy leads to *action* of the body, which leads to *interaction* of the body with other bodies, which leads to the *symbol* of the experience of "satisfaction" and "validation." In that this "interaction sequence" is a gestalt, it follows that the energy can *produce* the action, *predict* the action, or *recognize* the action which is appropriate from the array of possible actions. In turn, action can *produce* or *predict* the interaction or it can *recognize* the interaction. The utility of this interaction sequence and its Gestalt dynamic will become clear when the actual procedures are described below.

So, the aim is not to make energy (i.e., tension, emotion, feelings) go away, but to move in the direction of the tension permitting it to become overt action, and in turn, to allow it to become interaction which brings satisfaction and validation to the self. As Pesso (1973, p. 8) wrote,

> many emotions are not experienced or actions expressed by people because the family setting or circumstances ... did not provide satisfactory accommodations or "matching" responses to their feelings or behaviors. By offering accommodation to as yet unexpressed emotions and behaviors, the psychomotor process taps the reservoir of repressed, inhibited and unconscious feelings and permits those aspects of one's being that have yet to be discovered, to be expressed and hopefully, to be integrated into one's life.

The basic technique of psychomotor is "accommodation." And, accommodation is interactive; it involves interaction with "target figures." The target figures are archetypal, and are role-played by actual participants. The role-play situation in which accommodation of the patient's energy, action, interaction provides satisfaction and validation is called a "structure." In the "structure" target figures are often polarized so that there are a negative mother and a negative father who symbolize the negative aspects of the literal parents, and there are the opposites, or a positive mother and a positive father. The positive figures represent idealized or archetypal parents who perfectly satisfy the growth needs of the symbolically regressed patient. In the role play setting of the "structure" the accommodating figures, positive and negative, do exactly and say exactly the words which are given to them by the therapist.

The therapist is the director of the role play, and consults with the adult (nonregressed) part of the patient to find out the exact actions and words which would accommodate the actions of the patient, making those actions into satisfying and validating interactions. The negative figures are, of course, the accommodating figures for the patient's negative energy. So as the patient expresses negative energy, the negative accommodators fall down, writhe, scream in pain, "die," or whatever feels validating to the patient. The literal action of the patient may be yelling in anger, striking a pillow, kicking a cushion, biting a towel or whatever action expression his energy takes. This literal action is given symbolic meaning via the accommodation by the target figures. The positive figures, then, are the accommodating figures for the patient's positive energy. Through his interactions with them, his literal touching, holding, sucking, being held, being touched, or whatever his energy dictates, and the words spoken to him become the symbolic carriers of nurturance, support, protection, limits, or some combination of those needs. "A structure provides an opportunity for symbolic rebirth in a perfect setting that matches his need for expression and personal growth" (Pesso, 1973, p. 8).

The versatility of the "structure" is considerable, and although positive and negative parents are almost always present as target figures, other target figures may also be included. These other target figures run the gamut of the personified archetypes.

Pesso (1973) sees interactive energy as having five arenas, each one having its own sensory-motor apparatus and its own type of target. These are reflexive body righting, metabolic-vegetative, interpersonal, material (impersonal), and verbal-symbolic. "Experience in psychomotor therapy has led me to believe that there are archetypical pathways for the expression of interactive energy which result in archetypical patterns of behavior" (Pesso, 1973, p. 54).

To summarize the technical task of the therapist in a "structure," the therapist must track interpersonal interactive energy. He looks for where the energy shows up in the patient's body, helps it to become a concrete motoric action, and helps direct it towards appropriate interactive targets.

> If the energy does not show up as overt action, his function is to find its symbolic expression in the realm of thought or fantasy and to assist in translating it back to action. If the energy shows up as pain, somatic disturbance, or tingling, he must help to translate it back into action ... [Pesso, 1973, p. 79].

The key is the spontaneous, concrete interaction which carries symbolic meaning via the accommodation by target figures.

Earlier, I mentioned that energy can predict, produce, or recognize action and action can predict, produce, or recognize interaction. Therefore, the therapist has prediction, production, and recognition as options in facilitating the patient's becoming. Prediction is the choice to asking the patient to guess what the energy wants to do. Production is the choice of asking the patient to "go with his body," to let his body do whatever it wants to do. Pesso (personal communication, 1976) prefers a flow back and forth between prediction and production, thus integrating the cognitive with the body action. If production is overly emphasized in the therapy work, the patient can be overwhelmed by powerful actions devoid of an accompanying cognitive grasp. At times, when prediction and production are not furthering the patient's work, recognition can be used as a second choice. In recognition, the therapist suggests the action-interaction and invites the patient to do it and see if it "fits." The drawback of using recognition is that it introduces the therapist's distortions and biases and may lead the patient away from his own knowing. Interestingly, the incongruity between the patient's ability to predict and to produce can be seen as an index of repression.

Early in his work, Pesso (1969) distinguished three types of movement: reflex movement, voluntary movement, and emotional movement. Reflex movement pertains to the relationship of the self with gravity and the ground. Voluntary movement involves the self with the outside world in intentional ways. With emotional movement the self is expressing the inside world. For the exploration of these three types of movement, the Pessos have developed a very elaborate schema of exercises. The early material appears in *Movement in Psychotherapy* (Pesso, 1969), but the more recent elaborations which Diane Pesso has been developing are not yet published.

Psychomotor therapy is a coming-together of intricate role play and a careful focus on the body and its energy.

My discussion of body-oriented therapists is not exhaustive of those who have made or are making theoretical and procedural contributions. I have included the people whom I see clearly as pioneers. Each of the people discussed above has made a major impact on the evolution of the focus on the body in psychotherapy. Many more people whose contributions are definite but of less magnitude will be cited in the following pages.

2. An Organismic Perspective on Personality Dynamics

Psychobiological existence is based on need cycles, the cycles of contacting other people and other things in one's world for the satisfaction of needs and the withdrawal that follows. There is a rhythm to the process: a periodicity as needs arise, are satisfied, giving way to other needs, and arise again after a while. The cycle of contact-satisfaction-withdrawal has a certain integrity and can be seen as a "unit of living." Each unit emerges as a particular need becomes prepotent, and an organismically lived figure takes shape within the context of the environmental background. This is a Gestalt, forming, dynamically playing out, and de-forming. From the organism-in-environment background a dynamic organism-in-living emerges and recedes in figure-ground formations. The choice of which need is to be given prepotency at any given moment is based on the "wisdom of the organism."

I am presenting here a model for the description and understanding of this psychobiological unit of living, the contact withdrawal cycle (Smith, 1979). The model, of course, is a gross simplification. However, it does facilitate understanding.

A convenient starting point in the contact withdrawal cycle is the person's want. The want may be a need or a preference. Needs are those things which are necessary for survival. This includes *receptive* needs such as certain nutrients, water, air, heat, love, cognitive stimulation, and esthetic stimulation, as well as *expressive* needs such as elimination of metabolic wastes, elimination of excess heat, love, sex, cognitive expression, and esthetic expression. The ultimate need, which subsumes all of the above needs is "self-actualization," that urge for the realization of one's potential self. A preference is the specific choice one makes given that there are several options any one of which will meet a given need. In a sense, the needs are the "what" or content of living and preferences are expressed in the "how" or style of living. The needs are existential givens, part of what being a human is. Preferences involve choices, how I want to

29

Figure 1.

CONTACT / WITHDRAWAL MODEL

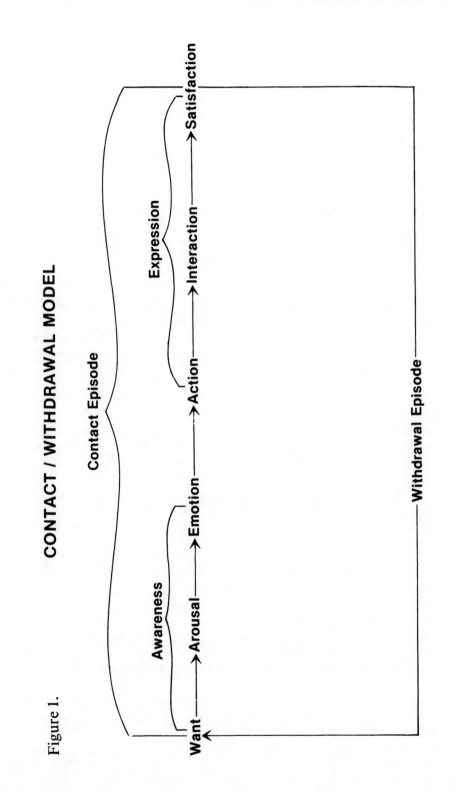

meet a given need. Fritz Perls called attention to the fact that needs are set, but we always have choices in what he termed "the means whereby."

Several steps can be described between the arising of a want (need or preference) and the satisfaction of that want. When a want arises, a state of physiological arousal follows. This arousal is a state of tension and excitement. The organism has become physiologically mobilized to a state of higher energy.

This heightened energy state which results from arousal is differentiated and subjectively experienced as an emotion. Emotion, also termed "feeling" or affect," is subjective experience of the flow of energy in the body.

The emotion, in turn, implies and calls for an action or movement of the flowing energy into the musculoskeletal system. Action is concrete movement of parts of the body or even the whole body.

Action implies and calls for interaction with someone or something in the environment. Interaction occurs at the "contact boundary" between organism and world.

The final stage of the contact episode is satisfaction of the want. The contact episode consists of these several steps delineated above, and is followed naturally by an organismic withdrawal episode. The contact episode and the withdrawal episode jointly constitute a contact/withdrawal cycle.

The first half of the contact episode (Want ►Arousal ►Emotion) is, psychobiologically speaking, under the auspices of awareness. In other words, the first half of the contact episode requires that one is organismically aware of wanting something (a need or preference), of being aroused (excited), and of feeling an emotion. This awareness serves as a focusing of energy for the second or expression half of the contact episode (Action ►Interaction ►Satisfaction). Satisfying contact requires both awareness and expression.

The steps in the contact withdrawal cycle are cumulative, each one depending for its success on the full and effective development of all previous steps. If a given step is not allowed to develop in full form, the proceding steps will be less well formed and the ultimate satisfaction will be diminished or missed completely. There are also feedback loops such that later steps may enhance earlier steps. For example, taking action may enhance the felt emotion, or if the action is not appropriate to the emotion, the action may reveal to the person what the actual emotion would be if it were allowed into awareness. It's as if there were a reverberating wave which further enhances the previous steps as each new step is taken. As long as these contact/withdrawal cycles emerge and recede smoothly, maintaining the organism and serving the pre-eminent need — self-actualization — there is a state of psychobiological health.

Figure 2.   Expansion and Relaxed Contraction

Expansion	*Relaxed Contraction*	*Anxious Contraction*
Contact Episode	Withdrawal Episode	(This column will
Pleasure	Centered quietness	be delineated in
Target has + valence	Target has 0 valence	the later discussion
Elongation, dilation	Shortening, relaxation	of psychopathology)
"Yes"	Disinterest	
Movement toward world	Withdrawal into the self	
Peripheral excitation		
Central discharge		
PANS dominant		
Anabolism dominant		
Muscular action	Muscles in relaxed tonus	

The contact/withdrawal rhythm is one of expansion and contraction. The contact episode involves a movement out into the world with the expectation of satisfaction. The person or thing targeted for the contact is given a positive valence. With satisfaction, the targeted person or thing is given a neutral valence and the organism withdraws in indifference. The withdrawal is a contraction or relaxation away from the source of satisfaction.

Reich (1973) identified a primary antithesis of organismic life: pleasure (expansion) and anxiety (contraction). The movements are distinguished by the direction of energy; "you reach out with your life energy when you feel well and loving, and ... you retract it to the center of your body when you are afraid" (Reich, quoted in Mann and Hoffman, 1980, p. 91). In this, Reich is identifying the expansive, pleasurable movement of the contact episode. But, he does not distinguish between the relaxed contraction which follows satisfaction and the anxious contraction which come from fear. I think it is more accurate to distinguish three poles: Expansion (pleasure, the successful contact episode), relaxed contraction (quiet, withdrawal episode), and anxious contraction (fear, blocked contact episode or avoidance). In the present chapter, my focus is on healthy personality dynamics (successful contact/withdrawal cycles), so I will reserve most of the elaboration of the dynamics of psychopathology (blocked contact/withdrawal cycles) until the following chapter.

Referring to the psychobiological level, Reich (1973, p. 288) states, "all biological impulses and organ sensations can be reduced to *expansion* (elongation, dilation) and *contraction* (shrinking, constriction)." These functions Reich (1973, p. 288) relates to the autonomic nervous system, "the parasympathetic (vagus) always functions where there is expansion, dilation, hyperemia, turgor, and pleasure. Conversely, the *sympathetic* nerves function whenever the organism contracts, blood is withdrawn from the periphery and pallor, anxiety, and pain appear." Reich (1973) provides a very detailed discussion of the neurochemical level of organismic expansion and contraction.

Saeger (1980) also provides a very good discussion of the basic physiological activities involved in this movement toward the world and withdrawal from the world. Stimuli, whether actual or imagined (symbolic) are processed through central integrating mechanisms involving the limbic and the hypothalmic centers, which send impulses to the autonomic nervous system. After central integration, the stimulus leads to an integrated response of the autonomic nervous system (ANS) which involves every system of the body. "The ANS-stimulated release of hormones through the endocrine system serves to either stimulate or inhibit the energetic functions of specific target tissues and organs, and to potentiate direct effects of parasympathetic or sympathetic innervation" (Saeger, 1980, p. 40). The endocrine effect, in general serves either to mobilize or to conserve energy. At the level of tissues or organs, the endocrine response and the effects of the sympathetic (SANS) and para-sympathetic (PANS) combine to create a specific metabolic and bio-energetic activity profile for basic emotions. The final pathway of mobilization of the emotional energy is in the muscle action potential.

I have suggested elsewhere (Smith, in press) that the organismic expansion is a psychobiological statement of "yes" and organismic contraction is "no." The chart in Figure 2 summarizes the main points of the present discussion.

3. An Organismic Perspective on Psychopathology

As long as the contact/withdrawal cycles emerge and recede smoothly, maintaining the organism and providing for self-actualization, there is a state of psychobiological health. There are two categories of problems which may, however, interfere with the cycles. The first category is the absence in the environment of the person or thing necessary for the satisfaction of the need. This is a problem of politics, economics, technology, ecology or some such realm, but not a question of personal psychopathology *per se*. The second category of problems which interfere with healthy contact and withdrawal is one of personal psychopathology. This category is concerned with one's stopping one's self in the contact/withdrawal cycle so that a rhythmic flow does not occur. For example: if I am alone in a remote and isolated location, I will not be able to get my interpersonal needs met (positive regard, esteem, love, sex). The literal, interpersonal meeting of these needs will be impossible and my humanness will suffer if a long time passes. And this is regardless of my level of psychological functioning. If, on the other hand, I fail to get my interpersonal needs met when there are adequate and appropriate people available, this is a psychological problem. If, out of my fears of reaching out, asking, contacting, I don't get my needs met, I am functioning pathologically. I define psychopathology as *any pattern of habitual self-interruptions in the contact/withdrawal cycles* (Smith, 1979). These habitual self-interruptions obscure the inner voice which speaks the "wisdom of the organism" and lead to a cumulative self-alienation.

There are several points in the contact/withdrawal cycle where a self-interruption can occur. This situation is one of the factors which contributes to the myriad forms which psychopathology can assume.

I want now to elaborate on the "what" of psychopathology, the self-interruption of life process.

First is the choice of being aware of one's wants or not. To be unaware of one's wants is to stay in the withdrawal episode even after the want has arisen. This is the patient who is blank or says, "I don't know," when asked, "What do you want?" or "What would you like?" Often, the increasing agitation bespeaks the fact that a want is present even though its existence has not been allowed into awareness. This is the essence of boredom: I want, I don't allow myself awareness of what I want, so I feel lacking and agitated.

An interesting variation of the awareness problem at the point of the want is the failure to differentiate needs and preferences. The usual form which this takes is to mistake a preference for a need. This, of course, "ups the ante" in that needs are necessary for survival of one's organism and humanness. If one thinks that a preference is a need, he or she will react strongly and out of proportion to what is in fact only the inconvenience of having preference denied. Much extreme behavior, demandingness, and violence results from this incomplete or low-level awareness. This confusion of a preference for a need can be labeled an addiction. The addicted person proceeds as if he or she *must* have the want satisfied at almost any cost. A tragic example of such addiction is the person who wants a lover, but believes that his preference for a particular person is a need. He then is "hooked" on that person, and if she does not agree to his demand for love, affection, attention, he may in desperation kill himself and even kill her. Such addiction is strongly reinforced by the lyrics of popular songs (e.g., "It had to be you..." "I can't live without you..."). For a thorough and inspirational exploration of the relationship, dynamics, and implications of needs, preferences, and addictions I recommend *The Handbook to Higher Consciousness* by Ken Keys (1972).

The second point for self-interruption is the juncture between the want and arousal. With self-interruption at this point the person is not aware of the physiological arousal which is present. So, when asked what he or she is aware of, the patient says, "Nothing," even though there may be external indications of excitement.

The transition from arousal to emotion is the third point of possible self-interruption. In this case the lack of full awareness involves a failure to differentiate the excitement into a specific affective experience. This patient, when asked what he or she is feeling, will report some version of, "I feel tense," or, "I feel nervous."

The fourth point for self-interruption, the transition from emotion to action, is a movement into the realm of expression. In blocking movement from the awareness half of the contact episode into the expression half, energy is not allowed to flow in the musculoskeletal system. This decision to self-interrupt at this junction and remain in the realm of pre-action is especially common in oversocialized patients, those who ruminate and obsess rather than risk "misbehaving."

Once the transition into the realm of expression is made, the next

Figure 3. CONTACT / WITHDRAWAL MODEL (With Avoidances)

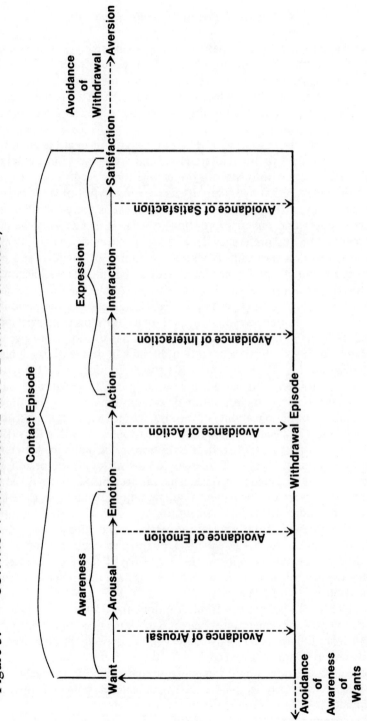

decision is whether to make the action interactive or not. The fifth point of self-interruption is here, not allowing the action to become an interaction with a target which would allow satisfaction. The choice might be not to interact at all, or to interact with a target unsuitable for providing satisfaction.

The sixth point of self-interruption is between interaction and satisfaction. The patient who blocks at this juncture does not allow satisfaction, even though all of the previous steps have been taken appropriately.

Whether or not to move into the withdrawal episode following satisfaction is the seventh decision point in flowing or self-interruption. If the contact episode is prolonged beyond the point of satisfaction, the contact becomes forced, unnatural, and what would have been satisfying becomes noxious and disgusting. This is the situation with patients who "hang on" in the various forms from overeating to staying in bad relationships or work situations. Perls (1969) termed this the "hanging on bite."

To summarize the above, it is impossible to effect a self-interruption in a contact/withdrawal cycle at any one of the seven junctures of the cycle. Such a self-interruption is a short-circuiting of the ongoing flow of the psychobiological life process. The issue is, do I allow a natural flow in my energy process, or do I override the wisdom of my organism and interrupt my flow? The decision to self-interrupt means leaving a need or a preference unmet, and thus the accumulation of "unfinished business." The self-interruption is an avoidance, an avoidance of the next step in the cycle, or ultimately an avoidance of being fully alive.

The discussion above, explicating *what* psychopathology is, invites two important questions. The first is, *why* would one want to interrupt the natural contact/withdrawal cycles? Given that one wants to do so, the second question is *how* does one accomplish the self-interruption?

First, I will address the "why" of self-interruption. As early as *in utero* the human organism is responsive to the adequacy-inadequacy of its environment and responds to the atmosphere as one of nurturance, support, protection, and limits or the lack thereof. Depending on the adequacy of the environment provided by the mother, the fetus expands or anxiously contracts from life. Organismic patterns are being set. The birth process itself, that initial excursion into the post-natal world, then has its impact on the organism, again inviting expansion and aliveness or the converse.

To the basic patterning set *in utero* and in the birth process, there is then added the early learning history of the child. The treatment of the child by the parents, again, in general or in specific ways, encourages natural aliveness or discourages or even forbids it. During early development, most importantly the first five years or so, children are told not to express a certain feeling in a particular way, or not to express that feeling at all, or not to feel that feeling, or not to get excited, or sometimes not even to have certain wants. These prohibitive messages may be expressed verbally or non-verbally. Due primarily to the profound dependence of the child on the parenting figures for its very survival, the prohibitive messages are "swallowed-whole," introjected. Secondarily, the process of introjection is facilitated by the fact that the child has little life experience, relative to the parenting figures, against which to judge the prohibitive messages. During this phase of the socialization process, many of the introjected messages are bionegative, that is, they are socially arbitrary messages which do not support the child's aliveness. The bionegative message is, then, a toxic introject.

There are two components to the toxic introject. First, is the content, or the specific prohibition. Second, is the threat that if the toxic introject is not obeyed love will be denied. The threat is experienced as if something awful, terrible, even catastrophic will happen. An example is the message to a little boy, "Big boys don't cry. Don't be a sissy." The content of this message is, "You should not cry," and the threat is, "If you cry I won't love you any more." Such toxic introjects are usually maintained, unexamined and unchallenged, throughout one's life. The result is lifelong internal conflict between the natural urge for aliveness and the toxic, introjected message which calls for deadness. Once the toxic message has been introjected, the threat of loss of love for disobeying becomes a conditioned phobic belief in imminent catastrophe whenever the toxic message is not honored. The toxic introject carries a "should" or "should not" (the content) and a catastrophic expectation.

The greater the number and severity of toxic introjects, the more phobic the person is, and the less aliveness the person allows. The self-interruption of contact/withdrawal cycles is the essence of limiting aliveness. Which contact/withdrawal cycles (based on which needs or preferences) I interrupt, and at which of the seven points of possible avoidance I choose to enact the interruption, are dictated by the details of the content of the toxic introject.

Now, having described why one would choose to self-interrupt contact/withdrawal cycles, I turn to the second question, the "how" of self-interruption. Avoidance is accomplished by means of four pathological mechanisms. These mechanisms work in combination and in synergy to block the organismic flow very effectively. Since satisfying contact involves: (1) arousal of the organism, (2) focusing of the aroused energy through awareness, and (3) enactment with that energy (action and interaction guided by awareness), the four pathological mechanisms focus on the quieting of arousal, the clouding of awareness, the nonenactment of action, and the nonenactment of interaction, respectively. The result of the use of these mechanisms of avoidance can be either a complete stoppage of flow, or just a diminishing of that flow. The Polsters (1973) have suggested the term block for a complete stoppage of the impulse and inhibition for the diminished expression.

The first mechanism for self-interruption is focused on inhibiting or blocking arousal. The primary method for quelling excitement is to limit breathing. By means of tightening the diaphragm, and thereby limiting its excursion, and tightening the muscles of the rib cage, breathing becomes shallow. This shallow breathing involves use mainly of the upper chest on inhalation and an incomplete exhalation, the result being a diminished oxygen supply. This leads to a diminished level of energy. This mechanism of blocking or inhibiting excitement is a reflex action in response to a scare, in the pathological context of self-interruption, the scare is in response to the voice of the toxic introject. The role of limited breathing in psychopathology is strongly emphasized in Gestalt therapy as well as in the Reichian and neo–Reichian approaches. There are several adjuncts to this primary method of limiting excitement which can be built into one's lifestyle. These include smoking (for some people, smoking has the opposite effect and actually energizes), use of alcohol and other quieting drugs, poor nutrition, lack of exercise, lack of sufficient sleep and rest, lack of play, and lack of sexual activity.

The second mechanism is focused on the clouding of awareness. No matter how energized the person is, without the focusing of that energy through awareness (What do I want; What am I feeling; What do I have to do to get what I want; With whom or with what do I have to do what I have to do; When am I satisfied and ready to withdraw?), the likelihood of satisfaction is nil. Awareness is the guide. The specific processes which interfere with awareness are introjection, projection, confluence, deflection, and desensitization. The first three create *confusion*. In the case of introjection I believe something is mine when it really is yours. That is, I have taken in your idea, value, belief, moral guideline, whatever, and act on it without having examined it thoroughly and decided if I really wanted to incorporate it into my overall system. Projection is the opposite process in that I attribute something (idea, belief, value, feeling, or the like) to you when it really is mine. Confluence involves a blurring of the ego boundary so that I do not differentiate "you" and "me," and recognize only "us." Perls' (1973, p. 40–41) summary of these three processes is, "The introjector does as others would like him to do, the projector does unto others what he accuses them of doing to him, the man in pathological confluence doesn't know who is doing what to whom..."

With deflection and desensitization there is a *dulling* of awareness. "Deflection is a maneuver for turning aside from direct contact with another person ... by circumlocution, by excessive language, by laughing off what one says, by not looking at the person one is talking to, by being abstract rather then specific, by not getting the point, by coming up with bad examples or none at all, by politeness instead of directness, by stereo-typed language instead of original language, by substituting mild emotions for intense ones, by talking *about* rather than talking to, and by shrugging off the importance of what one has just said" (Polster and Polster, 1973, p. 89). Deflection can be used either by the sender of a message or by the receiver. In either case the message is diluted, thus resulting in a dulled level of awareness.

"Desensitization ... is the sensory analog to motoric retroflection. Scotomata, visual blurring, chronic 'not hearing,' sensory dullness, frigidity, etc..." (Enright, 1970, p. 112). Any dulling of awareness by decreasing the acuity of a sensory modality is a desensitization. For those who do not want to develop skills at desensitization, breweries, distil-leries, and pharmaceutical houses offer products which can be put to this use quite effectively.

The next focus in self-interruption of contact/withdrawal cycles is the enactment of the expression of energy, or the action►interaction sequence. I have termed the processes of non-enactment "retroflection of action" and "retroflection of interaction."

The juncture between the awareness portion and the expression portion of the contact episode is of special importance because it involves the movement of energy into the musculoskeletal system. During the awareness portion most of the energy is in the vegetative nervous system, but with the expressive portion the voluntary muscles become the main loci of energy. Retroflection of action, or the diminishing or total blocking of muscular movement, is then an important process of self-interruption. Enright (1970, p. 112) stated, "Retroflection describes the general process of negating, holding back, or balancing the impulse tension by additional, opposing sensorimotor tension. ... Since the net result of all this canceled-out muscular tension is zero—no overt move-ment—there is no particular increase in activity at the contact bound-ary...." Enright (1970) also pointed out that this retroflection, as it is termed in Gestalt theory, when chronic, is what Reich identified as char-acter armor. About this action-deadening form of retroflection Perls (1969, p. 229) said, "We repress vital functions (vegetative energy, as Reich calls their sum) by muscular contractions. The civil war raging in the neurotic organism is mostly waged between the motoric system and unaccepted organismic energies which strive for expression and gratifica-tion. The motoric system has to a great extent lost its function as a working, active, worldbound system and, by retroflection, has become the jailer rather than the assistant of important biological needs. Every dissolved symptom means setting free both policeman and the prisoner — motoric and 'vegetative' energies — for the common struggle of life."

Self-interruption, as has been shown already, may be at the juncture between action and interaction. The action is allowed, but the inter-action is retroflected. The essence of retroflected interaction is the absence of an environmental object. In describing this, Perls, Hefferline and Goodman (1951, p. 146) said of the retroflector of interaction, "He stops directing various energies outward in attempts to manipulate and bring about changes in the environment that will satisfy his needs; instead he redirects activity inward and *substitutes himself in place of the environ-ment* as the target of behavior. To the extent that he does this, he splits his personality into 'doer' and 'done to'."

The Polsters (1973, p. 82) were explicit in distinguishing two forms of what I later labeled retroflected interaction, "retroflection is a her-maphroditic function wherein the individual turns back against himself what he would like *to do to someone else* or does to himself what he would like *someone else to do to him*."

In the latter case, the paradigm content is love. Self-patting, self-holding, self-stroking, self-preening, and masturbation all can bespeak the doing to one's self what one would like someone else to do to one. Verbal statements of liking or loving one's self and self-complimenting may accompany the physical activity. In classical mythology we are in-structed about retroflected love by Narcissus. The curse put upon Narcis-sus by Nemesis, goddess of righteous anger, was "May he who loves not others love himself" (Hamilton, 1942, p. 88).

Two elements are involved in retroflected love: the impulse to love (the "doer" role) and the need to be loved (the "done to" role). Since the same self is both "doer" and "done to" in retroflected love, the "doer" fails to have the experience of loving another, and the "done to" fails to have the experience of being loved by another.

Self-hate (anger) is the paradigm content of the other type of retro-flected interaction (doing to one's self what one would like to do to an-other). This retroflected anger can be identified by any act of hurting one's self such as scratching, hitting, biting, kicking, cutting one's self or so forth. Frequently, retroflected anger is expressed in diminished form so that little or no pain or damage is experienced. If, however, the biting of one's lips or pounding of one's fist on one's leg is exaggerated, the meaning becomes clear. Verbal statements of greater or lesser subtlety may accompnay the retroflected anger. Examples are: "I hate myself," "I could kick myself for that," "I'm so dumb," or "I'm such a klutz." Any self-derogation is a retroflection of anger. Doing to one's self what one would like to do to another is a comico-tragic event, a case of mistaken identity.

Perls (1969) saw self-control, self-hate and narcissism (self-love) as the three most important retroflections. In that statement I see the basis for what I have termed retroflected action and retroflected interaction of the two types discussed above, respectively. Obviously, there are healthy occurrences of retroflected action — self-restraint in situations of genuine danger. An elaboration of this idea is presented by Perls, Hefferline, and Goodman (1951, p. 455): "Normally, retroflection is the process of reforming oneself, for instance correcting the impractical approach or reconsidering the possibilities of the emotion, making a readjustment as the grounds for further action. ... And more generally, any act of deliberate self-control during a difficult engagement is retroflection."

Retroflected interaction of the form, "Doing to oneself what one would like another to do to one" also can be manifested in biopositive form. When a need is present and the appropriate target person is not, self-holding, self-stroking and such self attentions are appropriate second preferences. This is an aspect of self-support, a highly valued process in Gestalt therapy. Zinker (1977, p. 103) viewed both the positive and negative sides, "The price he pays — among other things — is that of using his own energy rather than being replenished by another person. His rewards are independence, self-reliance, doing better for himself than another can, privacy, and the development of his individual capacities and talents."

The key point is that retroflected action and retroflected interaction are pathological when they are an avoidance, a self-interruption of the contact/withdrawal cycle. As I see it, retroflected interaction of the form, "Doing to myself what I would like to do to you," is always an avoidance, and hence, pathological.

Figure 4 summarizes the psychopathology material presented above.

Just as the healthy contact episode involves aggressive expansion into the world and withdrawal involves relaxed contraction into the self, the self-interruption is an anxious contraction away from the world, an avoidance of aliveness. Quoting Reich (1973a, p. 288) again in reference to the psychobiological level "all biological impulses and organ sensations can be reduced to *expansion* (elongation, dilation) and *contraction* (shrinking, constriction)." In relating these functions to the autonomic nervous system (ANS) Reich (1973a, p. 288) stated, "the parasympathetic (vagus) always functions where there is expansion, dilation, hyperemia, turgor, and pleasure. Conversely, the *sympathetic* nerves function whenever the organism contracts, blood is withdrawn from the periphery and pallor, anxiety, and pain appear."

In discussing the sympathetic nervous system response Saeger (1980, p. 42) states: "The blood is literally withdrawn 'away from the world' in a SANS response: there is peripheral vasoconstriction with concomitant stimulation of the heart (in extreme cases, palpitation and tachycardia).... The opposite occurs in PANS activation." Following further discussion of

Figure 4.　　Psychopathology Summary

What is psychopathology?	Psychopathology is any pattern of habitual self-interruption in the contact/withdrawal cycle.
Why does one choose to self-interrupt?	Self-interruptions are in response to the toxic introject which forbids full aliveness. The toxic introject contains both a content (what is forbidden) and a threat of catastrophe if it is disobeyed (the catastrophic expectation). The self-interruption is to avoid the next forbidden step in the contact/withdrawal cycle.
How can one self-interrupt?	Self-interruptions are accomplished through a synergestic combination of the following four mechanisms: 1) Lowered arousal (through insufficient breathing) 2) Clouded awareness 　　a) Confused awareness (through the processes of 　　　1. Introjection 　　　2. Projection, or 　　　3. Confluence) 　　b) Dulled awareness (through the processes of 　　　1. Deflection, or 　　　2. Desensitization) 3) Retroflected action (through body armoring) 4) Retroflected interaction 　　a) Doing to one's self what one would like to do to another, or 　　b) Doing to one's self what one would like another to do to one. Self-interruption may be partial (inhibition) or complete (a block).

ANS profiles, Saeger concludes that the ANS profile determines the direction of flux of body liquids of the whole organism, and that SANS hyperactivation (having norepinephrine as its main neurotransmitter at synapses) describes the anxiety response. Pleasure is described by PANS activity (having acetylcholine as its main neurotransmitter at synapses) or flux of fluids toward the world. Fluid and electrical charge flows are hard to separate, since electrical charge is carried by electrolytes in the fluids of the body. Both fluid and electrical charge flow are governed by ion flux.

Anxiety is experienced at the point of self-interruption. The avoidance precludes the full processing of energy, and it is this unprocessed energy which is experienced as anxiety. This is the psychobiological "unfinished business." Orgone is released through muscular activity or it is bound (inhibited or blocked) by muscular tension (armoring). The energy is *pleasurably* expressed through muscular action or it is nonenacted by virtue of the body armor with a feeling of displeasure or *anxiety*. The anxious contraction of the armored body is an exaggeration of the normal relaxed contraction of the withdrawal episode. As Baker (1967, p. 9) has stated, "Anxiety is actually a contraction against expansion."

The chronic tension of muscular armoring requires a constant energy supply, thus an elevation of catabolic metabolism and a chronic SANS activation with related catabolic endocrine activity. As Saeger (1980, p. 44) states, "muscular armor represents a chronic ANS and endocrine skew towards SANS activation and catabolic metabolism." The result is, then, not only displeasure and the unfinished business of an incomplete contact/withdrawal cycle, but a bionegative state of the organism. Reich termed this unhealthy state a biopathy. The biopathic state created by chronic body armor can be seen as the condition for degenerative disease and vulnerability to pathogenic organisms with which one may come in contact. Reich (1973a, 1973b) and Baker (1967) offer discussions of the relationship between various diseases and body armor.

Figure 5 provides a summary of the relationship among organismic expansion (contact episode), relaxed contraction (withdrawal episode), and anxious contraction (blocked or inhibited contact episode—avoidance).

A final point about psychopathology which I want to make pertains to symptoms. Very often psychopathology is identified and classified on the basis of symptoms. This approach is misleading and usually has little meaning in terms of implications for treatment. What is of greater importance than the symptoms is the underlying process, which I believe is elucidated in a meaningful and useful way in the present chapter. When the process is understood, therapeutic procedures are implied and at times even obvious. The myriad of symptoms arise from the dynamics of "unfinished business." With avoidance the contact/withdrawal cycle is left

Figure 5.   Expansion, Relaxed Contraction,
and Anxious Contraction

Expansion	*Relaxed Contraction*	*Anxious Contraction*
Contact Episode	Withdrawal Episode	Blocked Contact Episode (Avoidance)
Pleasure	Centered quietness	Anxiety
Target has + valence	Target has 0 valence	Target has − valence
Elongation, dilation	Shortening, relaxation	Shrinking, constriction
"Yes"	Disinterest	"No"
Movement toward the world	Withdrawal into the self	Movement away from the world
Peripheral excitation		Peripheral discharge
Central discharge		Central excitation
PANS dominant		SANS dominant
Anabolism dominant		Catabolism dominant
Muscular action	Muscles in relaxed tonus	Muscular armoring

incomplete. The energy does not just go away, and unmet needs do not disappear. The primary impulse in question, when blocked or severely inhibited is diverted into a secondary impulse. As Reich (1973a, p. 294) put it, "The inhibition of the primary impulse produces a secondary impulse and anxiety." Baker (1967, p. xxiv) offers the following elaboration, "Natural strivings, when they pass through armor, change from soft to harsh." It is the natural impulse, thus perverted, which manifests as many of the well-known symptoms. The first task of understanding psychopathology is to see beneath the symptom and recognize what impulse is being blocked and at what point in the contact/withdrawal cycle. The locus of self-interruption reveals which of the four pathological mechanisms or combination of mechanisms is being used. In actual practice, the pathological mechanism is what is first discerned and that implies the locus of self-interruption. The partial stopping of the self-interruption then reveals clearly the content of the blocked or inhibited impulse. The assessment task and therapeutic task will be attended to in later chapters.

4. An Organismic Perspective on Psychotherapy

In making the body a focus in psychotherapy Reich (1949, 1973) looked to the body as both a locus for the assessment of psychopathology and a locus for therapeutic intervention. Some psychotherapists focus on the body, at least at times, for assessment, but don't intervene at the body level. This approach is not fully organismic. A psychotherapy which is truly organismic not only focuses on the body as a way of understanding the person, but actually works with the body therapeutically.

As I conceive of it, therapies which consist only of *patient and therapist* talking have their major impact on the awareness half of the contact episode. Through skillful verbal interventions the therapist can facilitate heightened awareness in the patient. That is, the patients can come to know better what they want, what they feel, how they inhibit their expressions, and why they inhibit in terms of both current, and more importantly, historical reasons. The patients can come to a clearer understanding or insight. Having the insight can be comforting and can point the direction for growthful change. When used skillfully the verbal level of intervention may expose the memory of the events which led to the patient's avoidance or self-interruption of process. At times, the *memory* leads to the experience of the *feeling* which accompanied the event. It is, of course, the reexperiencing of the feeling which is necessary for psychological growth to take place. (The other condition which must accompany the reexperiencing of the feeling will be discussed below.) Sometimes the talking will lead to feelings and then memories, but more frequently the verbal channel runs through memory (thinking) on its route to the feelings. The talking path:

Talking ►Memories (thinking) ►Feelings

The talking sometimes gets mired in the thinking about-talking about memories. One rationale for body work in psychotherapy is that the body

46

intervention more predictably gives access to the feelings. This access is more direct through the body. To quote Reich (1973, p. 301), body intervention offers "the possibility of avoiding, when necessary, the complicated detour via the psychic structure and of breaking through to the affects directly from the somatic attitude. In this way, the repressed affect appears before the corresponding remembrance." The body path:

Body work ►Feeling ►Memory

The rationale for body work presented above is that it provides more direct access to the affects which are connected with the past, the unfinished business. Even more importantly, body work tends to evoke the feelings in their full power. Feelings accessed strictly verbally by the therapist frequently appear in diminished form and often are brought to their full intensity only with great difficulty. There are, of course, some very skillful therapists who readily invite and are met with the patient's feelings in full form. Body work does this with greater reliability. As to the importance of facilitating the reexperiencing of the unprocessed feelings in their full intensity, Reich (1973, p. 316) states, "the effects of a psychic experience are determined not by its content, but by the amount of vegetative energy which is mobilized by this experience."

Further rationale for body work in psychotherapy follows from the point made earlier in the present chapter, that talking between therapist and patient serves primarily the awareness half of the contact/withdrawal cycle. The patient is then left to do the expression of the uncovered emotions on her or his own out in the world. Body work in therapy allows the expression half of the contact/withdrawal cycle to be done in the safety of the psychotherapy setting. The body-oriented therapist can arrange a situation in which it is physically and interpersonally safe to experiment with and practice new expressions, previously avoided. This means allowing organismically appropriate action and interaction in safety so that previously interrupted cycles can be completed to satisfaction. Thus the necessary and sufficient conditions for growth are provided in the therapy situation.

It follows from the previously discussed theory of the contact/withdrawal cycles in healthy functioning and in psychopathology, that the therapeutic task is to restore the spontaneous rhythm of contact and withdrawal. The task of the therapist is to recognize what, where and how the patient is self-interrupting in the contact/withdrawal cycle and to intervene in a manner which facilitates the patient's stopping the self-interruption. The therapist is the facilitator with her or his talking and body interventions, while the patient has the responsibility (response-ability) for growthful change. Ultimately, the patient chooses whether or not to avoid being alive. So, the skillful therapist for the most part tracks the patient in the contact/withdrawal cycles and intervenes at the point of the patient's self-interruptions. During periods of smooth organismic flow, the therapist needs only to be supportively present. But, at times of self-interruption the therapist's skills are called for to frustrate the patient's avoidance. Perls (1973) identified these two tools of the therapist as "support" and "frustration": "the therapist must frustrate those of his patient's expressions which reflect his self-concept, his manipulatory techniques, and his neurotic patterns. He must satisfy those of the patient's expressions that are truly expressions of the patient's self" (Perls, 1973, p. 114).

The obvious question is, how does the therapist support and how does he or she frustrate? Another way of stating this question is, what does the therapist do to intervene? Basically, the therapist has two options, talking and physical contact. So, the therapist can intervene verbally (and with those nonverbal communications which carry communicative meaning) or bodily (touching the patient). And the therapist's verbal and body interventions can be to support an ongoing flow or to frustrate self-interruptions in the patient's process.

The therapist can *talk* to the patient in several important ways, including (1) interpretations (explaining the meaning of a dream or some other symbol, explaining present feelings or behaviors in terms of historical patterns, etc.); (2) reflections (stating phenomenological observations); (3) confrontations (stating what the therapist believes is happening, as in pointing out a probable avoidance); (4) sharing a personal reaction (the therapist shares his emotional response to something the patient has said or done); (5) sharing one's own history, experience, beliefs, values; (6) strategic statements (paradoxical statements, intentional manipulations); and (7) statements of support (encouragement, empathy).

In terms of *body interventions* the therapist, again has several options, including (1) expressive work (the patient carries out the concrete actions and interactions with a symbolic target which allow for satisfaction in a contact/withdrawal cycle. The therapist "directs" the work of this psychodrama and provides appropriate body contact, e.g., holding, rocking, physical resistance); (2) soft techniques (the therapist uses light touch to the patient's body, or places the patient in various postures which have a particular meaning, e.g., fetal posture, spread eagle, standing up straight); and (3) hard techniques (the therapist applies deep pressure or places the patient in stressful positions, e.g. bioenergetics stress postures).

Each of these three major forms of body interventions will be presented in detail in Part III of the present volume.

The artistry of psychotherapy is well served by the wide variety of interventions, both verbal and physical, which are available. Through the person of the therapist these interventions are given life and become the vehicles which carry the relationship between the participants.

In terms of the patient, there are several levels at which he or she may work in response to the therapist's interventions. The first level is "talking about," the level at which the patient relates things to the therapist. This level is the safest level at which to work in that the patient stays at some distance from the material talked about, and usually at some distance from any strong emotional reactions. This also means that this level of work is not very potent. Although, as mentioned in Chapter 1, Perls was rather disparaging of this level of work, referring to it as "mind-fucking," I see it as a valuable option. The "talking-about" is important when caution is in order, as in the initial bringing up of an anxiety-producing issue. "Talking about" is also useful in the initial getting-acquainted between therapist and patient, the presentation of the patient's "story" which gives an overview. The getting-acquainted may be repeated time and again as the patient opens up new areas by which to be known. So when a highly charged issue is first addressed, or when an overview of one' story is wanted, or when there is need for a cognitive framing of expressive work after the work has been done, "talking about" is valuable. "Talking about" is wasteful at those times when it is done in order to avoid experiencing. The term "counseling" seems to me appropriate for this level of work. "Psychotherapy," in contrast may be an appropriate term for the other levels of work where experiential happenings are sought, emotions are elicited and processed.

The next level at which the work can be done is the "fantasy" level. At this level the patient moves from the more emotionally distant "talking about" to imagining, which is a here-and-now experience. With the introduction of fantasy activity, the patient is able to experience the processing of energy in terms of imagined sights, sounds, tastes, smells, as well as imagined actions and interactions. It is this imagining that allows, then, an enhancement of awareness and a safe rehearsal for expression in the interrupted contact/withdrawal cycle. In that the mental images function as elements in a *symbolic reality*, and are happening in the here-and now, the organismic involvement can be dramatic. The psychophysiological experience can be as profound as in the experiencing of a *literal reality*. Put another way, an altered state of consciousness may be involved at this fantasy level of work. The upshot is that working at the fantasy level is more organismically involving, more experiential, and therefore, holds more potential for the patient's growth than "talking about" the same issue. The two major advantages of fantasy work are that awareness can be expanded by virtue of the experiencing of a symbolic reality in the here-and-now, and that expression can be rehearsed and tried out with the safety provided by the symbolic reality, but which would not be guaranteed in literal reality. What I term the fantasy level of work includes a major application of hypnosis and also includes much of what is referred to in the literature as imagery, guided imagery, and guided fantasy. The imagery literature is considerable, not to mention the extensive literature on this application of hypnosis.

If the fantasy is psychodramatically acted out, a profound enhancement is added to the experience. The symbolic reality is further vivified by virtue of concrete use of the musculoskeletal system. So at this third level of work, action and interaction are actualized, not just fantasized and the organism expresses in concrete form. This can allow satisfaction, symbolically. By use of the "enacted fantasy" level of therapy, awareness is further cleared and sharpened. This is because of the reverberating circuits in the contact/withdrawal cycle which were discussed in Chapter 2. The model here is to provide a literally safe situation in which the patient can act out her or his heretofore blocked or inhibited expression, concretely. The concrete action and interaction with a concrete target (person or object) which carries the needed symbolic meaning provides the needed experience for satisfaction. This is a step in finishing unfinished business. By virtue of the musculoskeletal involvement, the *acting* on the symbolic reality, this level of work often brings about a profound altered state of consciousness (Smith, 1975, 1978). Sometimes the extent of musculoskeletal involvement is the use of the vocal apparatus. But the talking, at this level of work, is a "talking to" the symbolic target as opposed to the "talking about" which was discussed above. "Talking to" is organismically involving and emotionally immediate, whereas "talking about" can occur with minimal organismic experience and with great distance from feelings. Usually, however, "talking to" leads to or is concomitant with other musculoskeletal activity. It is this enacted fantasy level of work which is the forte of expressive therapies such as Gestalt and Psychomotor, and for which they are best known. A later chapter will focus on the technical aspects of expressive body work.

The final level of work is "literal activity." At this level concrete action and interaction occur, but with the literal target rather than with a symbolic target. This includes actual engagement by the patient of the person or object with whom or with which satisfying contact has been avoided. This level of work has the obvious advantage of literalness in facilitating the patient's growth and aliveness, but has the disadvantage of being complicated by the reactions of the other person involved. The other person may not cooperate in the patient's processing through the contact/withdrawal cycle, but may thwart that out of his or her own needs and preferences. So literal work has the danger of backfiring by not providing satisfaction, thereby reinforcing the patient's old pattern of avoidance. In such cases the catastrophic expectation has come true. Another disadvantage of literal work less serious in its outcome but frequent in its appearance is the obfuscation of the patient's work by the introduction of the other person's dynamics. This disadvantage is from the perspective of individual therapy, and this disadvantage fades and transforms into the grist for the mills of couples and family therapy as well as group process-oriented group psychotherapy. An obvious limitation of this level is that sometimes the literal target person is not available due to death or some logistical impracticality.

All four of these levels of working are of value, and at any given time one of them will be the level of choice. Even within a particular therapy session any number of these levels may be used as the patient moves in her or his process.

Figure 6 shows in summary form some of the important characteristics of the four levels of working. As one moves down the list from "talking about," to fantasy, enacted fantasy, and to literal activity, there is an increase in the potency of the work. In other words, the levels of work increase in the impact which they have on the patient. The other side of the issue of potency is the issue of safety, so as one moves down the levels there is a decreasing safety. Just as the increase in the "realness" of the experience makes it more potent, this "realness" makes the experience that much more reinforcing of the patient's avoidance if the work is not carried through to a satisfying end. One of the responsibilities of the therapist is to judge at which level of work a patient will be facilitated best at any given moment, considering the two-sided issue of potency/risk. The self-interruption can be addressed at any one of the four levels.

The first two levels are *abstract* in the sense that there is only minimal involvement of the musculoskeletal system. In "talking-about" the focus is on "head stuff." The muscles of the vocal apparatus are used, of course, and there may be meaningful posturing and gesturing. All of these actions, though are in the service of the "talking about," not in the service of experiencing and expressing. At the fantasy level there is the addition of muscular micro-movements as the drama is played out in the patient's head. These muscular micro-movements are well known to psychophysiologists and represent attenuated actions. If these micro-movements are sufficiently exaggerated, the patient would be acting out the fantasy and would be, then, at the next level of work.

By virtue of the heavy musculoskeletal involvement the third and fourth levels of work are *concrete*. The action is not any longer in the abstract, but is now an actual, concrete, observable here-and-now event.

There is also a progression in the use of the target figure for one's energy. At the level of "talking about" the energy is not directed to the target. Instead, the patient tells the therapist about interactions with the

Figure 6.   Levels at Which the Patient Works

Increasing Potency and Decreasing "Safety"	1. Talking about (not directed at a target) 2. Fantasy (Directed at a symbolic target)	Abstract (Minimal musculoskeletal involvement)
	3. Enacted fantasy (Directed at a symbolic target) ("Talking to") 4. Literal activity (Directed at a literal target)	Concrete (Heavy musculoskeletal involvement)

target. In fantasy one directs the energy at a symbolic target, but in the abstract (minimal musculoskeletal involvement). The target remains symbolic at the enacted fantasy level, but with concrete action (heavy musculoskeletal involvement). At the final level, literal activity, energy is directed at a literal target.

The increasing potency as we move down through the four levels of work is a function of the increase of "realness" in dealing with the appropriate target of one's energy. The movement at each successive level is toward more immediacy of contact. The greater immediacy of contact, or "realness" is based on the cumulative effect of three related factors: increasing musculoskeletal involvement (abstract to concrete), increasing focus on the target (not directed at the target, to directed at a symbolic target, to directed at a literal target), and increasing emotional involvement (vegetative-visceral involvement).

Having discussed the therapist's options for intervening, and the levels at which the patient can be worked with, I now want to analyze the task of psychotherapy at its several levels and clarify where the therapeutic options can be applied optimally. I will start with the whole and step by step differentiate that whole into increasingly specific sub-units for clarity.

At its highest and most abstract level the task of psychotherapy is defined in terms of philosophical bias, a notion of what is good or what is valuable in life. My starting point is to see this level as the facilitation of a richness and meaningfulness in the patient's living. The richness and meaningfulness follows directly from the second level, facilitation of self-actualization. That is, as one becomes that which one can be, there is meaning to one's life. There is richness in actualizing potential. This level of viewing psychotherapy is discussed at length in the humanistic and existential therapy literature.

The third level of the task introduces a practical dimension, the beginnings of a guide as to what is to be done in psychotherapy. This level of conceptualization is, stopping the interruptions in the contact/withdrawal cycle. Since the patient's self-interruption is a stopping, the task is to facilitate the patient to stop stopping, or to allow the natural organismic flow to be. I referred to this level earlier in the present chapter when I defined the task of the therapist to be to recognize what, where and how the patient is self-interrupting in the contact/withdrawal cycle and to intervene in a manner which facilitates the patient's stopping the self-interruption.

Since the reason for the self-interruption is the presence of a toxic introject, the therapy task can be viewed at the next level as one of removing toxic introjects.

The previous four levels of conceptualization represent an increasing precision and specificity of the therapy task. The following levels become the guides for what actually to do.

In Chapter 3, I discussed the four pathological mechanisms which in synergistic combination bring about the self-interruption in the contact/withdrawal cycle. The next level of the therapy task branches into four tasks, corresponding to those mechanisms of avoidance. The tasks, then, are to facilitate awareness, facilitate breathing, melt body armor (stop the retroflection of action), and stop the retroflection of interaction. These are, as I see it, the four focal tasks in an organismic psychotherapy.

Facilitating awareness can be specified further by dividing that task into those of clearing confusion and sharpening dulled awareness. Clearing confusion, in turn, further differentiates into reowning projections, externalizing introjections, and separating confluences. These three tasks correspond to the three mechanisms which confuse one's awareness. In the case of sharpening dulled awareness, there are two tasks which correspond to the two mechanisms of dulling. These tasks are stopping deflections and stopping desensitizations.

Seeing the therapy task in terms of this multi-level conceptualization gives a clarity and a useful orientation. With this orientation we can see where the options of therapeutic intervention apply. As I see it, there is an optimal category of intervention for each of the four focal tasks of organismic psychotherapy. That does not mean that other types of interventions would not have some effect, and sometimes other forms of intervention serve as adjuncts. But there is a category of intervention that is optimal and paradigmatic for each of the four tasks.

Awareness is facilitated mainly through the therapist's *verbal interventions*. The patient may work at any of the four patient levels. The exemplary work on awareness involves the patient at the level of enacted fantasy with emphasis on "talking to" a symbolic target. To appreciate the power and elegance of this work I invite the reader to sample Perls'

Figure 7.   **LEVELS OF THE THERAPY TASK**

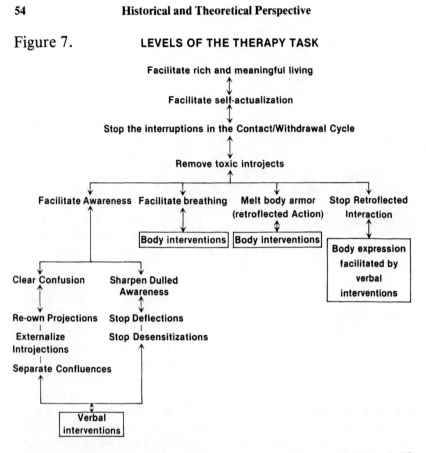

masterfulness as reported in *Gestalt Therapy Verbatim* (1969) and *The Gestalt Approach and Eye Witness to Therapy* (1973).

Facilitating breathing is optimally done by the therapist's direct *body interventions*. There may be effective verbal intervention to support the body work. The patient could be at any of the four patient levels, but often the breathing work is conducted just prior to inviting the patient to the level of enacted fantasy.

In working to *melt body armor* or facilitating the patient to stop retroflecting action, again direct *body interventions* by the therapist are the paradigm. This work is frequently the prelude to the patient's enacted fantasy.

To facilitate the patient to *stop retroflecting interaction* the paradigm is the patient at the level of enacted fantasy and the therapist intervening with *body expression* work. (Body expression is from the therapist's intervention side synonymous with enacted fantasy on the patient's side. The therapist is directive and supportive of the work of the patient using talking and sometimes body contact.)

In summary, the organismic approach in psychotherapy involves somatic interventions as well as organismic methods of assessment. To facilitate the patient in stopping the avoidance of her/his aliveness, it is optimal to deal with the four mechanisms of self-interruption — clouded awareness, inadequate breathing, retroflected action and retroflected interaction — to the extent that each is present. Verbal interventions are best suited to facilitating awareness, direct body contact interventions for facilitating breathing and facilitating the melting of action-blocking armor, and directed body expression work for facilitating the stopping of retroflections of interaction. Figure 7 offers a graphic summary of the levels of the therapy task.

What we are about in organismic psychotherapy is getting the person alive and functioning as a holistic unit. In terms of the contact/withdrawal model of functioning, awareness without expression is not enough. Often psychotherapy gets stuck in over-valuing insight and the patient understands more and more but does not take the action which would lead to satisfaction. Some therapists in reaction to this have gone to the other extreme in their work and have over-emphasized expression, without giving sufficient attention to the development of awareness. These two extremes tend to produce people who are alienated from parts of themselves. The first extreme produces someone alienated from their soma, the second produces someone who doesn't think but acts without the wisdom of awareness. Obviously, neither extreme leads to creative and satisfying living. In therapy there must be a balance between awareness and understanding on the one hand and expression on the other. To guide this balance the therapist must use both verbal and body interventions as appropriate, not either to the exclusion of the other.

Part of the process of facilitating awareness is identifying the toxic introjects and understanding their dynamics in one's current functioning. The work of externalizing and defeating the toxic introject involves the early remembrances of introjection and the feelings which were concomitant. In working, then, the patient is dealing with a nonconcensual reality, a reality for her or him from the past. This procedure is *presentification*, defined by Naranjo (1970, p. 53) as "an inward attempt to identify with or relive past events, or, most often, a reenacting of the scenes with gestural and postural participation as well as verbal exchanges, as in psychodrama." He mentions further that presentification may be of the past, or the future, or of fantasy in general. I draw the distinction between presentification with regression, or *regression* for short, as involving the patient as if at an earlier age, and *presentification* as involving the patient as he or she is at the present literal age (or anticipates being at some later age). The advantage with presentification is that the patient can deal with the historical event with all the wisdom, skills, and power which he or she has accumulated during the extent of her or his literal life. So what may have been overwhelming for the child can now be said or done by the adult in response to the toxic introject.

In both presentification and regression the patient creates a here-and-now experience, feeling the emotion of the historical incident as the incident is remembered and relived. In the case of regression, the patient is encouraged to "go back" to the age at which the incident in question occurred, feeling and being as much as possible that age. (With presentification, on the other hand, the patient brings the past forward in time so that the old incident is relived with the patient being as he or she is now).

Regression is called for when the task is to let the patient gain awareness by reexperiencing how it was to be a child in the historical situation. In this way the patient may get in touch with childhood fear, frustration, deprivation, and so forth. Regression is also appropriate when the task is to give the patient the experience of getting a childhood need met, which in literal childhood was not met adequately. The regressed patient could then experience receiving satisfaction of the need for nurturance, support, protection or limits from a symbolic parent in the form of the therapist (or a group member if the therapy is taking place in a group context). A special case of this is the form of retroflection of interaction in which the patient is doing to herself or himself what she or he would like to have done to her or him. In general, regression is called for when reexperiencing of an earlier age is necessary or desirable for the movement through a block or inhibition.

Organismic growth is through emotional expression where once it was not allowed. The toxic introject becomes irrelevant when the contact/withdrawal rhythm is reestablished and the organism flows with life energy. Awareness is the guide, and emotional expression (action ► interaction ► satisfaction) is the proof of growth. On the psychophysiological level, growth is the giving up of anxious contraction against expansion. It is finding and allowing the natural rhythm between expansion and relaxed contraction.

In the chapters which follow I will cover in more detail the techniques of personality assessment from the body and techniques of therapeutic intervention with the body. I want to make a couple of essential points clear, however, before proceding to technique. First, techniques are of value only as they are brought to life through the person of the therapist. Psychotherapy does not involve an "I-It" relationship, but rather takes place in the context of an "I-Thou" relationship. Whatever "technique" the therapist uses must, in order for it to have impact, be an expression of the person of the therapist. Succinctly put, techniques must be egosyntonic to be effective.

My second point is that all change stems from dissatisfaction (Perls, 1969). What this means is that a person does not make changes, does not want to change unless he or she is dissatisfied with his or her way of being. It is this dissatisfaction which serves as the motivation in psychotherapy, the displeasure which the patient experiences in living. The therapist is a facilitator who then works with the patient to move from unsatisfying to satisfying ways of being.

Part II
The Body as Locus of Personality Assessment

Part II is concerned with a major use of the body in psychotherapy, that of personality assessment. In this part we will explore how the physical activity of the patient can be examined as a way of coming to know that person's way of being in the world. Earlier, in Chapter 3, I presented an organismic perspective on psychopathology. Part II is designed to address the application of that theory.

In Chapter 5, "Communication with the Body," we will look at how the body is presented to the therapist. This is the realm of posture and gesture, an aspect of what has come to be known as nonverbal communication.

Chapter 6 is devoted to how the patient has structured her or his body. The focus is on how one can "read" the patient's personality from the physical structure. Included are the level of phenomenological reading and the level of interpretation. Interpretation is dealt with both from the perspective of nontypology and typology. The nontypology interpretation includes several approaches which I have found useful in clinical practice. In terms of body reading with typology I have focused on Sheldon's somatotyping and the Reichian/bioenergetics reading of character types.

Chapter 7 addresses the methods which can be used to facilitate and enhance the patient's awareness of her or his body. This chapter is concerned with how the patient's body presents information to the patient, and how that information reveals personality dynamics. A variety of specific methods which I have found fruitful are outlined and arranged in a hierarchy of potency.

5. Communication with the Body

In terms of understanding personality functioning via the body, the area which has been researched most extensively and with the greatest scientific rigor is the area of postural and gestural communication. But even prior to the scientific interest in the communicative meaning of posture and gesture, this channel of expression was thoroughly explored by the writers of poetry and prose.

The frequent and detailed descriptions of body positions and gestures which appear in the world's literature bear testimony to the recognized importance of these behaviors in the understanding of man. For centuries authors have devoted great care to the development of postural and gestural portrayals of their subjects so as to create and express the personality of the character. And perhaps of particular significance, is the fact that the author, master of the verbal, chooses to employ her or his skill to attend to the character's nonverbal, as well as verbal expression. It is the postural and gestural portrayal of the character which is largely responsible for inviting the reader to have a visual image of the character. These images of the character give her or him life and extension in space. It is through these carefully worked out descriptions that the author presents the character embodied and thereby concrete.

Further support for the importance of posture and gesture in the understanding of the person is provided by our "lived language." Many of our basic experiences are graphically reflected through body descriptions, including descriptions of posture and gesture. Understanding, then, may follow from this more basic phenomenological description. A few moments' pondering provides a host of phrases which reflect a phenomenological description pressing hard toward understanding. The reader is invited to enter into and thereby experience the following examples. This may be done by enacting each of them with one's own body and reflecting on the body sensations and feelings which accompany each one.

He holds his head high.   He puts his finger on it.
He has a tight jaw.   He meets one with open arms.

He does not hold his head straight.
His head is cocked.
He looks down his nose.
He keeps a stiff upper lip.
He does not look one in the eye.
He is down in the mouth.
He turns away.
He has shifty eyes.
He has a stiff neck.
He sticks his chest out.
His shoulders are stooped.
His arms are outstretched.
He is heavy-handed.
He puts his best foot forward.
He drags his heels (see Griffith, 1966).

He is tight-fisted.
He waved me away.
He is shady.
His shoulders are square.
He stoops low.
He sits tall.
He sits straight.
He is tied up in a knot.
He is backward.
He is forward.
He leans on people.
He wants to sit on it.
He is weak in the knees.
He put his foot down.
He is a high stepper.

And this list could be greatly extended. The point is that our language reveals that at some level we are aware of the communicative meaning of postures and gestures.

In contrast to the author's frequent and long-standing interest in postural and gestural behavior, the scientist, with a few notable exceptions such as Charles Darwin (1898), has been a relatively recent attender to these forms of expression. Darwin's work on the body's expressions in emotional states stands as a classic.

The pioneering work of researchers such as Birdwhistell (1952, 1970), Critchley (1939), Deutsch (1947, 1952), Efron (1941), Hall (1959), James (1932), Krout (1931, 1935a, 1935b), Maranon (1950), Reusch and Kees (1956), and Weiss (1943), however, has led to an impressive burgeoning of research during the last two decades. Postural and gestural behavior, as channels of communication, have become prime targets for a variety of research strategies, as reviewed by Duncan (1969). Further recognition of the importance of postural and gestural communication, in the context of psychotherapy, is attested to by the inclusion of a chapter by Ekman and Friesen (1968) entitled "Nonverbal Behavior in Psychotherapy Research" in Volume III of *Research in Psychotherapy*. Inspiration for much of the research reviewed by Ekman and Friesen probably derived from the writings of practitioners such as Feldman (1959), Fenichel (1945), Ferenczi, Freud, Fromm-Reichmann (1950), Perls (1969), Reich (1949), and Sullivan, all of whom have given attention to kinesic behavior.

A thorough coverage of the research in kinesiology is provided by Harper, Wiens and Matarazzo in *Nonverbal Communication: The State of the Art* (1978).

The American Academy of Psychotherapists acknowledged the relevance and importance of understanding postural and gestural communication in psychotherapy by devoting a special issue of its journal to that topic (*Voices*, 1970, 6). That issue was titled "Unspoken Behavior" and contained contributions by communication experts such as Ray Birdwhistell, Jay Haley, and Albert Scheflen.

Closely related to the psychotherapy literature is the literature concerning "awareness training," or techniques whereby one can gain or regain intimacy with one's body. Some of the techniques used in awareness training involve carefully focused attention to areas of muscular tension, postures and gestures. Sources which contain material on body awareness and postural freeing include such classics as Jacobson's *Progressive Relaxation* (1938), *Anxiety and Tension Control* (1964), and *Biology of Emotion* (1967), and Feldenkrais' *Body and Mature Behavior* (1949), as well as several more recent sources (Lewis and Streitfeld, 1970; Otto and Mann, 1958; Peterson, 1971; Schutz, 1967; 1971; Shatan, 1963; Stevens, 1971). The most detailed statement in this area is that of Charles Brooks (1974). In his *Sensory Awareness*, he presents in depth the work of Charlotte Selver and himself. The care and subtlety of understanding which is presented make this an important work for anyone who wants to know human posture and movement.

In addition to the scientific and professional literature on postural and gestural behavior, this area has had considerable coverage in popular sources. For example, articles have appeared in *Playboy* (Blazer, 1969, "The Language of Legs"; Hall and Hall, 1971, "The Sounds of Silence"), *Picture Magazine* (Parkinson, 1970, "What Does It Mean When You Gesture"), and *My Baby Magazine* (Penn, 1971, "Talk to Your Baby in Body Language"). *Psychology Today*, in addition to publishing articles on nonverbal communication, even marketed a game called "Body Talk." Several popular books on the subject have been published. Noteworthy among them are the "best-seller" by Julius Fast, *Body Language* (1970) and the encyclopedic work of Desmond Morris, *Manwatching*, (1977). Morris' book, subtitled "A Field Guide to Human Behavior" is profusely illustrated, containing 470 photographs and 250 drawings, prints, and diagrams, and is over 300 pages in length. The examples of popular handling of communication with the body could go on and on.

Turning, now, from an overview of the postural and gestural domain, let us look at some more specific and technical aspects of postural and gestural communication.

A number of recent investigations of the relationships among the various channels of communication have demonstrated that nonverbal channels are oftentimes more important than the lexical channel in the expression of emotional meaning (Levitt, 1964; Mehrabian, 1968a;

Shapiro, 1966). In extending this line of research, Mehrabian and Ferris (1967) discovered that *when there is an inconsistency between the emotional tone expressed in the lexical and nonverbal channels, the nonverbal channels may override the lexical one and determine the meaning of the communication.* There have even been attempts at the quantification of the relative strengths of the components of a communication. For example, Mehrabian (1968a) reported in one study that the total impact of a communication was equal to weighted verbal, vocal and facial components, with the respective weightings being .07, .38, and .55.

Consistent with the above concept is Shapiro's (1965) theoretical discussion of "neurotic styles," in which he suggested that any communication can be seen as having both a contentual and a stylistic aspect (this amounts to a special case of G. Allport's [1937] distinction between coping behavior and expressive behavior). Shapiro suggested that if one's purpose is to *understand* a given personality, it is more important to attend to the style than to the content of his communication. In a somewhat different context, psychotherapy, a parallel point is made by a number of writers such as Fromm-Reichman (1950), Kaiser (Fierman, 1965), and Reich (1949). Reich (1949, p. 45), for example, stated, "The how of saying things is as important material for interpretation as is the what the patient says.... Past failures with many cases of neurotic characters have taught us that in these cases the form of the communication is, at least in the beginning, always more important than their content."

By virtue of the complexity of the multi-level, multi-channel communications of humans, the lexical channel serves best for communication of content. Or, as Scheflen (1965, p. 35) stated it, "The interchange of new information ... is largely through speech, while simultaneous regulation of deviancy and pace are generally kinesic." Watzlawick, Beavin, and Jackson (1967, p. 66) explained this situation in terms of the mode of codification involved, "Human beings communicate both digitally and analogically. Digital language has a highly complex and powerful logical syntax but lacks adequate semantics in the field of relationship, while analogic language possesses the semantics but has no adequate syntax for the unambiguous definition of the nature of the relationship." As further elaborated by Mehrabian (1968a, p. 53), "Language ... can be used to communicate almost anything. By comparison, nonverbal behavior is very limited in range. Usually it is used to communicate feelings, likings and preferences, and it customarily reinforces or contradicts the feelings that are communicated verbally. Less often it adds a new dimension of sorts to a verbal message...." In brief, the postural and gestural behaviors help define the style or "how," while the lexical behavior defines the content or the "what" of the communication.

That *posture and gesture are better vehicles for the expression of emotion than are words* is substantiated for the phenomenologist by his experience. This experience is alluded to in our language when we declare that "actions speak louder than words," but is really known only to him who has had a really "moving" experience. Words are about experience, and, by being about, lead to a distantiation from the immediate experience. *Emotion compels action while words about the action may serve as its substitute.*

That nonlexical communication is more primitive than verbal communication, both on a phylogenetic and an ontogenetic dimension (Darwin, 1898; Fossey, 1970; Ruesch and Kees, 1956) is almost a truism, but deserves emphasis for its aid in clarifying at least one aspect of kinesics. "Feedback is learned by the child first in the nonverbal mode, and only later does he become aware of the signifying property of words which then are fitted into this ready-made nonverbal bed (Reusch, 1959, p. 898)." Consistent with this, Needles (1959) has said of gesticulation that it bears all the earmarks of regressive behavior. That is, speech (which is a more recently acquired mode of communication, executed in a circumscribed area) may be augmented or replaced by a more primitive mode of expression which is more diffusely executed. Furthermore, Needles has suggested that gesticulation is most likely to make its appearance at a time when speech is "emotionally charged." This last notion has received rather wide support from clinical observations (Deutsch, 1947; 1952; Mahl, 1966; 1967).

One expression of emotional tone which has received considerable attention in discussions of psychotherapy is rapport, concerning which Scheflin (1965, p. 245) stated, citing research evidence, "the structure we clinically know as rapport shows the same basic elements of posture ... regardless of who the participants are." So once these basic postural attitudes are attended to, it is possible to evaluate rapport.

Of particular fascination is the fact that so much of one's postural and gestural behavior occurs outside awareness, or with only vague awareness. One typically concentrates primary attention on his lexical performance, thus ignoring the position and motions of his body. This situation suggests that kinesic behavior, being relatively less carefully monitored or edited, therefore may be a more accurate index of genuine feeling. For as one pays careful heed to his words, picking and choosing for just the right nuance, he is inattending to his postures and gestures, affording himself opportunity to "live-out-into-his-world" more authentically.

Based upon my own research experience, (Smith, 1972), I believe that the various classes of kinesic behavior arrange themselves along a continuum with respect to the performer's awareness of their "meaningful" occurrence. Going from greatest to least awareness, the classes seem to be

Figure 8.   Levels of Kinesic Behavior

Increasing Awareness and Conscious Control During Ordinary Interpersonal Interactions ↑	Pantomimes
	Gestures
	Non-Pantomime Communicative Gestures
	Information Bearing Movements
	Postures

as follows: pantomimes, nonpantomime communicative gestures, information bearing movements, postures. (These classes will be explained later.)

An impressive array of evidence for such unconscious expression of feeling is afforded by several psychotherapists, perhaps the most explicit being Deutsch, Mahl, Perls, and Reich. Deutsch (1952, p. 199), for instance, states, "Asynchronous postural behavior represents a partial loss of ego control.... The appearance and disappearance of a posture represents, it would seem, the attitude of the ego toward a certain impulse with which the specific movement is associated."

Mahl (1966, 1967) has presented evidence for the nonverbal anticipation of subsequently verbalized material in interviews, and suggests that the temporal delay between the two may be an index of the strength of resistance. The body reveals first, and then, after editing, the material is put into verbal form.

Perls has gone much further in that he does not stop at the point of interpreting a postural or gestural performance, but rather may use the performance as a launching point for the patient's self-exploration. That is, the performance may be called to the patient's attention and he is then invited to exaggerate and thereby magnify the performance. Encouraged to focus on the now magnified performance, the patient is often able to get in touch with a dynamic meaning of his behavior of which he was previously unaware (Levitsky and Perls, 1970; Perls, Hefferline and Goodman, 1951).

Reich (1949) deserves credit for the early exploration of psychomotor defenses, that is, the role of muscle tension in the binding of anxiety. This defensive state of muscle tension exists in Reich's phraseology as the "body armor." One's posturing and gesturing will, of course, be influenced by the pattern of body armor.

The Reichian position has found support and enhancement within other therapeutic orientations as well. A very fine example of this is found in the book by Corlis and Rabe (1969), *Psychotherapy from the Center: A Humanistic View of Change and of Growth*. The authors state, "An impulse impels action and an act is performed through the motion of musculature. If an impulse must be curtailed or interrupted then the musculature will have to implement the curtailment of motion. And if the defense against the impulse becomes habitual then the somatic equivalent must be an habitual, characteristic way of bodily movement. For this reason we can speak of resistances implemented by the musculature. We feel that all resistances are located in the musculature.... Our posture, gait, articulation of movement, our talk, laugh, and tilt of the head all reflect in some way our habitual conflict solutions (p. 64)."

In a consistent vein, Braatoy (1954) demonstrated clinically that habitual postural hypertension helped patients to maintain composure. He referred to this as an "imprisoning of anxiety," thus seeing the habitual posture as an affect-fixing attitude.

I want to focus now on the classification of kinesic behaviors and the meaning which various postures and gestures may convey. I have found that careful classification is extremely helpful in understanding. The array of postural and gestural behaviors is complex and the placement of a grid over this constant flux simplifies the task of understanding greatly. My grid is based on elements drawn from many sources. This classification system can be useful clinically and it is reliable enough to be used in laboratory research (McNatt, 1973; Paulk, 1973; Schlosser, 1977; Smith, 1972).

Birdwhistell (1952) distinguished three subdivisions of kinesics: (1) Prekinesics (the general physiological bases for the study of body motion); (2) Microkinesics (the isolation of kines, or least particles of abstractable body motion); (3) Social Kinesics (the functioning of motion as related to social performance).

Scheflen (1964) has found it convenient to distinguish three hier-archical levels of kinesic behavior — point, position, and presentation. The *point* consists of a head nod, an eye movement, a hand gesture, or any such expressive movement which occurs within the context of a relatively unchanging posture. The *position* includes a sequence of several points and is marked by a gross postural shift involving a major portion of the body. And, finally the *presentation* consists of the totality of the positions of an interaction and is marked by a complete change of location. He also drew attention to three basic postural relations between two persons: (1) *Inclusiveness to noninclusiveness* (legs and arms open or closed to the other); (2) "*Vis-à-vis to parallel*; (3) *Congruence to non-congruence of postures*. In an earlier publication, Scheflen (1963) em-phasized the importance of attending to gestures in a quite detailed manner and to the use of a time-sequence analysis of the kinesic behaviors. By means of tracing the points and positions through time it is possible to do a sequence analysis and to look for shared behaviors between the partners.

Lists of specific movements which have proven to be important are offered by Geller (1968) and by Rosenfeld (1966). Geller, in his rather detailed discussion of movements of the hands and arms, distinguishes "information bearing" movements which may occur whether one is alone or with someone (stretching, scratching, fingertapping, etc.) and "communicative gestures" which comprise a bonafide channel of communication. A subcategory of the "communicative gestures" are the pantomimes, which, within a given culture, carry a more or less universally recognized meaning (smile, head nod, head shake, wave "goodbye," the "fica," etc.).

Several lesser suggestions have been incorporated into the following structure as well: Deutsch (1952) discussed asynchronous postural behavior (poorly coordinated discharge of energy) as an indication of anxiety. Dittman (1962) called attention to frequency of movement in each of four body areas—head, arms and hands, legs and feet, trunk. Hall (1963) suggested a series of useful symbols for shorthand recording of postural and proxemic behaviors. And, finally, Blazer (1966, 1969) discussed empirically derived personality correlates of several preferred leg positions.

Postural and gestural behaviors are, of course, a nonverbal mode of communication, and often are carried out without awareness, or with only partial awareness. Since we all engage in these behaviors, but often are only marginally aware that we do so, it takes a concerted effort to pay careful attention to the movements of the person being observed.

The task of attending to a person's postures and gestures in a detailed fashion at first sounds extremely complex, but a couple of factors reduce this task to a manageable size. First, the human anatomy places certain mechanical limits on one's movements. That is, structural factors serve to delimit the range and type of motion of the various body parts. And secondly, our culture has presented detailed guidelines for permissible posturing and gesturing. Just as one's individual verbal behavior consists of only minor variations on culturally-defined themes (language), so one's individual nonverbal behavior consists of combinations of basic elements inherent in one's culture (nonverbal "language"), or "language community." So, one's postural and gestural behaviors reflect both anatomical and cultural underpinnings.

Within the limitations presented above, what, then, are the possible nonverbal behaviors to which to attend? The first categorical distinction of such behaviors is between postures and gestures. "Posture" refers to the relative arrangement of the various parts of the body, a pose. And, as such, it is static; that is, we move from posture to posture, but pause to rest in a given pose. A "gesture" is a motion of the body, or more frequently, the limbs, which occurs within the context of a given posture.

And now for the *gestures*. As is also the case for postures, certain gestures occur whether one is alone or with others. These sometimes nonsocial and thus, sometimes noncommunicative gestures, may be called "information bearing movements" or more descriptively, "self-manipulations."

Self-manipulations: scratch, lick the lips, adjust glasses, stretch, cough, yawn, pull up one's socks, tap the fingers, tap the feet, swing a leg, adjust clothing, brush back one's hair, etc.

In addition to the self-manipulations, "gesture" includes a bonafide channel of communication, the *communicative gestures*. Most of these gestures concern the arms and hands.

There is an additional type of communicative gesture, the *pantomime*, which carries a nigh-on universal meaning.

Pantomimes: smile, nod the head "yes," shake the head "no," laugh, wink, frown, shrug the shoulders, wave, stick out the tongue, shake the fist, raise the eyebrows, the "fica," etc.

I want to emphasize that a person cannot refrain from postural behavior, but at any given time he or she can refrain from gestural behavior.

Empirical evidence suggest that certain categories of posture and gesture seem to reflect a positive, engaging, or affiliative attitude toward another person. I have termed such behaviors "conjunctive" (Smith, 1972).

Conjunction: (1) "Quasi-courtship" behaviors (Scheflen, 1965; Smith, 1972), e.g. pulling up one's socks, straightening one's necktie, brushing back one's hair, adjusting one's clothing, preening, primping, licking one's lips, and such behaviors, usually performed slowly; (2) Shared gestures (Scheflen, 1963), i.e., people making the same gesture; (3) Inclusive posture (Scheflen, 1964); (4) "Vis-à-vis" postural orientation (Mehrabian, 1958b; 1970; Scheflen, 1964); (5) Congruence between trunk and extremities (Scheflen, 1964); (6) Postural congruence between persons (Scheflen, 1964); (7) Smiling and laughing (Fretz, 1966; Rosenfeld, 1966); (8) Positive head nods (Fretz, 1966; Rosenfeld, 1966); (9) Leaning forward (Fretz, 1966; Mehrabian, 1968b; 1970; Rosenfeld, 1966; Smith, 1972); (10) Frequent gesticulation (Fretz, 1966; Rosenfeld, 1966; Smith, 1972); (11) Eye contact (Mehrabian, 1968b; 1970).

Absence of the above behaviors, or opposite behaviors from these, of course, suggest an attitude which is less positive, or less engaging, or less affiliative. I have termed such behaviors disjunctive. Additional suggestions of *disjunction*: (1) Self-manipulations (Rosenfeld, 1966; Smith, 1972) e.g., stretching, scratching, tapping fingers or feet, yawning, coughing, biting the lips, etc.; (2) Frequent postural shifts (Deutsch, 1947; 1952; Jourard, 1964; Mehrabian, 1968b; Rosenfeld, 1966; Smith, 1972). (Note the difference between manipulations of self which are the disjunctive

behaviors described by Rosenfeld as "self-manipulations," and the manipulations of self which are the conjunctive behaviors described by
Scheflen as "quasi-courtship" behaviors. The latter concerns one's manipulation of his "plumage," i.e., his hair and clothing, in a manner suggestive of preening, whereas the former refers to "nervous fidgeting.")

There are considerations which complicate the above scheme,
however. Mehrabian (1968b) has found that certain of these behaviors are
curvilinearly related to attitudes toward another person. He also has
demonstrated that both relative status and evaluative attitudes toward the
other person affect certain postural and gestural behaviors. Furthermore,
the two groupings above contain several dimensions (positive vs. negative
evaluation of the other, intense vs. nonintense relationship with the other,
engaging vs. nonengaging attitude toward the other, etc.). It is certainly
conceivable that these dimensions may arrange themselves in a manner
other than that listed above, for example a positive but not intense relationship, or a negative but intense relationship. For these reasons and
others, the postural and gestural behaviors listed above cannot be
assigned definite, simple, and universal meanings. They do, however,
serve as guidelines.

The dimensions discussed above which may comprise the conjunc-
tive-disjunctive continuum sound reminiscent of the primary dimensions
of semantic space, i.e., evaluation, activity, and potency (Osgood, Suci,
and Tannebaum, 1957). And, indeed, Mehrabian (1970) has presented
evidence that these three dimensions (evaluation, activity, and potency)
account for the bulk of the variability of the referents of postural and
gestural behavior. Mehrabian's evidence suggests that *increases in positive
evaluation* are denoted by greater postural immediacy (forward lean, eye
contact, direct orientation, etc.), *increases in activity*, by greater gestural
movement, and *increases in potency or status*, by greater postural relaxation.

A further important distinction between two categories of muscular
tensions is drawn by Shatan (1963). Reminiscent of the personality trait —
personality state dichotomy, drawn by personality theorists, Shatan has
called attention to fixed (habitual) postures and attitudes versus transi-
tory tensions (arising from immediate emotional conflicts) which may
result in "slips of the body." These "slips of the body" are inadvertent
affectomotor communications. Shatan's idea is consistent with Darwin's
(1898) view that feeble or repressed emotions are unwittingly expressed
through, slight, involuntary movements.

Understanding kinesic communication is a valuable skill for the psychotherapist allowing her or him a major access to patients' feelings. It
also gives the therapist a channel for expression to the patient, one which
is powerful and more basic than spoken words.

6. Reading the Body

Body reading is based on the concept that *structure is frozen function*. What this means is that a person's physical structure is a statement of that person's psychobiological history and current psychobiological functioning. Think of the physical structure as being molded by the experiences of living. That is a continuous process, with the body structure always evolving as experiences in interacting with the physical and social worlds impact upon it. So, those parts of the body which are used and nourished grow toward their genetic limits. Those parts which are not exercised and nourished do not develop fully, or may atrophy, become diseased, or even stop functioning altogether. The principle here is *if you don't use it, you lose it*. Behind the use, nonuse, or misuse of the body are the organismic decisions made in response to the parental messages given. When these messages are toxic, and have been introjected, the result is nonuse or misuse of the body. Either part of the body becomes deadened, armored, and to some degree out of use, or it will be used in ways which are not natural and biopositive. Certain parts may be damaged by physical trauma, those scars being the physical legacy of the mistreatment from others, the intentional "accidents," the subintentional accidents, and the true accidents which may come from worthy attempts to exceed one's previous limits.

What we can see in a person's physical structure is the current point of evolution of the interaction of a genetic base and the living out of a "body script." The body script consists of all of one's permissions and prohibitions concerning the living of one's body (using, nonusing, misusing).

The task for the therapist in reading a patient's body is to see the physical structure, note the physical phenomena present, and generate hypotheses as to that patient's psychobiological dynamics based on the phenomena seen. Clothing, by its very design, tends to dissimulate body phenomena. Therefore, body reading is more easily done with the patient clad only in underwear or a brief swimsuit. The more skin which is covered and the more attention-getting the fabric used (color, patterns of print), the more difficult the body reading.

Since body reading is almost always uncomfortable for the patient, some preliminary work is helpful. Before doing a body reading, I always explain the theory and rationale, as well as the actual procedure. If the patient seems more than mildly uncomfortable with the reading, I never proceed until that discomfort is allayed. That requires a thorough exploration of the discomfort and whatever therapeutic work to resolve the discomfort. Although I prefer doing a body reading as part of the intake process, strong discomfort in the patient sometimes means waiting for several therapy sessions. On occasion I work with patients who do not get comfortable enough with the body reading procedure to do it until we are so far into therapy that most of the information which would be gained by a body reading has already been revealed. Body reading is most useful as part of the early assessment of the patient and planning of treatment. Secondarily, it serves as a means of assessing therapeutic change.

After explaining the theory and rationale of body reading and having gotten the patient's agreement, I offer the option of proceeding in the present session or doing the reading the following session. This decision obviously intersects with what clothing the patient wants to wear (i.e., underwear or swimsuit). Once we are ready for the reading, I use instructions such as:

> Stand here and relax as much as you can. Breathe comfortably and relax. Let your arms hang to your sides. Now, I am going to look at you from the front, the back, and each side, and just see what I can. I will write down what I see, and then when I am through looking I will share with you what observations I have made. And then, I will try to tie those observations together and come up with some guesses about your psychobiological history and present psychological style. (Pause) Now turn with your back to me. Turn to one side. (Pause) Now the other side. (Pause) Now I'm going to run the back side of my fingers along your skin to see if there is a temperature differential. (Pause) Now we can talk about what I see. You may put your clothes back on if you want to, or you can stay as you are and look in the mirror as I describe what I see in your body.

The next logical question seems to be, what do I look for? This question brings up the styles of body reading. Body reading may be done with or without a typology. I want to describe several levels of body reading, both with and without body/person typologies.

Body reading without a typology includes, at the most basic level, a phenomenological viewing of the patient's body. This means looking carefully at the patient and naively seeing what appears. By naively, I mean without evaluations or interpretations of what is seen. For example, the therapist might see that the patient's left shoulder is held higher than the right, or that the knees are locked, or that the legs are thick relative to the upper body. Such phenomenological observations have value as information which can be given to the patient. As impartial, naive observer, the therapist may see that which the patient has missed, but upon having it called to her or his attention can now see. So, awareness of body has been served. Even more importantly, these phenomenological observations serve as the initial step before moving to the interpretive level of body reading. So, skill at phenomenological observation is basic. First, the phenomena of the body are seen. Then, if one wishes, one can move to the level of interpreting the meaning of those phenomena, that is, hypothesizing elements of the patient's history and current dynamics.

One way of interpreting a body phenomenon is for the therapist to do to her or his own body what the patient is doing, and then experience that. For instance, upon seeing that the patient holds the left shoulder higher than the right, the therapist can elevate her or his left shoulder and see what that is like. The therapist's own experience with the phenomenon in question can be the basis for understanding the meaning for the patient. In the situation where the therapist cannot actually mimic the patient, such as the thick legs relative to upper body, the therapist can imagine that in her or his own body and again experience what that is like. I have labeled these two closely related methods of interpretation "empathic body mimicry," and "fantasized empathic body mimicry," respectively.

The use of intuitive metaphors is another means of interpretation. The intuitive metaphor may pertain to a particular body phenomenon, or to the patient's body as a whole. The body or body part is translated into some metaphor, very often an animal metaphor. The translation is done intuitively, not by any analytic process or deliberate searching for the metaphor. One way to assist the process is to look at the patient's body and take the first association that comes to mind. Sharing the metaphor with the patient usually leads to fruitful discussion of issues for therapy. An interesting variation is to have several people pick a metaphor in response to a particular patient's physical structure and then look for the consensual meaning in the several metaphors. For example, the following metaphors might be offered in response to a patient: a thick oak tree; a stone wall; a big bull. The people offering these metaphors might then give their associations to those images and the emergent meaning can be explored for fit by the patient.

Keleman (1979) has suggested a dimension which I have found to be very useful in finding meaning in body phenomena. He begins with excitement, the basic pulse of life. It is in how we choose to let excitement expand and how we express it or how we choose not to let it expand and not express it that we reveal ourselves.

Keleman (1975) sees expansion as "going public," while withdrawing is "keeping excitement at home." There are breathing styles which correspond to the extremes of expansion and contraction (Keleman, 1975). The overly-expanded person tends toward overexcited breathing, which results in an alkaline state and overreactivity. The overly-contracted person, on the other hand, tends toward tight, restrained breathing. Contracted breathing makes the person stiff and dense and inhibits oxygenation, thereby creating a buildup of carbon dioxide. The resulting acid state can invite vivid fantasy or even delusional thinking.

Upon closer examination, this dimension of how one handles excitement can be differentiated into two "somatic descriptive parameters," to use Keleman's (1981) term. Keleman (1981) refers to the first parameter as "how people form boundaries." One end of the continuum is too much restraint, a boundedness. Such people look tight, constricted, rigid, or compressed. Such a person will be overly restrained, reach out little, and tend to be overly-orderly and overly-restrictive in their living. This over-bounded person curtails excitement. The other end of the continuum is the person with weak boundaries and no restraint. This is the person of impulse. These people have weak and toneless shapes. This person tends to be always active and overdoing. The examples which Keleman (1979) uses for the overbounded and the underbounded person are Laurel and Hardy, respectively.

In reading a body, then, I may look in terms of where the person is located on a continuum from bounded to unbounded. I look for evidence in the physical structure of being too tight, stiff, contained, or of being undertoned, weak, without containment. A tendency to either role suggests to me some guesses as to how that person functions.

In considering how a person tolerates excitation, I think in terms of a continuum from hyperactive to passive. Keleman has used the terms "overcharged" and "undercharged" for this second parameter. The somatic features which reveal an overcharge include constant motion which is nonfunctional in terms of any environmental interaction; jumpiness; hot, flushed skin; and rapid heavy breathing. At the other pole, an undercharge, one might see a stillness; cool, pale skin; and slow, quiet breathing.

A metaphor which I use to understand the relationship between the dimensions of charge and of boundedness is that of an automobile's drive train. The engine provides the charge. An engine may run at a wide range of revolutions per minute, representing an overcharge of produced energy at one extreme to an undercharge at the other. The engine's charge of energy is transmitted to the wheels through a gear box. The gear box "contains" the energy and transmits it in a focused manner. This containment is analogous to boundedness. If the gear ratio is too low for the speed that one wants the car to go, the car is, by analogy, overbounded. If the gear ratio is too high, the car goes too fast—it is underbounded. So, the performance of the car is determined by the interactions of how "charged" the engine is (from idling to racing) and how "bound" the transmitted energy is (from low gear to high gear). Think of a car, engine racing at top speed, with the transmission in low gear. The car moves with power, but very little speed. It can climb a steep grade, but it will not cover much ground before it runs out of fuel. It is not efficient and wastes energy. By analogy, this is a case of being overcharged and overbounded. If, keeping this analogy, the car is undercharged and underbounded (engine idling, transmission in high gear), it will stall easily and will not be able to climb a grade. So, getting started will be difficult, as will situations calling for power. This car will move along on level ground, but when "life" is other than smooth, it will tend to stall out and come to a standstill. I invite the reader to play with this metaphor in order to get a feel for what might be expected with a person when in the situation of various combinations of the levels of charge and boundedness.

Relating these somatic descriptive parameters to the contact/withdrawal model, charge pertains to the development of arousal which can then develop into a specific emotion. It is the level of charge which determines how much energy one has for going about life. Charge is potential for action. Boundedness, on the other hand, pertains to how much of the charge is allowed to manifest in action. Boundedness determines how much charge is allowed to build, how much is contained until the right moment for action.

In terms of the pathological mechanisms discussed earlier (Chapter 3), the natural level of charge can be interfered with by certain breathing patterns. This was discussed a few paragraphs back. Boundedness is a function of muscular condition. With chronic muscular hypertonus, or body armoring, there is an overbounded condition. If the opposite is true, muscular hypotonus, then the person will be underbounded. An optimal level of muscular tonus allows for a spontaneous build up of charge until it is sufficient for the action ►interaction intended, and then a spontaneous expression of that charge.

Figure 9 summarizes some aspects of the interaction of the extremes of level of charge and level of boundedness. Additionally, Keleman (1981) has named several other "somatic descriptive parameters." These include relationship to gravity, patterns of movement and gesture, and the tendency of thought, feeling and action toward organization or disorganization. These have been less useful to me than charge and boundedness.

Another thing to look for in reading a body is the presence of asymmetries. Look for parts of the body which do not seem to go together. These "splits" often reveal important organismic information. Such

Figure 9. Interaction of Charge and Boundedness

	Overbounded	*Underbounded*
Overcharged	High energy held back, with periodic eruptions into action. Irregular rhythm, spurts. "Sprints through life." May "burn out" if the path is long. Gets up early; goes to bed early.	High energy constantly flowing. Regular rhythm. "Life is a marathon run." Doesn't like to rest; goes until he/she drops. Gets up early; goes to bed late.
Undercharged	Low energy; held back. Constant level of low vitality. "Sits life out." Trouble getting started; often doesn't get started. Gets up late; goes to bed early.	Low energy; constantly flowing. "Life is a slow walk." Slow start, gradually fades out; may not finish. Gets up late; goes to bed late.

"splits" in the body have been acknowledged and interpreted by many writers. One such writer, who has done a particularly thorough job, is Dychtwald (1978). He identifies five major body splits: right-left, top-bottom, front-back, head-body, and torso-limbs.

A right-left split can be recognized either by a different appearance of the two sides of the body, or by observing differences in activity on the left and right sides. In looking for structural differences, imagine a midline running down the body and dividing it into a left half and a right half. Then, look for differences. In terms of activity, notice what is done by the right side and what is done by the left side. Dychtwald (1978) noted that the most obvious differences in right and left activity is in the expression of emotions.

In terms of attributing meaning to the right and the left, as they appear in relative development or as they are relatively expressive, important and consistent suggestions can be found in several sources. Jung, Perls, Kurtz, Schutz, Lowen, and Dychtwald, to name a few, all have had something to say about left and right. My summary of this material is in Figure 10. In reading a body, one can hypothesize on the basis of these suggested meanings the relative aliveness, development, and expression of the "left" and of the "right." One can look for structural and kinesic evidence for how the person lives out into the world with the two sides. Several writers have suggested that these right and left meanings prevail regardless of handedness.

The second split, top-bottom, is sometimes referred to as a "segmental

Figure 10.   Meanings of Left and Right

Left	*Right*
Controlled by right hemisphere of the brain (primarily responsible for orientation in space; has a holistic, integrative cognitive style for the purpose of pattern recognition and orientatation; output by expressive movement and gestures, manipulation of objects and drawing; sensory perception; spatial relationships; visual memory; musical perception and expression).	Controlled by left hemisphere of the brain (predominantly involved with logical, analytic thinking; verbal and mathematical thought; output by speech and writing; comprehension of language; association of names with objects; language memory).
"Feminine."	"Masculine."
Yin.	Yang.
Anima.	Animus.
Feelings, emotions, intuition.	Reason, logic, thinking.
Relations with mother.	Relations with father.
Receptive, passive.	Expressive, aggressive.

displacement." On a large scale the person's energy has developed differently between the top segment of the body and the bottom segment. One can recognize segmental displacement by a top half and bottom half which do not seem to go together. One half may seem overblown, built up with an accumulation of static energy. The opposite segment may appear relatively less well-developed, thin, and less alive. There may be differences in skin color and temperature, too, which evidence an unequal energy distribution between the two segments.

Segmental displacement can also be detected by observing the person's kinesic behavior. One segment may appear more active and graceful, more "lived" than the other.

Dychtwald (1978) has suggested that the less alive segment may more frequently be the locus of disease. This seems consistent with Reich's discussions of biopathies resulting from blocks in the flow of orgone. The observation has been made by Kurtz and Prestera (1976) that displacement in men is more often upward (top-heavy) and displacment in women is more often downward (bottom-heavy).

When there is a segmental displacement, the functions which are related to the overdeveloped segment are also exaggerated. Conversely, there will be an impairment of the functions of the underdeveloped,

Figure 11. Meanings of Top Half and Bottom Half

Top-half Functions	*Segmental Displacement Upward*
Social contact (speaking, touching, holding, hitting). Contact with objects (manipulating). Sensory functions (seeing, hearing, smelling, tasting). Breathing (energy charging). Thinking. Public parts (face, hands, etc.).	Overdeveloped in the outgoing, social expressive aspect of life. Difficulty with grounding of energy and with support and stability (may be emotionally labile and impulsive, may be dependent). More an "action" person than a "being" person. Exaggerated hunger for recognition, importance, achievement through action.

Bottom-half Functions	*Segmental Displacement Downward*
Contact with the earth (grounding of energy, rooting, stabilizing, support). Moving about in the world. Sex (energy discharge). Private parts.	More comfort with the grounded, stable, private, homey aspect of life. More a "being" person than an "action" person. Difficulty with taking aggressive action; problem with passivity and inenertia.

undercharged segment. The meanings which can be hypothesized in top-bottom splits are summarized in Figure 11.

An imbalance can also exist between the front side and the back side of a person. There may be a lack of front-back symmetry, suggesting that the psychological qualities corresponding to the two halves may be relatively more or less developed. The front side is, indeed, one's "front." It is this front side that one presents to others and which one is usually more aware of and consciously controlling. So, the front may reflect the social self and the conscious self. The soft emotions – happiness, sadness, loving, longing – are reflected in front side development. The front side is also the side that participates more in nonverbal communication.

In contrast, the back side has more relationship to the private and the unconscious. So, unwanted or socially disapproved feelings may be given bodily encoding on the back side. These are the things which one may hide or put "behind" one. Anger, cruelty, hardness, and hatred may be reflected in the development of the back. (Keep in mind that the "hard" side is as important as the "soft" side. Wholeness comes only with the

Figure 12.   Meanings of Front and Back

Front Side

One's "front."
Social self.
Conscious.
Soft feelings (happy, sad,
    loving, longing, caring).
Communicates more.

Back Side

What one puts "in back."
Private self.
Unconscious.
Hard feelings (anger, hatred,
    assertiveness, drive).
Holds "back" more.

development of both; creative living involves the appropriate use of both, singularly and in combination.) Figure 12 summarizes suggested meanings of the front and back.

Perhaps the most striking in its appearance, and frequent in occurrence is the head-body split. The contrast between the development of the head and face and the body is often overlooked, but when attended to is obvious and suggestive of important meaning. Since the body from the neck down is mostly covered in most situations, it is the head and face which are most social. It is the head and face that are most presented to the world for visual contact. Most people attend much more to the head and face to create the desired impression (hairstyling, cosmetics, shaving, orthodontics, cosmetic surgery, and so forth) than they do to their bodies below the neck. In body reading, look for the relative development, aliveness and attention given to the head and face versus the body below the neck. Meanings of a head-body split can be hypothesized from Figure 13.

The final split is between the torso and the limbs. Look for unequal aliveness and development between these two areas. We can hypothesize a difference to reflect the psychobiological split between "being" (the torso) and "doing" (the limbs). The torso is the core. It is within the torso that the life processes take place. In terms of the contact/withdrawal cycles, withdrawal is into one's core, or body. The limbs are in the service of making contact. As mentioned above in the discussion of the top-bottom split, the legs and feet give support or grounding contact and allow for movement of the organism as a whole toward those people and things in the environment which may provide satisfying contact. The legs and feet may directly make contact in the expression of anger if one chooses to kick. The arms and hands allow for manipulation in the environment — reaching out, pulling in, holding, pushing away, and striking. The arms and hands also play a major role in communication. They make interpersonal contact by means of gesturing.

In expansion of the organism, energy moves from the core to the periphery, from the torso into the limbs. In contraction (either the

Figure 13.   Meanings of Head and Body

Head and Face	*Body*
Social.	Private.
Mask (artificial).	Natural.
More conscious of this part.	Less conscious of this part.
Mind.	Body.
Intellect.	Passion.
Thinking.	Feeling.
Highly developed.	Animal.
Sensing (see, hear, taste, smell).	Intuiting ("gut reactions").
In the clouds.	On the earth.

relaxation of withdrawal or the contraction against expansion which occurs in avoidance) the energy moves back from the limbs and into the torso (periphery to core). The question is, has the expansion or the contraction predominated so as to be reflected in a structural asymmetry, a torso-limbs split. Figure 14 is a summary of the torso-limb relationship.

In addition to recognizing the presence of these major splits, one can look for an asymmetry between any body part and the rest of the body. The meaning can be hypothesized by thinking of the function of that body part and seeing the function as relatively overdeveloped or underdeveloped as reflected by the overdeveloped or underdeveloped structure.

Now I want to shift to *body reading with a typology*. A typology is a system of classification based on certain characteristics. In body reading the presence of certain combinations of structural features can define body types. To the extent that there are psychobiological characteristics which correspond to the body types, then body reading can disclose an organismic syndrome.

The early work on relating physical characteristics and behavior consisted of compiling dictionaries of folk beliefs concerning these relationships. Examples of this approach were offered by Lavater in 1804 and by Gall and Spurzheim in 1809. The next step was to observe carefully and see if, indeed, such relationships between physical characteristics and behavior exist. Such early empirical work and further cataloguing was done by Rostan (1824), Viola (1909), Sigaud (1914), Naccarati (1921), and Kretschmer (1925). Interestingly, the work of these men did not find much of an audience in the United States. Hall and Lindzey (1970) suggest that these "constitutional" theories conflicted with the strong environmentalism of American psychology. They say that since it is commonly accepted that physical characteristics are closely linked to genetic factors, to suggest a relationship between the physical and the psychobiological seems to imply a championing of genetic determinism.

Figure 14.   Meanings of Torso and Limbs

Torso	*Limbs*
Core.	Periphery.
Being.	Doing.
Withdrawal after satisfaction.	Contact for satisfaction.
Contraction.	Expansion.
	Support and motility (legs and feet).
Vegetating.	Manipulation and communication (arms and hands).
Time alone.	Time with others.
Attention on self.	Attention on environment.

Genetic determinism seems at odds with the ideals of American democracy, the Protestant ethic, and the dogma of the self-made man. (The work of Reich and the neo–Reichians on character structure does not support the position of genetic determinism. Instead, physical structure is seen to reflect one's psychobiological history. This will be presented in detail later in the present chapter.)

A brief overview of constitutional psychology will be helpful for putting the characterology of Reich and the neo–Reichians in perspective and appreciating it more fully. By way of definition, Hall and Lindzey (1970, p. 340) say, "the constitutional psychologist is one who looks to the biological substratum of the individual for factors that are important to the explanation of human behavior."

Constitutional views antedate the existence of academic psychology by many centuries. One of the earliest known is that of Hippocrates. He suggested a typology of physique, a temperament typology, and a conception of humors (body fluids) which is consistent with current thinking about the role of endocrine secretions in human behavior. Hippocrates' body typology consisted of two types, the short and thick versus the long and thin. The first type was prone to apoplexy, while the long, thin type was prone to tuberculosis. In terms of temperament, Hippocrates suggested four basic types, the type being determined by which of the four body humors was predominant (Hall and Lindzey, 1970). The two extreme types are the "choleric" and the "melancholic." Between these two extremes are two more moderate types, the "sanguinic" and the "phlegmatic." These types correspond to a predominance of yellow bile, black bile, blood, and phlegm, respectively. (An interesting note is that Pavlov divided his experimental dogs into the four types suggested by Hippocrates, using the terms "excitatory" and "inhibitory" for the extremes, and "lively" and "quiet" for the less extreme or "equilibrated" types. Pavlov believed these four types applied to temperament of animals and man. Furthermore, Adler in 1927 interpreted Hippocrates' four temperament types in light of his "individual psychology." In 1935 Adler introduced his own typology based on two dimensions: degree of activity and level of social interest. Adler's "dominant" or "ruling" type corresponds to the choleric, the "getting" type to the phlegmatic, the "avoiding" type to the melancholic, and the "socially useful" type to the sanguinic. [Wolman, 1960]).

Rostan (1824), in France, suggested a fourfold body typology: digestive, muscular, cerebral, and respiratory. This system included Hippocrates' body types, and added more specificity. Rostan's digestive, muscular, and cerebral types are the core for later body typologies (Hall and Lindzey, 1970).

The Italian anthropologist, Viola (1909), simplified Rostan's system, suggesting three body types. The "microsplanchnic" was characterized by a small body and long limbs, the "macrosplanchnic" by a large body and short limbs, and the "normosplanchnic" was in between (Hall and Lindzey, 1970). Viola introduced a new emphasis in constitutional psychology — careful, objective, standard bodily measurements.

The move toward precision and objectivity in body typing continued with the work of the German psychiatrist, Kretschmer (1925). His method consisted of having the subject stand nude in front of the investigator while the latter filled out an elaborate checklist consisting of descriptive phrases for each of the major parts of the body. This was a very systematic and painstaking procedure. A complex analysis of these ratings and objective measurements yielded three basic body types. The first is a frail, linear physique, the "asthenic." The second is muscular and vigorous, the "athletic." And third is the "pyknic," the plump type. Kretschmer added a fourth type to cover unusual body structures which are "rare, surprising, and ugly." This he called the "dysplastic." From a study of 260 psychotic patients, Kretschmer concluded that there is a "clear biological affinity" between the pyknic type and manic-depressive psychosis and between the asthenic, athletic, certain dysplastic body types and schizophrenia. Kretschmer viewed psychotic and normal on a continuum, so he spoke of degrees of these dimensions as follows: (normal) schizothymic-schizoid-schizophrenia, and (normal) cyclothymic-cycloid-manic depressive. In keeping with this view of a continuum from normal to psychotic, Kretschmer believed there is a relationship between body type and behavior in normal persons (Hall and Lindzey, 1970).

The person who developed this line of theorizing and investigation to a level of high achievement was William Sheldon (1940, 1942, 1949, 1954, 1969). His constitutional psychology is complex, but for our purposes here I will present a brief overview. If you want more detail, I refer you to

Hall and Lindzey (1970) or to Sheldon's own writings which I have referenced above.

In Sheldon's view there is a "morphogenotype" or hypothetical biological structure underlying the "phenotype" or observable physique. The morphogenotype plays a key role both in determining the development of physical structure and in influencing behavior. By measuring the phenotype an indirect assessment is made of the morphogenotype. The measurements identify a "somatotype."

Somatotypes were first identified by means of the "Somatotype Performance Test" (Sheldon, 1954). This consisted of photographing the subject in a standard posture from the front, the rear, and the side before a standard background. A careful analysis of 4,000 photographs revealed three primary components of physique. Each body type represents, then, some combination of degrees of each component.

The first component of physique is *endomorphy*. A person high in endomorphy and low in the other two components is characterized by softness and a spherical appearance. There will be an underdevelopment of bone and muscle and a low surface-mass ratio (thus, the person has a low specific gravity and therefore will float high in water). The digestive viscera, derived from the endodermal embryonic layer, are highly developed. So, the vegetative system is predominant and this person puts on weight easily. This person depends on the digestive organ system in dealing with the world.

Mesomorphy is the second component. When this component is heavily predominant, the person is hard and rectangular, having well-developed bone and muscle. Such a person tends to be strong, tough, and equipped for strenuous physical activity. Bone and muscle have derived primarily from the mesodermal embryonic layer. Their skin tends to be thick. They tend to deal with the world through the motor organ system.

The third component is *ectomorphy*. When a person is high in ectomorphy and low in the other components, he or she will be linear and fragile, characterized by a flatness of the chest and an overall delicacy. Being thin and light of muscle, the ectomorphic person shows a dominance of mass over surface. Because of their proportionately large surface area they are easily overexposed to stimulation from the environment. They are not well-equipped for strenous physical activity. The brain and nervous system, derived from the ectodermal embryonic layer, are large and well-developed. They depend most on the sensory organ system for dealing with the world.

Sheldon developed a method of deriving somatotypes by using seventeen anthropometric measurements which could be taken either from the subject or from a photograph. The measurements were expressed as ratios to the person's height. This resulted in a score of one to seven on each of the components. Thus, a somatotype score contains information as to the extent (from a minimum of one to a maximum of seven) to which each of the primary components of physique is present in a specific phenotype. In addition, Sheldon has provided a system for rating each of the three components for five specific body areas: head-neck, chest-trunk, arms, stomach-trunk, and legs.

In actual practice somatotypes can be derived by knowing the subject's height, weight, and age and then entering tables prepared by Sheldon (1954). The subject's height is divided by the cube root of his weight and the tables entered by age groups. Additionally, photographs are given for various somatotypes with the derived score to allow visual comparison and placement. Sheldon also has provided a completely actuarial method of somatotyping, based on three objectively measured variables: height, ponderal index (height divided by cube root of weight), and trunk index (ratio of upper torso to lower torso).

The somatotype, then, is expressed by three numerals from one to seven with the first numeral referring to endomorphy, the second to mesomorphy, and the third to ectomorphy. For example, a rating of 1-7-1 represents a person with an extremely mesomorphic physique, having a minimum of endomorphy and of ectomorphy. A 4-4-4 would be balanced with an average amount of each of the three primary components.

Sheldon suggested several secondary components of physique which allow for a more complete description. One of these, *dysplasia*, he borrowed from Kretschmer. Dysplasia refers to an inconsistency in the mixture of the three components in different body regions. It is calculated by taking somatotype ratings for the five regions of the body and then summing the differences for each component among the five regions. A dysplasia score can be derived for each of the three components as well as a total score. It has been found that there is more dysplasia associated with the ectomorphic component than with either of the other two primary components, more dysplasia with female physiques than male physiques, and more dysplasia mong psychotics than among college students (Hall and Lindzey, 1970).

Another secondary component of physique is *gynandromorphy*, also referred to as the "g index." This index is related to the extent to which a physique possesses characteristics which are usually associated with the opposite sex. The range is from one, no sign of the opposite sex characteristics, to seven, hermaphroditism. Examples of gynandromorphy in the male include softness of the body, wide pelvis, large hips, long eyelashes, and small facial features. Sheldon has distinguished primary gynandromorphy which can be seen in a photograph and secondary gynandromorphy which is inferred from direct examination, including facial expression, voice quality, and kinesic behavior.

The *textural aspect* is seen by Sheldon as perhaps the most important of the secondary components of physique. It is also the most subjective to rate, being essentially an index of esthetic pleasingness. It is a dimension of coarseness to fineness, and Sheldon likens the person high on the t index to a purebred animal, fine featured and pleasing to look at. Primary t can be observed from a photograph, whereas secondary t is inferred from close examination. Sheldon (1954) offered illustrations of somatotypes rated between one to six on the g index and the t index. No "perfect seven" had been observed.

Similar to the manner in which Sheldon derived the primary components of physiques, he also derived primary components of temperament. Starting with 650 human traits which he found in the literature on personality, Sheldon reduced the number to 50 by eliminating apparent overlap. He then had subjects rated on a seven-point scale for each of the 50 traits as they were observed in their daily routines. A correlational analysis of these ratings revealed three main clusters of traits. Sheldon then added new traits to each cluster and again performed a correlational analysis. From this he finally selected traits which define three primary components of temperament.

Termed *viscerotonia*, the first component involves a general love of comfort, sociability, and gluttony for food, company, affection, and social support. Assimilation and conservation of energy are primary. Viscerotonia is characterized by relaxed posture and movement, slow reactions, even flow of emotions, toleration of others, complacency, extraversion, deep sleep, orientation toward childhood and family.

The second component is *somatotonia*, characterized by assertiveness of posture and movement and desire for muscular activity. Action and power are primary. Somatotonia involves love of physical adventure, risk-taking, courageousness, loud voice, aggressiveness, ruthlessness and callousness toward others, overmaturity of appearance, extraversion, need for action when troubled, and an orientation toward youthful goals and activities.

Cerebrotonia, the third component, involves restraint in posture and movement, inhibition of both viscerotonic and somatotonic expression, and overconsciousness. Avoidance of overstimulation, and hence, concealment are primary. Cerebrotonia is characterized by self-consciousness, secretiveness, fearfulness of people, youthful appearance, overly-quick reactions, poor sleep patterns and chronic fatigue, preference for solitude when troubled, introversion, vocal restraint, physiological overresponse, love of privacy, mental overintensity, agoraphobia, resistance to habit, unpredictability of attitude, hypersensitivity to pain, and orientation toward the later periods of life.

Sheldon (1942) has presented the scale for temperament, containing

20 defining traits for each of the three primary components of temperament. This scale can be used for rating a person on viscerotonia, somatotonia, and cerebrotonia.

Considerable research by Sheldon and his colleagues has shown a strong relationship between the primary components of physique (structure) and the primary components of temperament (function). Endomorphy and viscerotonia are related, as are mesomorphy and somatotonia, and ectomorphy and cerebrotonia. Sheldon (1949) has presented an intricate and fascinating "psychiatric index" in which he interprets psychiatric categories in terms of interactions of the overpresence and underpresence of the primary components of physique/temperament.

The work of Sheldon and his collaborators is thorough and methodologically respectable (Hall and Lindzey, 1970). His orientation was that of a scientist, a careful research of personality, or more specifically, constitutional psychology. His work represents the paragon achievement of the constitutional psychologists.

In terms of clinical use, Sheldon's methods may be too time- consuming. His findings, however, lend themselves to the artistry of body reading. The task is to look at the patient's body and estimate the relative components of endomorphy, mesomorphy, and ectomorphy. From these estimates one can then predict the corresponding presence of viscerotonia, somatotonia, and cerebrotonia. One can then hypothesize those traits which Sheldon found to correspond to those components of temperament. In addition, one can be alerted to the secondary components of physique (dysplasia, gynandromorphy, and the textural aspect) and when seen in a remarkable degree, one can hypothesize what factors in the patient's psychobiological history may have contributed to that structural feature and how might that structural feature be manifested in current psychobiological functioning.

Because of the relationships which Sheldon demonstrated between somatotypes and temperament, I can speculate about how somatotypes might relate to functioning in contact/withdrawal cycles. Viscerotonia involves "indiscriminate amiability," sociophilia under the influence of alcohol, extraversion of viscerotonia, greed for affection and for approval, liking of polite ceremony, and a need for people when troubled (Sheldon, 1942). If viscerotonia is extreme, and not balanced by the other primary components of temperament, we have the picture of a person wanting an incredible amount of contact. This is consistent with what Karen Horney (1945) identified as the neurotic need for "movement toward people." This was one of the three neurotic solutions which she saw in people to the problem of feeling isolated and helpless. Such a solution or strategy may assume the character of a drive for that person when under stress. In viscerotonia, then, we can expect a movement

Figure 15.   Summary of Constitutional Psychologies

Theorist	*Body Typology*	*Correlates*
Hippocrates	Short and thick body.	Prone to apoplexy.
	Long and thin body.	Prone to tuberculosis.
Rostan (1824)	Digestive type.	
	Muscular type.	
	Cerebral type.	
	Respiratory type.	
Viola (1909)	Microsplanchnic (small body, long limbs).	
	Macrosplanchnic (large body, short limbs).	
	Normosplanchnic (in between).	
Kretschmar (1925)	Pyknic (plump).	Affinity with manic-depressive psychosis.
	Athletic (muscular, vigorous).	
	Asthenic (frail, linear).	Affinity with schizophrenia.
	Dysplastic (rare, surprising, ugly).	
Sheldon (1940, 1942, 1949, 1954, 1969)	Endomorphy (soft and spherical).	Viscerotonia (assimilation and conservation of energy primary).
	Mesomorphy (hard and rectangular).	Somatotonia (action and power primary).
	Ectomorphy (linear and fragile).	Cerebrotonia (avoidance of overstimulation primary).

toward people for nurturance and support. I predict that in the contact/ withdrawal cycle the person who is highly viscerotonic will be able to flow through the contact episode (both awareness and expression halves), but not flow easily into the withdrawal episode. Such a person gets stuck at the point of satisfaction, being of great appetite. Others may find them draining and overstaying their welcome. This is the extreme endomorph.

In the case of extreme and unbalanced somatotonia, corresponding to the extreme and unbalanced mesomorphic physique, we would expect a "movement against people," to use Horney's term. This expectation is a summary term for what Sheldon (1942) found in the somatotonic temperament: love of dominating, bold and direct manner, competitive aggressiveness, callousness, ruthlessness, extraversion of somatotonia, assertiveness and aggression under the influence of alcohol, and need for action when troubled. I predict from this that the mesomorphic person flows well with the expression half of the contact episode and with the withdrawal episode. Her or his major trouble spot is with awareness. The problem for her or him is probably going to come most often from impulsive action, from not pausing long enough to allow awareness to develop and guide the expression. An expanded awareness would often tell this person that the action►interaction about to be taken is ruthless, uncaring, or callous, and ultimately is not in her or his best interest. But, too late. The expression is done and the person is already gone, leaving someone else feeling perhaps used or defeated, hopefully only frustrated. Movement against people is power-oriented.

The extreme ectomorph with corresponding cerebrotonia needs solitude when troubled. Sheldon (1942) also characterizes cerebrotonia as follows: love of privacy, secretiveness of feeling, sociophobia, introversion, and inhibited social address. This fits with Horney's third neurotic solution, "movement away from people." From this it seems like an obvious prediction that the extreme ectomorph is highly competent at the execution of the withdrawal episode. Additionally, though, Sheldon (1942) relates "mental overintensity," physiological overresponse, and hyperattentionality to cerebrotonia. So, the awareness half of the contact episode is also known territory. The extreme ectomorph, I predict, will tend to stay with awareness and withdrawal, being weak in the expression half of the contact episode.

Once again, as this discussion implies, creativity and richness of living come with wholeness and balance. With imbalance and incompleteness, there is a loss. Full satisfaction will not be experienced in any of the three imbalanced styles of life discussed above. Whether it is the endomorph's difficulty in withdrawing, the mesomorph's ruthless, awareness-deficient expression, or the ectomorph's restrained and inhibited expression, satisfaction will be partial at best. Under stress we

Figure 16.   Effects of Somatotype Imbalance
               on the Contact/Withdrawal Cycle

Balanced Type: Awareness ———————→ Expression
                                        ↑└———— Withdrawal ←———┘

Endomorphic Emphasis: Awareness ←———————→ Expression
(deficiency in withdrawal)
                                              Withdrawal

Mesomorphic Emphasis: Awareness   ┌———————→ Expression
(deficiency in Awareness)   │   │
                                              Withdrawal ←————————┘

Ectomorphic Emphasis: Awareness ————————┐   Expression
(deficiency in Expression)   ↑   │
                                       └———— Withdrawal

could expect that the manifestation of the imbalance would be more in evidence. Figure 16 is a summary.

Although not widely known even among clinicians, the system of body reading which has had the largest audience is that presented by Alexander Lowen (1971, 1975). This system is based on the work of Reich and is an elaboration of the observations Reich (1949) made concerning the pattern of body armoring found in the various character types. Being a clinical, diagnostic tool, rather than a precise laboratory tool, the Reich/Lowen system of reading character from the body is not based on body measurements. In this respect, it differs from Sheldon's somatotyping.

Unlike Sheldon's theory of somatotypes, the Reich/Lowen theory of character is not based on a genetic determinism. Instead, character is seen as developing from the early life experiences. The correlated body structure is a reflection of how the body has been used, not used, or misused as part of those experiences. To quote Lowen (1974, p. 3), "The character structure, seen both psychologically and physically, ... is regarded as representing a relatively fixed pattern of behavior determined by a given set of experiences in childhood."

In Chapter 1, I mentioned that Reich and Lowen differed slightly in their approach to body reading. In the Reichian approach the emphasis is on discovering the core armoring and thereby inferring the character style of the patient. Lowen, on the other hand, tends to observe the overall body structure and from that discover the character style.

To begin, I want to look at the Reichian approach as explained very nicely by Baker (1967). Character development depends on the degree of fixation at the various erogenous levels. Manifested on the somatic plane, character development depends on the degree of armoring in each of the erogenous zones. Symptoms "characteristic" of these levels are present when there is an energy block at an erogenous zone. Most people have a major block at one of the erogenous levels of development, with lesser blocking at some other level or levels. This means that muscular armor is greatest in one particular erogenous zone, with a lesser degree of armor in other erogenous zones in most people. There is usually armoring in other parts of the body (nonerogenous zones), as well, but as Baker (1967, p. 113) emphasizes, "it is *only* the armoring in the erogenous zones that determines the character type." The armoring in the nonerogenous zones creates the individual differences within a character type.

Baker (1967) speaks of four major erogenous zones, each one representing a stage of development. The zones are the eyes, mouth, anus, and genital, with the stages of development being the ocular, oral, anal, phallic and genital (the phallic stage actually being an early or incomplete phase of genitality). Note that the erogenous zones are located at the cranial and caudal extremes of the body, where contact with the environment is most important. One of the cranial pair, the mouth, and one of the caudal pair, the genital, allow superimposition with another person and are capable of initiating the orgastic convulsion (the mouth in the case of the infant and the genital in the adult). Development takes place from the cranial extreme (the eyes) down through the four zones to the genital. Therefore, the ocular, oral, anal, and phallic stages are referred to as pregenital.

In normal development each stage takes its turn as a primary focus of energy, and after the person's development has led to the next stage, the earlier zones remain important in the experience of pleasure. If, however, the person is traumatized at a particular stage, there will be a block or armoring at that erogenous zone. This arrest in development prevents the reaching of genitality and therefore prevents the person from access to full genital energy processing. The accumulation of energy at a pregenital erogenous zone produces clincial symptoms.

Baker (1967) goes on to say that an emotional trauma at any stage may have either of two results: (1) repression; or (2) lasting unsatisfaction. With repression the person never develops pleasurable functioning at that stage, never learns to enjoy the use of that erogenous zone. In the case of unsatisfaction, the person is insatiable, constantly trying to obtain the once-known satisfaction. In repression there is a more complete armoring than there is in the case of lasting unsatisfaction. In

Figure 17.   Character Types —
                 Repressed and Unsatisfied

Character Type (Developmental Stage)	Primary Armoring	Repressed Form	Unsatisfied Form
Ocular	Ocular segment	Confusion (doesn't "see")	Voyeurism
Oral	Oral segment	Depression	Overindulgence
Anal	Pelvic segment (especially posterior)	Restraint	Submission
Phallic	Pelvic segment (especially anterior)	Righteousness	Don Juanism
Genital	Pelvic segment	Flight or freezing	Frantic behavior

this latter case the striving is felt, but the armoring prevents sufficient expression to bring full satisfaction. The result is an almost constant urge for expression.

By means of recognizing the locus of heaviest armoring, one can identify the ocular, oral, anal, phallic, and genital characters. The recognition of armoring has been covered earlier in this chapter. In addition to reading the armoring by seeing or touching, one can ask for the patient's reports of symptoms which may then provide a convergence of evidence for the armoring. Where are the aches, pains, diseases, and malfunctions? When such phenomena involve erogenous zones they provide evidence for the character type. I have summarized this material from Baker (1967) in Figure 17.

From this schema of five basic character types, Baker (1967) delineates several specific syndromes within each. These syndromes, some of which correspond to traditional diagnostic categories, are based on the patterning of armoring in erogenous and nonerogenous zones secondary to the primary armoring of an erogenous zone by which the basic character type is defined. For a wealth of detailed discussion, I refer you, if interested, to *Man in the Trap* (Baker, 1967).

Let us turn now to Lowen and see how he developed Reich's reading of character from the body. The idea of character, briefly stated, developed as follows. In 1908, Freud wrote an essay, "Character and Anal Erotism," in which he pointed out the relationship between anal erotism and three traits which were often found in conjunction: orderliness, obstinacy, and parsimony. He postulated the idea of "character structure" from this, and saw it as based on the psychosexual stages of development:

oral, anal, phallic, latent, and genital. This line of thought was extended by Abraham in 1921 in a paper on anal character structure and its relationship to childhood experiences. Abraham offered theoretical treatments of the oral and genital character structures in 1924 and 1925. Although the psychoanalytic literature contained references to other character types (compulsive, hysterical, and masochistic), no integrated framework was presented. Interestingly, Freud moved in a different direction with his discussion of character types in 1931, identifying character with his structural theory of the psyche rather than with the pyschosexual stages of development and their respective erogenous zones. The schema was Erotic type (dominance of the id), Narcissistic type (dominance of the ego), and the Compulsive Type (dominance of the superego).

By 1933 Reich (1949) had written of several neurotic character types — hysterical, compulsive, phallic-narcissistic, masochistic, passive-feminine, and depressive — and a healthy type, the genital character. As discussed above, Baker wrote of ocular, oral, anal, phallic, and genital types of character structure. (In addition, Baker [1967] wrote at length about three "socio-political" character types. This writing is beyond the scope of what I want to cover here, however.)

Lowen (1971, 1974, 1975) did a great deal to systemize as well as to elaborate upon the theory of character. And with this, he defined the character types in terms of visible physical structure. As of 1971, (first published in 1958) Lowen wrote of the following character types: the oral, masochistic, hysterical, phallic-narcissistic, passive-feminine, schizophrenic, and schizoid. By 1974 he had brought further systematization to the study of character by defining five major character types and their relationships.

A "character" is a hypothetical syndrome. No one is a pure character type, but rather each person has elements of the various types. What we are looking for is which character type is dominant and which other type or types are secondary in a person's dynamics.

The five character types are in a developmental sequence in their etiology. The earliest type is the schizoid, then the oral, the psychopath, the masochist, and then the rigid types. The type of character developed depends on the stage of development at which the child is traumatized. If the trauma is relatively early, then the probability is that the person will have difficulty developing through the successive stages as well. Therefore, the character types are in descending order of complexity, as there will be a partial adding of type to type the earlier the initial trauma. Also, as one moves up higher in the developmental sequence of the character types, there is greater variety in the syndrome, since more personality differentiation has taken place prior to the trauma. By the time the rigid types are reached there has been a sexual differentiation, so the rigid type breaks down into male forms (phallic-narcissistic and compulsive) and a female form (hysteric).

The earliest character type is the *schizoid*. The trauma involved is feeling rejected, not welcome in the world. This rejection can be by the mother while the child is still in utero, perhaps. Certainly, the feeling of rejection can come during the first few months, largely from the mother, and either be reinforced or mitigated by the larger environment in which the infant is placed. The infant by being rejected is punished just for existing, and therefore begins to hold in all feelings, bind all energy. The schizoid is afraid of any expansion into the world; he or she is "antilife." Reality testing is not well-developed. And, not feeling welcome here, the schizoid is often away in a fantasy world. The real world is terrifying and to be avoided. Schizophrenia is the extreme of the schizoid character type. In terms of reading schizoid character in the body, the primary armoring is in the ocular segment. The eyes may seem weird, unexpressive, vacant, and it may appear that the schizoid is looking through you rather than at you. Often, there is tension along the ridge just below the occiput. This may extend as a band of tension around the head and through the eyes. Secondary to this armoring of the ocular segment there are several other bodily features common in the schizoid. The whole body may seem tense, with stiffness at the joints. This tight body, because of constant joint tension, may go off at angles. The head, especially, may be held angled to the side. The body may seem poorly coordinated. The facial expression may be cold with lips which are not full or sensuous. Energy will tend to be low in the face, hands, feet, and genitals. Sometimes the schizoid has an evil look and even an evil-sounding laugh. The top and bottom half of the body may look like they don't go together.

Developmentally, the next character type is the *oral*. For the oral character the trauma is deprivation and what is threatened is the right to feel secure. So he or she is afraid to have needs. The paradigm for the creation of the oral character is the child, hungry for food and contact, left crying alone until it finally gives up. The decision which the child makes is that needs are dangerous because they don't get met, and no one will be there for her or him. The result is that oral types have an issue around nurturance and support. They have a deep desire to cling, hold on, and be propped up. But, as much holding, cuddling, nurturance as they get, it is never enough because it is not taken in fully. The oral character usually has some form of eating disturbance and may have gastro-intestinal problems. Strong disappointment reactions are common and a sensitivity to feeling unloved is frequent. So oral characters have difficulty in asking for things. Clinical depression is pathognomonic of orality. Often the oral person is pale and thin and looks immature. The need for support and concomitant feelings of weakness is often evident in the oral character's locked knees and their narrow feet. Frequently the feet are flat. The head is often tilted forward, the chest collapsed, the belly soft and protruding. The overall picture is of an undercharged, collapsed body being propped up. The musculature is underdeveloped. There may be an appealing look for support in the eyes. The male often has reduced body hair and the female sometimes has overdeveloped breasts. Along with the thin, collapsed chest, there is often a characteristic indentation at the lower end of the body of the sternum. The oral apparatus itself may be characterized by full lips and a "reaching" mouth. The skin is often thin and easily bruised.

The *psychopath* is the next character type. The trauma involved here is being overpowered, overwhelmed, being made to feel weak and small. It is the child's right to be free which is threatened. So power is the issue. The child was required to hold onto feelings to keep from being enslaved. As a result the psychopath has a need to dominate and control. Feelings are denied. And, the psychopath has a great investment in her or his image. The mother has been covertly seductive in order to tie the child to her. The psychopath has learned, then, that sexuality is a realm for competition and power plays. So, the psychopath tends to be sadistic, using sex as an expression of power. The psychopath is in some ways a vague type, containing both some oral elements and some masochistic elements (the developmentally next character type). The psychopath expects that people are trying to control them and do not respect them. So, the psychopath denies her or his feelings and keeps cool. The psychopath rarely gets angry. He or she is heavily invested in an image of powerfulness and invulnerability. There are actually two types of psychopath: (1) the "bully" who overpowers others, ignores their feelings, and is opportunistic; and (2) the "seducer" who is gentle, overly-polite, and cunning, a real charmer who undermines others for control. In terms of physical structure, the bully often has penetrating, distrustful eyes. There will be tension along the base of the skull. The diaphragm is constricted. But most telling is the segmental displacement upward, the upper half of the body looking blown up, inflated. The seducer has a hyperflexible back and a highly charged, but disconnected pelvis. The diaphragm will be spastic. And, of course, her or his eyes will be soft and seductive, as will her or his voice.

Developmentally, the next character type is the *masochist*. The trauma involved is having love be conditional on obedience so that the child's right to be independent is violated. The paradigm is an overbearing mother who does not allow the child to be free and spontaneous. The child feels pushed and nagged and the mother teaches the child to feel guilty if he or she disobeys. The father, at the same time, is passive and submissive. This process begins during the second year and reaches full development after puberty. The result is a person who outwardly is submissive, but inwardly has repressed spite and rage. The masochist suffers, complains, whines, and stays submissive. He or she is self-effacing, but secretly feels superior. The masochist is limited in self-assertion and has difficulty being aggressive. The result is an almost constant sense of being under pressure and feeling anxious. Frequent collapses into a morass can be expected. The male may masturbate by squeezing of the penis. The masochist is usually hardworking. There is frequently an awkwardness about her or his behavior. Since the masochist is programmed to experience almost everything as a push, he or she is ready to resist, ready to say with her or his behavior, "I won't!" This can be recognized as a character trait of negativity. The masochist is also prone to get people angry with her or him and to feed on this energy. Their own energy is so bound, that to get beat on a little gives a sense of relief, a sense of being energized. And, masochists are usually quite skilled at defeating others in their attempts to help them. Physically, the masochist has a gorilla-like appearance. Included are thick, powerful muscles; a short, compressed body; increased body hair, a flat rear; a rounded back; a short, thick neck; and overdevelopment of the calves and front of the thighs. The hamstrings tend to be tight. Often the facial expression is innocent or naive, with soft, sad eyes showing the look of suffering. The voice of the masochist is often whining.

The last character type developmentally, is the *rigid* type. Since the trauma creating a rigid character structure occurs after sexual identity is set, there are female and male forms. The rigid character is a genital type, as opposed to the schizoid, oral, psychopathic, and masochistic types which are pregenital. Whereas the mother is the central figure in the trauma of the pregenital types, the father plays the major role in the formation of the rigid character. The trauma involved is the father's rejection of the child's love. The father rejects affection and in some way pushes the child away. The conflict is freedom versus wanting and loving. The message to the male child is "you're not good enough." The father makes his love contingent upon performance, and whatever the child does, he doesn't quite meet the standard. So the male child believes he has to perform and he gives up on reaching out in order not to be frustrated and hurt anymore. Under pressure the rigid male is prone to action. He wants structure and is attuned to the details. So the rigid male often seems self-confident, perhaps arrogant, and impressive in his action orientation. He will be ambitious and competitive, experiencing passivity as vulnerability. Inflexible, and determined, he may overwork in his striving for achievement or even perfection. There are two styles of the rigid male, both stiff with pride. The *phallic-narcissistic* tends to identify with the father and to be obsessive. He has a high emotional charge and strong genital activity (high erective potency with poor orgasic potency). Physically, the phallic-narcissistic has a small, narrow body, and will be proportionate, but stiff. The *compulsive* male, on the other hand, has had a threatening father and has identified with the mother. He is compulsive as a way of life, and therefore shows few if any compulsive symptoms. Genital activity is weakened by extreme anal tension. The ego of the compulsive is hard, inflexible, and cold. An outstanding trait is the affect block. Physically, the compulsive has a larger frame and heavier musculature than the phallic-narcissistic. The compulsive has a solid jaw, aggressively set forward. The body looks strong and hard with broad shoulders, narrow waist and tightly contracted hips.

Corresponding to the phallic-narcissistic and compulsive males, the rigid female character is the *hysteric*. The etiology is essentially the same as with the rigid male—rejection of the child's love. But, because of the male-female polarity between father and daughter, the rejection is sexualized. Often, the father has been loving earlier, but freezes up at the daughter's earliest signs of sexuality and pushes her away. This happens out of the father's fear of his own sexual feelings toward his daughter. The hysteric is characterized by being suggestible, emotionally labile with irrational emotional outbursts, and chaotic in her life style. She tends to be histrionic, overdramatizing her expressions and her experience of life. As part of this histrionic tendency, she may be prone to mendacity, or to use a phrase used by Lowen, she may be prone to "pseudologia phantastica." She is easily influenced and takes to expectations and fads. Attention is usually on the obvious, the striking, and her cognitive style is global and diffuse. Lacking in sharpness and in attention to subtle details, her cognition is impressionistic. This can lead to her being low in factual and technical knowledge. Her world is romantic and sentimental, so she is distractible and finds intellectual concentration difficult. Sometimes the hysteric is surprised at the outcome of her actions, when everyone else could see what was coming. She represses. There is a quality of wide-eyed innocence and immaturity. Given that this character structure is determined by a fixation at the genital stage, with its incestuous attachment, the hysteric tends to sexualize most of her relationships with men, thus leading to a split between tender feelings and erotic feelings. In an interesting way, the hysteric's genitality is a defense against sexuality. Her flirting is a way of raising her energy level in order to break out of her armoring. She can experience boredom and feeling in a rut easily, and her seeking excitement, usually sexualized, is a way of escaping. Physically, the hysteric is armored in the vaginal muscles and in the adductors of the thighs. This armoring in the pelvic segment may also include a tight lower back with a retracted and overcharged pelvis. The hysteric often has a stiff neck and jaw, showing her pride and determination. [Continued on page 100.]

Figure 18.   Schizoid Character

Physical Description:	Unexpressive, vacant eyes.
	Tension below occipital ridge.
	Tense body, stiff joints.
	Head held angled to one side.
	Arms and legs poorly coordinated.
	Top and bottom half of body don't look like they go together.
	Low energy in face (cold expression, thin lips), hands, feet, and genitals.
	Mechanical voice.
Time of Trauma:	In utero or first few months after birth.
Trauma:	Rejection. (Made to feel unwelcome).
Violated Right:	The right to exist.
Conflict:	Existence vs. need. (I can exist if I do not need).
Holding Pattern:	Holding together (against falling apart).
Personality:	Weak ego. Poor reality testing. Off in a fantasy world. Can't function under pressure. Holds in all feelings, with possible occasional outbursts. Withdrawn. Avoids intimate, feeling relationships. Thinking and feeling dissociated.

Figure 19.   Oral Character

Physical Description:	Pale, thin, underdeveloped muscles, immature.
	Thin, narrow feet (often flat).
	Head tilted forward.
	Chest collapsed. (Indentation, lower sternum).
	Belly soft and protruding.
	Thin skin, easily bruised.
	Reduced body hair in male.
	Soft, oversized breasts in female.
	Long, thin body.
	Weak, childlike voice.
Time of Trauma:	Within the first two years.
Trauma:	Deprivation. (Mother is not available).
Violated Right:	The right to be secure.
Conflict:	Need vs. independence. (I can need if I'm not independent).

Holding Pattern:	Holding on (against falling behind).
Personality:	"I can't." Difficulty asking straight. Strong disappointment reactions. Eating disturbances (possible gastro-intestinal problems). Depressed. Dependent, clinging. Low energy. Helpless and needy. Low aggressiveness. Tired. Fears abandonment.

Figure 20. Psychopathic Character

Physical Description:	The bully — upper half of body disproportionately large.
	Constricted diaphragm.
	Tension along base of skull.
	Penetrating, distrustful eyes.
	The seducer — hyperflexible back.
	Spastic diaphragm.
	Pelvis overcharged and disconnected.
	Soft, seductive eyes.
Time of Trauma:	By age four.
Trauma:	Overpowered. (Made to feel overwhelmed, weak, small).
Violated Right:	The right to be free.
Conflict:	Independence vs. intimacy. (I can be independent if I don't get intimate).
Holding Pattern:	Holding up (against falling down).
Personality:	Denial of feelings. Great investment in one's image. Drive for power. Need to dominate and control. Sexuality used for power. The "bully" who overpowers (ignores feelings of other, opportunistic, wants respect) or the "seducer" who charmingly undermines (gentle, overly-polite, cunning).

Figure 21. Masochistic Character

Physical Description:	Gorilla-like appearance (short, compressed body; thick, powerful muscles; rounded back; flat rear; short thick neck; overdeveloped calves and fronts of thighs; increased body hair).

Soft, sad eyes (look of suffering).
Innocent or naive facial expression.
Tight hamstrings.
A brownish skin tone.
Whining voice.

Time of Trauma: Begins in second year; full development after puberty.

Trauma: Pressured. (Overbearing mother, submissive father; love conditioned on obedience; not allowed to be free and spontaneous; feels pushed, nagged, and gulity).

Violated Right: The right to be independent.

Conflict: Intimacy vs. freedom. (I can be intimate if I am not free).

Holding Pattern: Holding in (against fear of self-assertion).

Personality: "I won't!" Suffers, whines, complains, and stays submissive. Suppressed spite and rage. Self-effacing. Anxious. Aggression reduced and self-assertion limited. Negativity. Sense of constant pressure. Hardworking. Awkward behavior. Collapse into brooding.

Figure 22.   Rigid Character — Male

Physical Description: Phallic-narcissistic:
　　Small, narrow body.
　　Proportionate body.
　　Stiff with pride.
Compulsive:
　　Larger frame, heavier musculature.
　　Solid jaw, aggressively set forward.
　　Strong, hard body.
　　Broad shoulders.
　　Narrow waist.
　　Tightly contracted hips (anal tension).
　　Stiff with pride.

Time of Trauma: Around five or six.

Trauma: Love rejected by father. (Father makes child feel not good enough).

Violated Right: The right to want and move toward satisfaction.

Conflict: Freedom vs. wanting (I can be free if I do not want).

Holding Pattern:	Holding back (against fear of surrender).
Personality:	"I will!" Has to prove himself. Doesn't reach out. Prone to action. Likes structure. Attends to details. Self-confident. Arrogant. Impressive. Ambitious. Competitive. Inflexible. Overworking. *Phallic-narcissistic*: Identifies with father. High erective potency with poor orgastic potency. Obsessive. *Compulsive*: Identifies with mother. Compulsive lifestyle. Weakened genital activity. Hard, cold, and inflexible.

Figure 23.   Rigid Character — Female (Hysteric)

Physical Description:	Pelvic armoring (overcharged pelvis, tense vaginal muscles, thigh adductors, tense lower back, retracted pelvis). Stiff neck. Stiff jaw. Rigid chest and upper abdomen (protecting heart). Small breasts. Upper body childlike, lower body womanly. Overly expressive voice, possibly shrill.
Time of Trauma:	Around five or six.
Trauma:	Love rejected by father. (Father rejects child's sexuality).
Violated Right:	The right to want and move toward satisfaction.
Conflict:	Freedom vs. wanting. (I can be free if I do not want).
Holding Pattern:	Holding back (against fear of surrender).
Personality:	"I will." Histrionic. Shallow, labile emotions. Chaotic life style. Suggestible. Global, diffuse, impressionistic cognitive style. Attends to the obvious, misses the fine details. Low in factual, technical knowledge. Intellectual concentration difficult. Romantic and sentimental. Wide-eyed innocence. Split between tender and erotic feelings. Relationships with men sexualized. Seductive. Believes no one listens or understands her.

The chest and abdomen tends to be rigid, restricting full breathing and therefore full feeling. Breasts are often small. Overall, her body is seductive, with the upper half childlike, the lower half more womanly. The hysteric's voice often is overly expressive, and may be shrill.

These, then, are the five basic character types which Lowen has presented. Most people are mixed types, their dynamics being a combination of two or more of the basic character structures. Figures 18, 19, 20, 21, 22, and 23 summarize the schizoid, the oral, the psychopathic, the masochistic, the rigid male, and the rigid female, respectively.

Of particular interest are the mixed types which combine a pregenital character type with the rigid character. In these types the pregenital and genital drives are fairly well balanced. Lowen (1971) has written of the passive-feminine male (oral-rigid mix or masochistic-rigid mix), the oral-rigid mix in the female (not named), and the masculine-aggressive female (masochistic-rigid mix).

The *passive-feminine* man is characterized by a soft, modulated voice, lacking in resonance and sharpness. His face is soft and plastic without strong lines. Often he is good looking in a boyish way. His movements are not brusque and lack in self-assertiveness. This man's hands are soft and have a weak quality. The body build is either rounded, with narrow shoulders, or it is v-shaped with narrow hips. The surface muscles are soft, while there is severe tension in the deep muscles. In manner, the passive-feminine man is gentle and humble and may be overly polite and considerate. He tends to have a passive-receptive attitude. He may be cunning. On the ego level he shows feminine tendencies while on the genital level he is masculine but passive, paralyzed with fear. The passive-feminine character is a combination of rigid and oral or masochistic strivings. Variations are in terms of the strength of the oral or the masochistic tendency. He feels hopelessness and despair, for his aggression is blocked by fear of castration and his regression is blocked by fear of homosexuality. Outstanding in the oral-rigid mix are oral deprivation at an early age (oral character etiology) and genital frustration which has paralyzed his aggression. In relationships with women he will tend either to be infantile or play father to a younger, dependent woman. Relating man to woman is difficult for him. He caricatures the hysteric and has been called the "male hysteric."

As is the case with the passive-feminine male, the female may show the mix of rigid dynamics and a pregenital masochistic disturbance or oral disturbance. First, the masochistic-rigid mix. Physically, such a woman is usually muscular and has a history of sports activities. Often there is facial hair along the jaw, heavy growth of hair on the legs and a male pubic hair distribution. The upper half of the body is rigid, well-charged, and aggressive, while the lower half is masochistic, weak, and passive.

Figure 24. Approaches to Body Reading

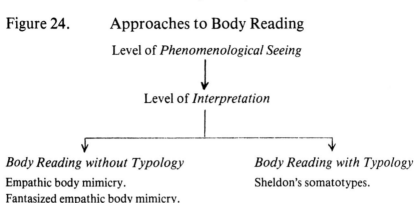

Level of *Phenomenological Seeing*

Level of *Interpretation*

Body Reading without Typology	*Body Reading with Typology*
Empathic body mimicry.	Sheldon's somatotypes.
Fantasized empathic body mimicry.	
Intuitive metaphors.	Reichian/Bioenergetics reading
	of character types.

Keleman's somatic descriptive parameters.
(Boundedness).
(Charge).
Body splits.
(Right-Left).
(Top-Bottom).
(Front-Back).
(Head-Body).
(Torso-Limbs).

The dominant conflict with the father (the rigid character etiology) is transferred to all men. This leads to a transferring of the masochistic conflict to men as well. She then develops an identification with the male, favoring aggressive tendencies and competition with the male. The failure of her aggressive receptivity to develop (the sexual receptive function of the female) results in a desexualized aggression. It is this aggression which characterizes the masculine-aggressive woman. The apparent sexual aggression is actually more an ego drive than a genital drive. This is the *masculine-aggressive* character. In a sense she caricatures the rigid male.

In the case of the woman with mixed orality and rigid character structure, there is a history of both oral deprivation and genital frustration. Such a person is characterized by oral dependency covered by rigid pride. As a young girl she transferred her oral longings to her father as well as having her need for acceptance of her sexuality focused on him. When such a person met with frustration on the genital level there was extreme hurt for it was felt on both genital and oral levels. This person is in a struggle between dependence and independence. Aggressiveness toward sexuality and toward life in general is lacking. The oral-hysteric type is characterized by dependency, passivity, and sensitivity. There is a childlike quality at times. At other times she is independent, rebellious, and filled with pride. Her body will reflect both her rigidity, more obvious in the upper half, and her oral weakness. Look for physical aspects discussed for the hysterical character and the oral character.

Lowen (1975, p. 170) wrote that "The character structure defines the way an individual handles his need to love, his reaching out for intimacy, and his striving for pleasure." The five basic character types form a hierarchy according to the degree that they allow contact and intimacy. Each character type represents the best compromise that the person was able to make in response to the traumatic conditions encountered in her or his early life. Each of the character structures is a defense against the one which is lower down on the hierarchy.

The theory of character structure is intricate and deserves considerable study. For a deeper understanding I suggest careful reading of Baker (1967), Kurtz (1981), Lowen (1971, 1974, 1975), Reich (1949), and Shapiro (1965). Each of these writers has made an important contribution to this area, and in the present writing I have dealt with much of their material in only a summary fashion.

Figure 24 outlines the approaches to body reading discussed in this chapter.

7. Methods for Body Awareness

Body reading, as described in the previous chapter, requires the therapist to be active. Her or his task is to observe carefully and to generate hypotheses about the patient's personality and functioning based on those observations of the patient's body. The patient remains inactive during this process. When *body awareness* methods are used, in contrast, the patient becomes active and the therapist is relatively inactive. The therapist offers some fairly simple directions and invites the patient to expand her or his organismic awareness. The task of the patient is to direct attention and allow awareness to develop.

In inviting an increased organismic awareness on the part of the patient what we are looking for are body phenomena which reveal the patient's energy dynamics. Otherwise stated, we are looking for those experienced body sensations which reveal body armoring. With body awareness we are asking the patient to become aware of and report specific body sensations which bespeak areas of diminished aliveness or blocks in the flow of that aliveness.

There are a number of advantages which body awareness work has, in contrast to body reading. First, by virtue of the active role of the patient, these methods are usually found interesting. It is more inviting of interest for the patient to be focusing on body sensations rather than standing still for several minutes while being observed. This also helps create a set for the patient to take an active role in her or his therapy. Many patients enter therapy with a passive set, expecting to be told about themselves and to be given advice. Using body awareness methods is a way of mobilizing the patient and bringing her or him to take an active responsibility for the therapy.

A third advantage of body awareness work is that it is less threatening than body reading. In my experience having a body reading has been anxiety-producing for every patient with whom I have worked, as well as for clinical psychology graduate students and professionals in body reading workshops. In contrast, body awareness may be done in such a way that the patient does not feel "on the spot" or stared at.

The metamessage of the body awareness techniques is that the patient herself or himself is the ultimate source of data for her or his therapy. This metamessage can help counteract the tendency to look to the therapist as the source of information, even the seer. Responsibility is clearly placed with the patient as the expert source of information on herself or himself.

A fifth advantage is that body awareness has an undeniable face validity. When the patient has revealed to herself or himself a body phenomenon, say a hot spot in a certain area, obviously something is going on there. This is the patient's own discovery, her or his own sensation.

Perhaps the most important advantage of body awareness is that the emergent phenomena are direct guides to body-focused therapeutic intervention. Whereas a body reading can lead to the therapist's understanding the patient's psychodynamics and to the predicting of growth issues to be dealt with, the body awareness work can reveal the precise locus for a body technique. The spot of tension or zone of heat guides the therapist, provides a map of the patient's energy blocks and status.

When the methods of body awareness are used, there are several body phenomena which we are looking for. These include hot spots, cold spots, tension, pain, numbness, paresthesias (prickling, tingling, or creeping, on the skin), energy streamings, and vibrations. The hypothesized meanings of these phenomena are as follows.

Hot spots, or areas on the skin surface which feel hot relative to surrounding areas, represent a high charge of energy, an area where energy has accumulated. Hot spots result when energy charge exceeds energy discharge, the energy accumulating at the skin surface and manifesting as heat. Consistent with this, Butler (1974) hypothesized that hot spots result from excess energy transmitted from overactive organs by means of their acupuncture meridians. The hypothesized meaning of hot spots is, then, that the organism has charged but held the energy in the hot area of the body not allowing it to be processed through to satisfaction.

Conversely, cold spots are areas on the body from which energy has been withdrawn. These areas are deenergized or deadened. We can hypothesize that cold spots result when the person withdraws energy from an area which if allowed full aliveness would be a threat to the person. "Going dead" is a way of avoiding the aliveness which is forbidden by the toxic introject operating in the person's dynamics. This meaning of cold spots seems to be clinically supported even in the case of Raynaud's disease (a disease manifested by a constriction of blood vessels causing impaired circulation in the hands, feet, ears, and nose) (Dychtwald, 1978, p. 174–175).

The biofeedback literature contains quite compelling evidence of the ability of people to learn voluntary control of skin temperature within a certain temperature range. This mechanism certainly could operate outside one's awareness. Other support for attributing psychobiological meaning to hot spots and cold spots is our "lived language." Consider for instance the experience of having "cold feet" in anticipation of making some expansive movement out into the world. And remember feeling "redfaced anger" and the explosion that was threatening at that moment. Even if you have not ever been "hot under the collar," surely you have had hot hands as you have been conflicted about touching some forbidden fruit.

As discussed in an earlier chapter, Reich equated expansion of the organism with vasodilation. When the expansion is partially carried out, then blocked, the result is an overcharge, heat. Reich equated vasoconstriction with contraction, or, what I referred to as contraction against expansion. This would be experienced as cold.

Tension is the direct subjective experience of body armor. Where one feels tense is where one is contracting a muscle or group of muscles to avoid the flow of a contact/withdrawal cycle.

If tension is strong enough and long enough in duration, pain is experienced. So, often, tension and pain are experienced together.

Numbness follows from nerve pressure which results from tension. With muscle tension in certain areas pressure is put on nerves resulting in a numbing or "going dead." Numbness is often accompanied by cold, since the tension may also be interfering with blood flow.

When a "deadened" area (cold and/or numb) begins to come back to life, there may be prickly feelings, tingling, or a creeping on the skin. These paresthesias are a note of optimism, in a sense. They indicate that the immediate crisis with the toxic introject is passed.

Reich used the term "streamings" to describe the deep, currentlike sensations which run up and down the body shortly before orgasm. To a lesser degree streamings may be experienced by relatively unarmored persons during very deep breathing. Streamings, then, can be taken as an indication that the body armor has largely dissolved and that the orgone has begun flowing freely.

Before streaming of orgone is possible there must be an increasing of the vibratory state of the body. As Lowen and Lowen (1977) have written, vibration is the key to aliveness. The healthy body is in a constant state of vibration, due to the energetic charge in the musculature. So, a lack of vibration can be taken to mean that the bioenergetic charge is greatly reduced or even absent. The quality of vibration gives some indication of the degree of muscular armoring. With heavy armoring, vibration in the affected body area will be completely arrested. With a somewhat lesser armoring, vibrations will occur, but with a gross quality. The vibrations will be irregular, and be of large amplitude. As muscular armor is nearly

Figure 25.   Body Phenomena
                        Revealing Energy Dynamics

Phenomenon

Hot spots	Overcharge. An accumulation of energy which has not been allowed to be processed.
Cold spots	Undercharge. A withdrawal of energy, a deenergizing or deadening.
Tension	Armoring. Contraction of muscles to avoid the flow of a contact/withdrawal cycle.
Pain	Armoring. A stage following tension, resulting from extreme and chronic tension.
Numbness	Armoring. A stage following tension or pain, resulting from extreme tension. A deadening.
Paresthesias	The return of energy to an area which had been deadened.
Streaming	Free flow of strong energy charge up and down the body, experienced as current-like sensations. Body armoring largely absent.
Vibrations	Presence of aliveness. A continuum from no vibrations (heavy armoring) through gross vibration (partial armoring) to fine vibration or purring (lack of armor).

absent, the vibrations will be more rhythmic and much finer. In a state of near freedom from armoring, the body will vibrate in a very fine steady way, in a constant hum or purr. The presence of this purring indicates a person well anchored in her or his body and a lack of anxiety about allowing the spontaneous flow of energy.

These, then, are the phenomena which we want the patient to allow into awareness. The therapist's task is twofold in this process. First, the therapist can offer the invitation to awareness, and second, he or she can suggest a body position to the patient which will magnify the body phenomena as much as is necessary for the patient to gain the awareness which is sought.

The invitation. In the invitation to awareness the therapist is facilitating the patient's focus of attention and is giving support for the patient's being aware. These two aspects of the invitation can both be of great importance. Many patients have very limited practice in the focusing of attention on themselves. To be invited to spend time just looking inside and noting happenings in their body may be quite novel, and is a step toward the ending of their body-alienation. Giving support for the awareness process can be important in countering the patient's learned clouding of awareness. Just as the patient learned to cloud awareness in response to the introjected toxic voice, the patient can begin to be more clearly aware in response to the therapist's encouragement.

In offering the invitation of awareness it is important for the therapist to use her or his own words and to find the appropriate pace and phrasing for the patient. Developing awareness takes time, so it is important not to rush the patient. In doing awareness work the most common error is moving through the exercise too quickly. I have found that it is better to err on the side of going too slowly.

Learning body awareness is a skill, and as it is developed by the patient, it can be accomplished with a simpler, abbreviated invitation and with less time involved. The basic form of invitation which I use, and which can then be modified to suit the patient's level of sophistication is as follows:

> Close your eyes and just relax for a few moments. Breath comfortably. (Pause) (Repeat the directions to relax and the pauses until the patient seems to be involved in the exercise.) Check out your body to see what you find. Note anything in your body which calls attention to itself. Just monitor your body, inch by inch, from the tips of your toes to the top of your head and down to the tips of your fingers. In particular, note any hot spots, cold spots, tight or tense muscles, pains, tingling, or anything happening in your body. Don't try to edit or change anything, just be aware and note what is happening. (Pause for a minute or two). Take your time. When you are finished, open your eyes. (Wait until patient opens her or his eyes).

Following this I ask the patient to describe to me what he or she discovered. If the patient reports awarenesses of body phenomena which can serve as material for therapy work, the awareness work is complete for now. If, however, the patient reports nothing, or reports something too vague to grasp, more awareness work is needed. This situation tells me that the patient is so body-alienated or repressed that the technique which I used was too subtle. The next step in this case is to use a technique which is less subtle, a technique which will magnify the body's voice to a level where it will come into the patient's awareness. This is accomplished by various body positions which can be assumed during the awareness work.

The body positions. There are several body positions which I use. The first three are simple and arrange themselves in order of increasing gravitational stress on the body. The increasing of gravitational stress has the effect of slightly magnifying the body phenomena which may occur. The first position is *lying* supine with the legs slightly apart and extended and the arms extended along the sides. This position minimizes gravitational stress and is comfortable for most people. Occasionally a patient may experience lower back pain in this position. In order to get beyond the pain and obvious lower back lesion, the lying position may be modified by having the patient bend his or her knees and place the feet flat on the floor. From this position, the work can be continued. The second position is *sitting* upright in a chair with knees bent, both feet on the floor, and arms bent with the hands resting on the chair arms or in the lap. To increase gravitational stress further, the third position, *standing*, can be used. For standing, I ask the patient to stand in a relaxed manner with weight equally distributed to both feet and arms hanging to the sides. Of the several body positions I use standing awareness most frequently.

When working with patients who have a high level of body awareness, the above three body positions may be adequate for tuning into body phenomena. If, however, the patient is more body-alienated, or if the body phenomena are very subtle (slight or partial armoring), then greater magnification of the phenomena is called for. In order to get this greater magnification, the body is stressed beyond that of the gravitational pull in normal lying, sitting, and standing.

I have found that the next level of body stressing occurs with the *species stance*. I learned the species stance from its originator, Albert Pesso. In his first book, Pesso (1969) described the species stance and referred to it as "a cornerstone of psychomotor training." This body position is a stance achieved by relaxing or attempting to relax all of the skeletal muscle short of falling down. The way in which I use the species stance is somewhat different from Pesso's way. The instructions which I use are essentially as follows. I demonstrate as I give the instructions:

> Stand comfortably. Let your feet be at a comfortable distance apart. Bend your knees slightly. Now first the head. Place your chin on your chest. (Pause.) Lift your head and place it again. Be aware of what happens throughout your entire body as you lift and place your head. (Pause.) (May be repeated several times.) This time let your head fall to your chest. Lift, let it fall. (Pause.) (May be repeated.) Now your shoulders. Lift them as high as you can, as if to touch your ear lobes. Now place them back down. Be aware of your entire body as you do this. (Pause.) (Repeat.) This time lift your shoulders and drop them. (Pause.) (Repeat.) Now arms. Lift your arms out in front parallel to the floor, palms down. Place them back at your sides. Be aware of your whole body as you do this. (Pause.) (Repeat.) Now lift them and let them drop. (Pause.) (Repeat.) Now the chest. Lift it up and stick it way out. Now place it back down. (Pause.) (Repeat.) Be aware of all of your body. This time lift it and let it fall (Pause.) (Repeat.) Now the

belly. Suck in your belly as far as you can, as if to touch your spine with your navel. And now place it back out. (Pause.) (Repeat.) Be aware as you do this. This time suck in your belly and let it fall back out. (Pause.) (Repeat.) Now we'll put this all together. Lift your head, lift your shoulders, lift your arms, lift your chest, suck in your belly. Now place everything back where it was. Be aware of anything that happens in your body when you do this. (Pause.) (Repeat.) This time lift everything and let it fall. Head, shoulders, arms, chest, belly. Let go and let everything fall. Now, one more time, but after you let everything go, stay in that position. Head, shoulders, arms, chest, belly. Let go and stay! (Pause.)

At this point, I would give the essence of the awareness instructions which I presented above in detail. Awareness is made easier with the species stance than with the simple lying, sitting, and standing postures. In the species stance we have added to the pull of gravity while standing, the elements of preliminary focusing on a body part at a time, intentional movement (lifting and placing), and giving in to gravity (lifting and letting go). These additional elements contribute considerably to the facilitation of an expanded body awareness.

At times even more is needed. The interaction of the patient's level of body alienation (level of inattention to body phenomena) and the sublety of the body phenomenon is such that the patient does not become aware through the previously described techniques. To obtain adequate magnification of the phenomenon great body stress is suggested. The technique, here, is the *stress posture.* Lowen and Pierrakos developed several stress postures and variations, making these central to bioenergetics. (A catalogue of these is provided by Lowen and Lowen, 1977). In the context of the present chapter, the use of body awareness techniques for personality assessment, I have found the "bow" to be the most useful of the stress postures. If, in using the bow, a body phenomenon is disclosed, and if I want to facilitate the patient's further exploration of that phenomenon (the focus still on personality assessment), I may suggest other stress postures which are more specifically designed for the body area in question. The bow, however, because it stresses almost all of the skeletal muscles simultaneously, is my usual choice. The stretching of muscles is in addition to the gravitational force while standing.

The body position you are about to get into is designed to stretch or contract most of your muscles. So this can be physically quite stressful. Be careful not to hurt yourself with it. If you feel any sharp pains, stop. The idea is to stress your body, not to injure it. Turn your toes in as far as you can wihout losing your balance. Bend your knees slightly. Now make fists and press them into the muscles in your lower back. Use the part of the fist that you would hit with — these first two knuckles. Keep your elbows pulled toward each other so as to stretch your chest and shoulders. Press forward with your fists so as to arch your body. Bend as far as you can. Keep your face looking straight ahead. Now let your mouth drop open. Breathe through your mouth. Breathe deeply. Let a vocalized sound come out when you exhale. Breathe hard, make the sound, and let your body vibrate if it wants to. Do this until you've had enough, and then rest.

I would now give the awareness instructions which I have used with the previous body positions. If the patient seems to have cut the experience short or not really entered into it fully, I would have her or him repeat the bow after a minute or so of rest.

These are the body positions which I frequently use in facilitating body awareness for the purpose of understanding the patient's personality functioning. My experience in using these body positions has suggested that they form a continuum from subtle facilitation of awareness of body phenomena to dramatic magnification of those phenomena.

A further method which I use is not a body position but rather the exaggeration of a body action. Frequently patients make minimovements or partial movements which suggest to me the action which follows from a present emotion. Upon calling attention to the diminished movement patients frequently report either that they were unaware of the action or that they do not know the meaning of it. Sometimes patients even deny that these movements have any meaning. My hypothesis in such situations is that this "slip of the body" is the attenuated expression of the emotion which is disallowed by the toxic introject. It is as if the healthy part of the person is trying to follow through with an organismically appropriate contact/withdrawal cycle while the toxic introject is keeping the action minimal and perhaps outside of awareness.

By inviting the patient to repeat the diminished action, but in exaggerated form, the meaning usually becomes obvious. Awareness is served both in revealing what emotion ►action sequence is present, and in revealing that it was inhibited. The fact of the revealed inhibition is evidence for the toxic introject in the patient's dynamics.

An example of this is the patient who, while talking about her ex-lover, begins slightly swinging her leg which is crossed over the other leg, knee on knee. The therapist asks her to be aware of her leg and she says, "Oh, I'm just nervous today." So the therapist asks her to exaggerate the movement. She swings her leg in a larger arc, with more force, and declares, "I must want to kick him. But I didn't know I was angry today. Oh, I just remembered what he said last week. I am mad at him!"

Figure 26.   Methods of Body Awareness

Lying awareness

Sitting awareness

Standing awareness

Species stance (added factor of
    stress by "letting go")

Increasing gravitational stress

Stress postures (added factor of
    stress by muscle stretching)

Exaggerated actions (magnification of
action to the threshold of recognition)

In a situation such as this the patient can be facilitated to the awareness both that she was repressing (unaware) and inhibiting and that the content of her repression and inhibition was her feeling and expressing anger. That is a good bit of potentially valuable information for the patient to have about herself. And, obviously, there are clear therapeutic directions for her and her therapist to take.

A further dynamic which, if present, may be revealed by the method of exaggeration is the retroflection of interaction. If, for example, in the situation described above the patient had been hitting her knee rather than swinging her leg, the exaggeration of the hitting would have told her: (1) I repress my feeling of anger; (2) I inhibit the expression of my anger; and (3) I turn my expression of anger back on myself. Again, with these issues clearly seen, the therapist can move into the therapeutic work.

The method of exaggerating actions is obviously a method of magnification. It is taking an action which was done outside of awareness or was done in such diminished (inhibited) form that the meaning was not in the patient's awareness, and making the action so big that it can not be ignored and its meaning becomes apparent.

The awarenesses which arise from these several methods are valuable guides for the therapist. They identify body areas as access points for therapeutic intervention. In addition, they contribute greatly to the patient's self-knowledge. The patient, with such new awarenesses, now knows what he or she as an organism has been doing. I remember from a workshop in the Feldenkrais method of body work his saying over and over: "If you don't know what you're doing, you can't do what you want."

Part III

The Body as Locus of Psychotherapeutic Intervention

In Part III, attention is given to the body as locus of intervention in the psychotherapy process. In this part we will explore various ways of interacting with the patient as embodied self which hold promise for promoting that patient's growth. In Chapter 4, I presented an organismic perspective on psychotherapy. Part III is an elaboration of that theory into the realm of actual application.

Chapter 8 is a presentation of what I term "soft technique." These procedures tend to be gentle and allowing rather than forcing.

In Chapter 9 the focus shifts to techniques which are highly potent and dramatic. These procedures, being uncomfortable and at times even painful, I refer to as "hard technique."

Chapter 10 is devoted to expressive technique, the forte of Gestalt therapy and psychomotor therapy. Expressive technique involves the embodied living out of the patient's psychodrama with symbolized meaning. It is in this psychodramatic acting out that previously incomplete contact/withdrawal cycles can be brought to completion.

Soft technique and hard technique have as their focus the charging of the organism through facilitation of breathing and the melting of body armor. In terms of the contact/withdrawal cycle this means the focus of the soft and hard body techniques is on arousal▶emotion▶action, with a feedback loop which may enhance awareness of the want. So, these techniques get energy flowing in emotion and take the patient to the point of taking action.

Expressive technique is designed for getting energy flowing in the action▶interaction sequence of the contact/withdrawal cycle. These techniques involve the musculoskeletal system in nonretroflected action and interaction with the world.

I think of two levels of awareness. There is awareness prior to

expression and there is awareness based on doing. The first level of awareness may be developed to an exquisite degree but still is of a different
level, a different quality from awareness which has a basis in expression.
Awareness based on doing is more complete and full, for it is an awareness not just of wanting and arousal and emotion, but an awareness of a
complete contact/withdrawal cycle. I term these level I awareness and
level II awareness. Expressive body work, when successful, moves the
patient to level II awareness.

A final thought concerning the body interventions about to be presented: there seems to me to be a phenomenon with techniques analogous
to the "halflife" phenomenon of atomic physics. Radioactive elements
decay or lose their radioactivity (i.e., energy or potency) at different rates,
but all radioactive elements follow the same decay pattern. At the end of a
certain period of time, that period being a peculiar characteristic of each
radioactive element, half of the atoms will have decayed. During the next
time interval of the same duration half of the atoms that are left will
decay, and so on with the passage of each of these time intervals. So,
halflife of a radioactive element is the time taken for one half of the
atoms present to decay.

There are three important implications. First, radioactive potency
decreases across time. Second, the decrease in potency follows a logarithmic curve. Third, radioactive elements can be compared as to their rate of
decay or halflife. I believe an analogous situation is true with the techniques of body work. First, a technique shows decreasing potency over
time if it is used repeatedly with a patient. Second, the loss of potency
seems to mimic, although without mathematical precision, a logarithmic
decay curve. And third, each technique (or more accurately each technique as brought to life through a given therapist) has a peculiar,
although not mathematically precise rate of loss of potency. Some techniques have such a long halflife that they can be used an almost unlimited
number of times with a given patient and still have dramatic yield. Other
techniques are of short halflife and may be effective only a few times with
a given patient, perhaps being of great value only once or twice. Halflife
does not seem to be related to the potency of the technique *per se*, but
only to how well the technique maintains potency with repeated use.
Some of the most powerful and dramatic techniques are in fact, as Reich
suggested, nonce techniques. I suggest that the reader explore this halflife
phenomenon as he or she practices the techniques which follow.

8. Soft Technique

Soft techniques of psychotherapeutic body intervention tend to be subtle. The interventions themselves are gentle and allow for things to happen rather than being forceful. The things which happen, such as increased body awareness, psychological regression, increased experience of emotion, and expression of emotion often do not happen as quickly or dramatically as is the case with the hard techniques or the expressive techniques to be discussed in the two successive chapters. It is these gentle and subtle characteristics which are the advantages of the soft techniques. Relative to hard techniques and expressive techniques, the soft methods are safe. In a sense they are of lower potency and therefore don't require the degree of caution and attention which is required with hard or expressive methods.

A very gentle technique is that of inviting the patient to assume a particular body posture. Postures can be chosen which are paradigmatic of emotions. These postures can be used for the patient to recognize a blocked feeling, short of expressing it. There are times when the therapist wants to facilitate the patient's recognizing and experiencing an emotion, but the time or circumstance may not be safe enough yet for the expression of the feeling. At such times, and if the patient is blocked, the therapist can suggest assuming an appropriate posture for what the therapist is guessing the blocked emotion to be. By assuming the posture the patient may recognize the emotion, he or she may feel the fit almost like a piece of a jigsaw puzzle clicking into place. With a bit of creative intuition the therapist can create postures which bespeak angers, fears, loves, joys, and sadnesses.

In addition to these postures designed out of the therapist's creativity, there are certain other postures which are more standard. These also can be used to see if the patient recognizes what the therapist intuits or predicts the patient is feeling and which is associated with the posture. These are the spread eagle (the person lies on her or his back, legs spread, arms spread), the fetal posture (lying or sitting), and the reaching posture (the person lies on her or his back and reaches up with the arms and hands towards someone). The spread eagle often evokes the feeling of vulnerability or insecurity. The patient who does not feel safe in the world may contact that feeling from this posture. The fetal posture, lying or sitting, is usually associated with feeling safe and alone. The reaching posture may educe a feeling of wanting or neediness and if continued longer, a feeling of abandonment or of a hopelessness in getting one's needs met.

If I notice that a patient is holding a body part in a peculiar way, I sometimes rearrange the holding pattern and ask her or him what it is like to be in the new position. To facilitate this awareness I may have the person go back and forth between the two postures several times for comparison. An example is the patient sitting in a closed posture (crossed arms, crossed legs, or both). I would invite the patient to uncross and see what that feels like, and then cross again. The meaning of the closed posture usually becomes quite clear to the patient from this. Another example is the patient with her or his shoulders rolled forward. In this case I would move the shoulders back by applying firm but gentle pressure to the front of the shoulder while stabilizing the patient's body with my other hand on her or his back. After thus moving both shoulders back, I would ask the patient how he or she experienced the world from this new posture. If this awareness was difficult I would repeat the two shoulder positions for comparison. So, by inviting the patient to move out of a particular posture, or by changing the posture by a physical manipulation of the patient, one can facilitiate the patient's awareness, experience and flow of emotion.

One more way that the therapist may use the deliberate choice of the patient's posture effectively is in the facilitation of evoking the desired ego state. In terms of the ego states (by now well-known through the extensive transactional analysis literature), there are times when the patient needs to be in a particular ego state for the therapy to proceed. In general, I believe that the postures of standing, sitting, and lying correspond to the parent ego state, the adult ego state, and the child ego state, respectively. I'm suggesting a subtle correspondence which certainly doesn't mean that the posture determines the ego state or vice versa. Rather, I believe that the desired ego state can be facilitated and supported by the posture assumed. In terms of clinical anecdote, I have seen patients shift in ego state as they have changed posture. At times I have suggested a particular posture when the patient was having difficulty in staying in an ego state, and this intervention has seemed helpful. For instance, in an empty chair dialogue (a technique to be discussed in Chapter 10), a patient may have difficulty enacting the part of a critical parent convincingly. By having her or him stand and look down at the imagined person in the empty chair, the critical parent may come alive. In addition to the anecdotal evidence, there is experimental evidence that suggests that lying down facilitates recall of early memories and the primary process components of psychological regression (Berdach and Bakan, 1967). Kroth (1970) demonstrated that in the supine position, as compared to sitting, experimental subjects free associated more effectively, and talked with greater spontaneity and freedom. His conclusion was that primary process characteristics are more dominant in the supine position, and therefore lying down supports regressive activities.

When working in a therapy group there are soft techniques requiring the participation of several people which can be used. Two which I have found useful are group touching and group lifting and rocking. If a patient is feeling emotionally raw or lonely, a profound healing can be experienced by having the patient lie down and be touched by the group. Simultaneously, up to nine or ten people can gather around the patient and with respect and love can gently lay their hands on the patient. The several hands cover most of the patient, except for any areas where touch is not soothing (genitals are rarely touched). The patient may lie either on her or his back or front. After a few minutes of this quiet touching (the hands staying still in their places), the group members very slowly remove their hands.

A similar feeling of nurturance and caring can be given the patient in the group lifting and rocking, but with the added element of support. This literal support of the patient's body against gravity can have a powerful impact of emotional support. If a patient is undergoing a difficult period in her or his life, and is feeling drained and raw, this experience of support and nurturance from the group of peers can have a powerful reconstituting effect, helping ready the patient to go back into her or his not yet finished struggle. The lifting and rocking is done as follows: Have the patient lie on her or his back. Have group members gather round and place their hands under the patient. Ideally, one person will lift each lower leg, one person under each upper leg, two persons on each side of the torso, and one person under the patient's head. It is very important that there are enough people so that they can hold the patient without strain. Any strain can be felt by the patient and this detracts from the experience. The nine or so people simultaneously lift the patient very slowly to about waist height. It is important that they keep the patient's whole body level throughout the exercise (especially keep the head from falling back). Once the patient is lifted, the group begins a very slow rocking of the patient's body lengthwise by swaying together back and forth. After several minutes the patient is very slowly lowered to the floor and the group members slowly remove their hands. In both the group touching and the group lifting and rocking the patient is invited to close her or his eyes and relax as fully as possible. He or she is invited to "take in the experience and let whatever wants to happen, happen." It is usually best for the group to be silent during both of these exercises, letting the patient focus on their touch and her or his responses to that.

Touching the patient's body in specific ways is central to soft technique of psychotherapeutic body intervention. The simplest level of such work is the therapist's touching the patient to communicate caring or support. This involves a loving hug, an encouraging hand on a shoulder, a supporting hand on a back, a warm encouraging holding of hands, holding a sobbing patient, and so forth. These are natural and spontaneous actions which bespeak the therapist's human involvement.

Another way of touching is the deliberate placement of the therapist's hands on the part of the patient's body where some feeling is being blocked or inhibited. So, one thing which I might do is touch the patient where he or she experiences some unusual phenomenon (a hot spot, cold spot, pain, tightness, numbness, etc.). For example, a patient might report an emptiness or hollow feeling in the center of the chest, along the sternum. I might respond to that by placing my hand on that exact spot, as shown to me by the patient. I would then say something such as, "Just breathe and let go. Feel my touch and let whatever wants to happen, happen. Focus on your body sensations." Or, similarly, someone might say that her or his abdomen is tight, so I would let my hand rest there, just where the patient shows me. I might keep the touch anywhere from a few seconds to several minutes, until there is some shift in the patient's experience. When something happens, I then take the new happening as a guide as to how to continue being with the patient in a way that will facilitate her or his therapeutic process. I find that in such touching, skin to skin contact is often more powerful than placing my hand over clothing. Here, the decision is directed by this consideration of potency of touch and by the patient's level of comfort.

Additionally, I use light immobile touch in a style similar to what Malcolm Brown refers to as "blood synergic" work (Brown's work was discussed in Chapter 1). The purpose of this form of touch is a mobilization of energy flow. This light touch often has the effect of a gentle melting of body armor, much like a thawing process, and thereby a flow of energy/feeling is restored. The positions on the patient's body where I make contact most often are (1) upper abdomen (between sternum and navel); (2) lower abdomen (between navel and pubic bone); (3) center of the chest; (4) back of the neck. Sometimes I contact a combination of two of these areas simultaneously. This work is done using skin to skin contact with the patient supine. The touch is anywhere from a few seconds to several minutes, whatever time is required for some effect.

There is a striking parallel between blood synergic work and a procedure in applied kinesiology known as the "pre- and postganglion" technique (Walther, 1976). The theory of this is that there are vortices of force in the body which correlate with the pubococcygeal plexus, the solar plexus, the splenic plexus, cardiac and pulmonary plexus, pharyngeal plexus, and the cervical plexus. The level of these plexuses along the spine are referred to as preganglionic centers. On the anterior surface of the body are postganglionic centers, which consist of points in the meridian (acupuncture) system at levels corresponding to the preganglionic centers. (These points in the meridian system are "alarm points." In classical acupuncture they are evaluated for tenderness or pain, such sensitivity taken as diagnostic of an energy imbalance in the acupuncture meridian corresponding to that alarm point.) The technique is to place one hand on a preganglionic center and the other hand on the related postganglionic center and maintain light touch. This procedure is believed by the applied kinesiologists to balance energy in the body.

Breathing work is a major focus of soft body technique. (As will be discussed in the following chapter, breathing work is a major focus in hard body technique as well.) In Chapter 3, I discussed the role of breathing in the self-interruption of organismic arousal and in Chapter 4, I identified the facilitation of breathing as one of the four major thera-peutic tasks (at that level of the therapy, the four tasks are to facilitate awareness, facilitate breathing, melt body armor, i.e., stop retroflected action, and stop retroflected interaction). The reason that breathing work is central in body oriented psychotherapy is revealed by Lowen (1965) in his statement that every emotional problem is reflected in a disturbance of breathing. Interestingly, Perls (1969) pointed out the connection of shallow breathing and sighing with depression, chronic yawning with boredom, and the fight for breath with anxiety. He stated emphatically that anxiety is the experience of breathing difficulty during blocked excite-ment. So, anxiety is experienced when more air is required for the support of a growing excitement and the lungs are relatively immobilized by muscular constriction of the thoracic cage. Whereas the healthy response with excitement of any kind is to breathe more deeply, the neurotic response is to stay in control and be calm, and therefore to restrict breathing (Perls, Hefferline, and Goodman, 1951). Since it is breathing that provides the source of oxygen for metabolism, insufficient breathing leaves the organism like a fire with an inadequate draft. The vitality of the whole organism is reduced. Symptoms of inadequate breathing include tiredness, exhaustion, fatigue, depression, coldness, and a dull, lifeless feeling. If this poor breathing becomes chronic, the arterioles become constricted and there is a drop in the red blood cell count (Lowen, 1965). There may also be feelings of anxiety, tension and irritability.

Normal breathing is an involuntary rhythmic activity under the control of the autonomic nervous system. On the average one breathes fourteen to eighteen times a minute, or between twenty and twenty-five thousand times a day. Just imagine, then, the cumulative effect if one's breathing is interfered with and not allowed to be deep and full. The interesting thing about breathing is that one can take over conscious control of it, increasing or decreasing both its rate and its depth. Normal breathing involves the whole body, it is a smooth and rhythmic action. With inspiration there is an outward movement of the abdomen as the abdominal muscles relax and the diaphragm contracts, and an expansion of the chest. The pelvis rocks slightly so that the sacrum moves back and the head lifts and the neck arches back slightly. This wave of inspiration, when deep, can be felt from the head to the genitals. After a brief pause, the wave reverses, and expiration occurs. As the diaphragm relaxes the abdomen relaxes back in place from its protrusion and the chest relaxes from its expansion. The pelvis rocks forward and the head lowers slightly. And, again a brief pause. This describes abdominal or diaphragmatic breathing. The contraction of the diaphragm causes an increase in the vertical diameter of the thoracic cavity and thereby reduces the intra-thoracic pressure. The result is the inflow of the air from outside where the pressure is higher. On the exhalation the diaphragm relaxes and the recoil of the stretched costal cartilages and stretched lungs and the weight of the thoracic wall increases the intrathoracic pressure forcing the air out. So, in quiet, normal respiration the inhalation is active (diaphragm contracts) and exhalation is passive (diaphragm relaxes).

In forced respiration such as during strenuous muscular activity or voluntary deep breathing, there will be costal or thoracic breathing in which the external intercostal muscles (and several synergic muscles) are responsible for expanding the chest cavity and thus bringing in air. With forced breathing, exhalation, too, is an active process. The abdominals as well as the internal intercostal muscles, serratus posterior inferior and quadratus lumborum contract, thus reducing the size of the thoracic cavity and forcing the air out (Steen and Montagu, 1959).

Lowen (1965) has identified two typical disturbances of respiration. The first is found in the schizoid character and consists of breathing with the chest, with the abdomen mostly excluded. The diaphragm is immobilized and the abdominal muscles are held in contraction. The chest itself is held in a deflated position and tends to be narrow and constricted. The result is a low oxygen uptake and therefore lowered metabolism.

The second disturbed pattern of breathing involves diaphragmatic action with the chest immobilized. The chest is held in an expanded position, the lungs thereby retaining a reserve of air even at the end of an exhalation. The diaphragm and abdominals are relatively free for activity. This pattern is associated with the neurotic character, where there is a fear of the surrender, or letting go, in the passive process of exhalation.

The diaphragmatic breathing of the neurotic character, with the chest held in inflated position is more effective than the thoracic breathing of the schizoid character, and is adequate for most purposes. The neurotic maintains an inspirational attitude, not allowing full exhalation. As Reich (1973, p. 333) has written, "There is not a single neurotic person who is capable of breathing out deeply and evenly in one breath." The schizoid character, on the other hand, maintains an expirational attitude. The neurotic is afraid to let go, give in, and the schizoid is afraid to be aggressive and to take in from the environment. In both cases, the unitary functioning of the body which occurs in normal respiration is lost, and in turn emotional flow is impeded.

The task of the therapist in working with breathing is to facilitate the patient in learning to breathe fully and deeply, as a body unit. Baker (1967) has stated that increasing breathing in itself may overcome minor armoring and will help both in revealing and overcoming more severe armoring.

The simplest breathing work consists just of calling the patient's attention to her or his nonbreathing. Frequently, when a patient reaches a point in a therapy session of feeling the forbidden aliveness he or she will stop breathing completely for several seconds, or if the breath is not held, the patient will decrease the rate and depth of breathing dramatically. This is done without awareness, so by bringing it into the patient's awareness the breathing is usually restored and the therapeutic process continues. This reminder to the patient, "breathe," may have to be used many times, even within a single therapy session.

Another soft technique which I use in working with breathing consists of having the patient supine and telling her or him to let go and breathe for a few moments. I watch the pattern of breathing, noting its rate and depth. I note whether the breathing is diaphragmatic or thoracic, and where in the body there is any interruption in its unitary undulation with the breathing. By placing one of my hands on the patient's upper abdomen and my other hand midchest I then instruct the patient in diaphragmatic breathing and in thoracic breathing, having her or him push up the appropriate hand on the inhalation while letting my other hand remain still. In the same manner I teach full breathing involving abdomen and chest. If simply raising and lowering the appropriate hand or hands is too difficult for the patient to do, I will apply pressure with the hand that is not to move while the patient moves the appropriate hand. For example, with someone who is breathing thoracically I would place my hands and tell the patient that I am going to teach her or him abdominal or diaphragmatic breathing. I would then ask her or him to raise the hand placed on the abdomen with the inhalation and let it fall on the exhalation, while leaving my other hand (placed midchest) still. If need be,

I would use pressure with the chest hand during the inhalation to discourage the costal breathing and pressure on the abdomen during the exhalation. This is slow and gentle work, but in a while the patient has learned to recognize and to produce costal breathing, diaphragmatic breathing, and combined breathing. Thereafter, when the patient is inhibiting breathing, I can call that to attention and invite the patient to shift to breathing appropriate to what he or she is about, and the patient will know how to produce that kind of breathing.

A more advanced stage of gentle breathing work which is useful after the patient is able to produce costal breathing, abdominal breathing, and combined breathing is production of the unitary undulation of the body. To teach this (or reteach it, since this is natural behavior which has been trained out of the person), I have the patient assume a supine position and breathe abdominally. I then invite any of the following which are not spontaneously present: "Breathe through your mouth." "Make a vocal sound as you exhale." "Rotate your head back as you inhale." "Rotate your pelvis back as you exhale." "Relax any part of your body which you are tensing."

I work with the patient until all of these conditions are fulfilled, and thereby the whole body undulated rhythmically with each breath cycle. A variation which is a little more difficult, and therefore may need to be reserved until the supine undulation is perfected, is the undulated breathing while standing. The instructions are the same, except that the patient stands while doing it. (This undulated breathing, supine and standing, is preparatory for the orgastic reflex work to be explored in the following chapter.)

If the patient's energy level is low and the previously discussed breathing work is not sufficient, or if one wants a very brief breathing exercise which can be used with the individual or a group to raise the energy level, I recommend the jump-up. Have the patient stand and relax for a few moments. Then offer instructions such as:

> "Breathe through your mouth. As you exhale, make a vocal sound. Now bend your knees and bounce slightly." (Continue for a minute or two.) "Now, exaggerate the bounce so that you come up on your toes. Breathe deeply and make the sound louder." (Continue for a minute or two.) "Exaggerate this even more. Come clear off the floor. Breathe deeply. Make loud sounds." (Continue until the patient is well-energized.)

Stretching of any tight places in the body is useful in inviting the patient's aliveness. Have the patient check out her or his body and gently stretch any part which feels tense. The neck, shoulders, pelvis, wrists, and ankles all can be rotated. Have the patient do this slowly, deliberately, and in as large arcs as possible. Rotate in one direction and then the other. Invite the patient to report any memories or emotional reactions which occur while doing this. If the tense body part is being tensed in order to limit aliveness, the loosening of that part may help the patient recognize the underlying issue, to feel anxious, or to begin to feel the forbidden emotion. So, to intentionally interfere with the armoring which is taking place outside awareness is a way of gaining access to the blocked feeling as well as the toxic introject which is responsible for the blocking.

There are soft techniques specifically designed for working on armoring in the ocular segment. In Chapter 1, in my discussion of the work on vision which is a central focus of Kelley's Radix work, I mentioned the Bates method. The Bates method, I believe, would be effective in softening ocular armor. Since I have not been trained in the Bates method or in Kelley's method, I will not try to present them here. One of the methods which I do use is based on Hatha Yoga principles and technique as set forth by Swami Satchidananda (1970). The technique is to contract and to stretch the extrinsic muscles of the eyes by moving the eyes in various directions and holding them as far as they will go in each direction for several seconds. In each position the eyes are moved as far as they will go without pain. This position is maintained for increasing periods of time as the patient's armoring relaxes and the muscles strengthen. The positions, with one exception, are paired; after looking in one direction, the opposite direction is used. Throughout the eye exercises deep, full breathing is to be maintained. The beginning time for each position may be only three to five seconds, and may be increased gradually until each position can be held for half a minute or longer. The positions are: eyes squeezed shut, then opened widely; eyes to the left, then to the right; eyes looking up towards the eyebrows, then down at the checkbones; eyes crossed looking at the sides of the nose (this crossed position has no opposite to be practiced, i.e., extreme divergence of the eyes). For variety the pairs can be done in any order and the opposite movements within each pair can be done in either order. My experience, however, has been that doing a movement and then its opposite feels much better than a random ordering of all of the movements. Following these stretches, I instruct the patient to rotate their eyes either in a clockwise or in a counterclockwise direction several times, making as large circles as possible. Then, an equal number of times in the opposite direction, while still breathing deeply and fully. As I instruct the patient in the eye exercises, either sitting or lying, I ask them to report any emotional reactions or vivid memories which are elicited. These eye exercises can also be offered to the patient as homework to be done between sessions, after they have been used in the presence of the therapist.

Use of a mirror can be helpful in mobilizing the eyes. With patients who have extreme distortions of body image, who "see" themselves very differently from how others see them, I often have them stand in front of a full-length mirror. While standing in their underclothes in front of the mirror I invite them to visually examine themselves inch by inch from one end to the other, reporting what they see. At this stage, I instruct them in making phenomenological observations, in simply describing what is there without making any judgment as to good or bad, pretty or ugly. I help keep them focused if they skip over parts or become judgmental. The next stage is to look again and find parts to appreciate and identify parts which are embarrassing or displeasing. We then can work towards appreciation and acceptance. (Often I use dialogues with the body parts. The Gestalt dialogue will be discussed in Chapter 10.) The use of the mirror is almost always a powerful experience and tends to stand out as particularly memorable when patients review their therapy history.

Another use of the mirror, and one which is related to the body stretching discussed above, is in grimacing. The patient can be invited to make faces as a way of softening armoring in the facial muscles. As the patient looks into the mirror and makes faces, ask for her or him to report what he or she is aware of. Slow and careful use of this procedure can reveal shyness and embarrassment, as well as emotions which are not allowed expression through the face. This technique can be extended by asking the patient to produce sounds with the grimaces.

9. Hard Technique

I use the term "hard technique" to refer to those methods of body intervention which are neither subtle nor gentle. They are uncomfortable, at times even painful, and tend to be dramatic in their releasing of blocked emotion and memories. The hard techniques are of high potency and therefore require considerable judgment and caution on the part of the therapist if they are to be used in growthful ways rather than traumatic ways. When judiciously used, the hard methods of working can contribute greatly to unblocking, disinhibiting, and to the resumption of flow in the contact/withdrawal cycles. Used carelessly, they may bring a flood of feelings and memories for which the patient is not ready, which he or she can not yet process and support. The result is a traumatic experience from which the patient recoils and erects stronger defenses. My experience has shown me that the view which some therapists proclaim, that the patient will not get into anything that he or she is not ready for, is naive and misinformed.

The bioenergetics concept of "grounding" is relevant here. In Chapter 1, I referred to grounding, indicating that this concept is central to bioenergetics. To quote Lowen (1975, p. 40), "Grounding or getting a patient in touch with reality, the ground he stands on, his body and his sexuality, has become one of the cornerstones of bioenergetics." My understanding of grounding is that it is the experience of being in one's body in contact with the world. Being in one's body involves body awareness, which comes from experiencing one's body. Contact with the literal ground involves awareness of the body at the zone of contact, known in Gestalt theory as the contact boundary. There are concepts in Gestalt therapy and in psychomotor therapy which are analogous to grounding in bioenergetics theory. The analogy is

Grounding:Bioenergetics::Self-support:
Gestalt::Containment:Psychomotor

In each of these therapy systems, the concept is central. The idea is that if a person is not adequately grounded, self-supported, or self-contained, he or she will not function well. He or she will not be able to build up a high level of "charge," "excitement," or "energy" and "ground" "support," or "contain" it until it can be discharged or expressed in a manner which will optimize satisfaction. Without adequate grounding, self-support, or containment, a rising charge or excitement will lead to feelings of confusion, disorientation, or being "spaced out." There is, however, a difference in emphasis among the three analogous concepts. In bioenergetics the emphasis is, if a person is not well grounded, he or she will have difficulty "holding her or his ground," will have difficulty in tolerating a high energy charge, and will have difficulty handling strong feelings. Ungrounded equals "up in the air" or "hung up" (Lowen, 1977). In Gestalt theory, lack of self-support often is maintained by a demand for environmental support. This may take the form of financial support (pay my bills for me), intellectual support (think for me), physical support (prop me up), emotional support (decide what I "should" feel), and so on. The essence here is the taking of responsibility for one's own life. Lack of self-support equals not taking responsibility for one's choices, decisions, and actions. The psychomotor emphasis is on containing energy so as to have a clear sense of one's power without feeling overwhelmed by it. Without containment of energy by one's ego that energy creates the delusion that if one feels all of one's energy he or she will be out of control and something awful will result. Lack of containment equals the delusion of omnipotence (Pesso, 1973). Now I will discuss specific techniques of grounding and containment.

The "jump-up" which I described in the previous chapter can evolve into a hard technique by extending it in time and in having the participants bend their knees more and more until the jump begins from a squatting position. Using this very vigorous jump-up for more than a few seconds can enhance a sense of grounding and also bring on a very high state of energy charge.

In the chapter on methods of body awareness I discussed the use of stress postures with emphasis on the "bow." I described the use of the bow step by step. The bow can also be used therapeutically for grounding and for the releasing of body armor. As a therapeutic technique the bow may be used for a longer period of time and a greater number of times within a therapy session than would be the case when its purpose is body awareness for assessment of personality. The goal, therapeutically, is to reach a level of fine rhythmic vibrations throughout the body while in the bow. In the case of working on grounding, the vibrations in the legs are of special importance.

Three other stress postures which are especially suited to enhancing the sense of grounding are the one-legged stance, wall sitting, and lying with the legs in the air. In the one-legged stance the patient is instructed to shift all of her or his weight to one leg, bend that knee, and extend the other leg with the heel only slightly touching the floor. The straight leg is for balance only. The intensity of stress is regulated by the amount of time the posture is held and by the degree of knee bend. When vibrations have been reached in the stressed leg, the position is reversed, now placing stress on the other leg. Wall sitting involves taking a seated position with the back against a wall and the thighs parallel to the floor, but without benefit of a chair. (This position has long been used by skiers for pre-season conditioning of their legs.) The tendency to brace the arms against the thighs is, of course, counterproductive. Again, this stressed position is held until the vibrations in the legs can be felt. The third stress posture consists of having the patient lie on her or his back and extend both legs into the air vertically. The knees are straightened and the heels extended toward the ceiling (toes pulled back toward the body). Again, this is held until the legs vibrate. With each of these stress postures full, deep breathing through the mouth and vocalized exhalations are important.

So, grounding through the legs and feet, experiencing one's self embodied and in contact with the ground can be enhanced by these several hard techniques: the jump-up, the bow, the one-legged stance, wall sitting, supine leg extensions. These are the methods which I find useful.

Grounding, anchoring in reality, is also a function of unarmored eyes. In the previous chapter I presented soft techniques for this. A hard method which I use to mobilize the eyes and thus soften ocular armoring is one reported by Goldenberg (Baker, 1967). The procedure involves the patient's tracking a moving light while in a darkened room. When I do this I have the patient assume a supine position and maintain deep, full breathing. I use a totally dark room and a pen light. I ask the patient to track the light as I move it in erratic patterns, keeping the light about a foot from her or his face except for periodic movements down toward the face to within two or three inches. I make sure that my movements of the light beam requires the eyes to move throughout their full range of motion. I ask the patient to report any emotional reactions or strong memories of which he or she becomes aware. I continue until the patient responds, or up to fifteen minutes or a little longer. Goldenberg has noted that there is frequently a strong emotional reaction after about fifteen minutes, and that this time span may be critical for the effectiveness of the technique. My own experience has been that sometimes strong feelings can be evoked even more quickly. Goldenberg has reported that in relatively unarmored persons this procedure can elicit a partial or complete orgasm reflex. In her opinion, Goldenberg believes there are two important factors at work in this procedure: First, there is a direct photic stimulation of the brain; and second, the patient is pushed beyond the visual stimulus threshold, thus forcing a giving up of holding with the eyes. She thinks this method goes beyond the methods which only mobilize the eyes, and actually gets at a deeper layer of armoring in the brain parenchyma.

A hard technique which can be useful in breaking up a holding pattern in the muscles of the throat and the diaphragm is the intentional elicitation of the gag reflex. To do this I have the patient drink a glass or two of water at room temperature and then stand over a toilet bowl as he or she extends a finger to the back of the throat. The gag response involves involuntary spasms of the throat and of the diaphragm, so that the rigidity of these muscles is broken down. In my experience this technique almost always brings access to strong feelings. Fear, anger, embarrassment, or sadness may be experienced, and often, then, a feeling of calm and well-being. A sense of having been purged may result. It is important that this technique be used in the therapist's presence to allow for a processing of the emotions which are accessed.

Central to the hard body techniques is the procedure of using deep pressure on spastic muscles. Reich used this technique extensively, as have most therapists in the tradition of Reich. The model is to mobilize the patient's breathing and then work on the armored muscles while the patient is in this highly charged state. Without the high charge of energy the deep muscle work is of limited value. But when the deep pressure is applied during a state of high charge, the energy brings life to the emotion which was previously held in check by the tense muscle, and dramatic expressions of feeling often occur. I will discuss the use of this deep muscle pressure or orgonomic massage focusing on one body segment at a time.

The ocular segment presents an unusual problem in that neither the intrinsic nor the extrinsic muscles of the eye are directly accessible. Direct pressure is therefore not an option. The eye muscles can, however, be affected by the soft techniques discussed in the previous chapter and the hard technique presented earlier in the present chapter. There is, however, an ample area for direct massage in the ocular segment. This includes the temples, the entire scalp, and the muscles just below the occipital ridge. All of these muscles can be massaged with the finger tips and the pads of the fingers. The muscles below the occipital ridge often require very heavy pressure, following which patients sometimes report a shift in their visual functioning. The shift may involve heightened awareness of seeing or even a sharper visual acuity. The eyes can be held open, thus stretching the muscles which close the eyelids and the sphincter muscles which squeeze the eyes shut. This is often very potent and is appropriately used with special sensitivity and caution.

In terms of orgonomic massage in the oral segment, my focus is on the masseter muscles, the strong, heavy muscles used for biting. These muscles can be massaged either relaxed or while the patient bites down. If heavily armored, the masseters require extreme pressure, and at the same time can be very painful. Care must be taken not to slip off the masseters and cause pain in the surrounding tissue or to put force on the temporomandibular joint which can cause injury to the tendons and ligaments.

Because of the delicacy of the structures on the anterior of the neck, I limit my orgonomic massage of the cervical segment to the posterior part. The back of the neck can be massaged with the finger tips for deepest pressure and with the pads for pressure not as intense. While following along either side of the cervical spine hard protrusions can sometimes be palpated. These are the transverse processes of vertebrae which are subluxated (misaligned) in the direction where the protrusion is in evidence. Never apply pressure to these spots, since it is painful and serves no purpose. If subluxations are found, a referral to a chiropractor or osteopath for a cervical adjustment is advised. When the neck muscles are spastic there is an uneven dynamic force on the neck. This is one of the possible causes for cervical subluxations. Once the vertebrae are misaligned, the uneven skeletal structure precludes a normal positioning and relaxation of the cervical muscles. Therefore, I see a cervical adjustment as important, when there are subluxations, as part of the process of reducing cervical armoring. Orgonomic work with the neck frequently brings about energy streamings.

The thoracic segment is very large and the back can be heavily muscled. For these reasons and the fact that the chest plays a major role in respiration, the work on the thoracic segment may involve a variety of soft and hard techniques. As for the back, deep muscle massage can be done throughout, from the base of the spinal erectors to the upper trapezius muscles. Pressure with the fingertips and pads of the fingers can be used for getting deeply into the muscles. The upper trapezius muscles can be kneaded or pinched with sufficient pressure to bring about a softening of the armor and oftentimes an experience of energy streamings. Another hard technique which is useful, especially if the back is heavily muscled, is pounding. Using the heels of the fist like hammers the back can be pounded, just hard enough to shock the muscles and invite them to let go. In using pounding care must be taken not to strike the kidneys and to use lighter strokes where there is bone closer to the surface.

With the chest, most of the hard techniques focus on the breathing process. The major technique is chest vibration. To do this have the patient lie supine and place your hands, one atop the other, along the sternum. As the patient exhales through the mouth apply pressure downward. The pressure can be slow and constant, slow and intermittent (slow vibration), or fast and intermittent (fast vibration). The point of vibration can be moved lower on the sternum or can be moved to the upper chest with one hand just below each of the patient's clavicles. The pressure is applied on the exhalation only, thus allowing the patient to inhale without external interference. The patient is instructed to vocalize during the exhalation. To be able to use chest vibration to facilitate deeper, less inhibited respiration, and not to be invasive of the patient requires considerable sensitivity as well as a good deal of practice of the mechanics of the technique.

Another hard technique which can support the reduction of armoring in the chest is the use of the breathing stool. In Chapter 1, I referred to Lowen's breathing stool and described it. Lowen and Lowen (1977) have discussed a number of variations for working with the stool. What I have found most useful is to have the patient lie back over the stool with her or his arms back over the head and breathe deeply. There is a considerable gravitational pull on the chest in this position, both longitudinally and transversely. If the patient will breathe deeply and relax into the gravitational force on the exhalations, an obvious opening of the chest will occur. As in other techniques focused on breathing, vocalization on the exhalation is encouraged. The gravitational effect can be enhanced by adding chest vibration while the patient is lying over the stool. Since the stool places acute stress on the back, it should be used with caution, and never with a patient with a history of back injury.

If palpation of the pectoral muscles or the intercostal muscles reveals tension, the pectorals can be kneaded or pinched as well as massaged by long strokes from their origin along the sternum to their insertion at the shoulder. The intercostal muscles can be stroked by running finger tips along the intercostal spaces from the sides to the sternum (or from the sternum to the sides). Pressure is not to be applied on the breast tissue.

I find that I involve the arms and hands (extensions of the thoracic segment) through expressive work rather than with orgonomic massage. Expressive technique will be covered in the following chapter.

And now, the diaphragm. Earlier in the present chapter I suggested the use of the gag reflex to soften diaphragmatic armor. Another hard technique is, with the patient supine, deep massage under the lower rim of the rib cage and up under the xiphoid process (lower tip of the sternum). The pressure may be steady as the stroke moves along the rim of the rib cage, or it can be intense pressure with a sudden release. The pressure and release can be applied at multiple points simultaneously (spreading the fingers out), or one point at a time. Vocalization on the exhalation is, again, encouraged. Bending the knees, with the feet on the floor, will help disengage the abdominal muscles and make the diaphragm more accessible.

I do not use deep muscle pressure on the belly. For softening armor in the abdominal segment I use the appropriate soft techniques discussed in the previous chapter and the stress postures already discussed in the present chapter.

In the case of the pelvic segment I do use orgonomic massage both on the muscles of the pelvis itself and the muscles of the legs (extensions of the pelvic segment). In the pelvic structure I focus the deep massage on the gluteus maximus and gluteus medius muscles (the latter open the legs) using finger tips and thumbs to apply the pressure. This thumb or finger pressure can further be applied to the legs wherever spasticity can be palpated. I feel for the tension in the calves, the hamstrings, the fronts of the thighs, outsides of the thighs, and the adductors of the thighs (insides of the thighs which close the legs). The large leg muscles can also be kneaded or shocked by grabbing them quickly and firmly and then releasing them quickly. An additional hard technique for the gluteus maximus is to have the patient lie prone and tighten the buttocks as much as possible. The therapist then leans her or his weight on the patient with one fist on each buttock. The patient supports the therapist's weight with the contracted buttocks, breathing deeply and vocally until the buttocks fatigue. This fatiguing can bring about a relaxation of the armoring throughout the pelvis.

The effective use of orgonomic massage requires a lot of practice, and certainly cannot be learned from a book. What I have wanted to do here is give a brief description of this hard technique. The learning of it is best done through supervised practice. For further intellectual under-standing of the orgonomic process, I recommend a case presentation by Konia (1975). In this case study, Konia describes the systematic appli-cation of Reichian techniques, including examples of what I have termed soft techniques, hard techniques, and expressive techniques. This case study is succinct and particularly clear in presentation.

I want to return now to the topic of grounding, or more specifically, grounding as containment of energy. When one has adequate containment for the amount of energy present, that energy can be experienced as an alive issue with which to deal. But if the containment is not adequate, that energy is experienced as an overcharge, as "too much," and something which threatens one's organismic integrity. With this feeling of "too much" is often an illusion of omnipotence. The patient believes that if he or she felt the emotion fully, then he or she would do destructive things on a grandiose scale. Patients have said things to me such as "If I let out all this anger, I'd go right through that brick wall" or

"If I let myself feel all this sexual energy, I'd go out there and fuck every-body in sight!" Behind these statements of omnipotence are primitive *beliefs* in such omnipotence. Another perspective on this fear of omnipo-tence is to identify it as a form which the "catastrophic expectation" (stated by the toxic introject) can take. It is as if the toxic introject says, "Don't feel angry or you'll destroy everything!" Although this omnipotent version of the catastrophic expectation can be experienced relative to any pure emotion or blend of emotions, there is a special technique well suited for dealing with it in the cases of anger and sexual energy. The technique is one which I learned from Pesso, which he invented and named the "limits structure." I will describe my adaptation of this technique.

The time to use a limits structure is when a patient begins to move in the direction of feeling or expressing anger or sexuality, but then dra-matically shrinks (a dramatic contraction against expansion). The dramatic shrinking can be seen in the body and sometimes is also given words by the patient with the recognition of omnipotence as mentioned above. At those times, when the patient acknowledges spontaneously or upon exploration by the therapist that he or she has fear of omnipo-tence with the emerging feeling, the limits structure is a powerful option, and may even be the technique of choice.

In the case of a limits structure for anger, a group setting is impera-tive. The patient is told that the group is going to assist in helping create a situation in which he or she can experience the full extent of her or his rage without anyone or anything getting hurt, including the patient. It is essential that the patient agree to the technique and agree that this is not a contest, but a cooperative activity in which the purpose is the growthful experience of the patient. The message is, "We will help you by containing your energy so that you can have the experience of feeling and expressing all of your energy without anything bad happening." An agreement is made between the therapist and the patient that if either of them per-ceives that something is going wrong, he or she will say "stop" and every-one (patient included) will stop immediately. The patient is asked to lie supine on the floor (carpeted or padded), arms at the sides. Group members gather around and contact the patient in a manner such that they may exert downward force to the patient's lower legs, upper legs, pelvis, shoulders, upper arms, lower arms, and forehead. In the course of the limits structure, the patient may request resistance on the chest. The therapist can maintain a better vantage point for directing the limits structure if he or she also shares in the physical containment. The par-ticipants place their hands as much as possible on fleshy areas (never on joints) and are careful not to cause pain by pushing hard over a bony surface. They are instructed just to meet, to neutralize the patient's energy and not to pin the patient down. One or two trials with the patient using less than full force will alert the participants as to any adjustments in their arrangement or body position which they need to make in order to do the job of safe containment. The patient agrees not to exert until the therapist indicates that everyone is ready. It is also important to have the patient exert with steady pressure, avoiding jerking or twisting motions which could easily cause injury. The patient can now rage, rest and rage again until he or she reports a new awareness, that her or his anger is not too much to be contained, that it is possible to rage fully without anything bad happening. It is essential that the limits structure be carried out with utmost care, for if it backfires (patient gets hurt, participants get hurt, or patient overpowers the limits), the patient will have been given an experience which validates the toxic introject. This is a very potent and dramatic technique, and also one of the most potentially dangerous if done carelessly. It is obvious from this description that the limits structure is all or none, to be done completely and with total commitment from patient and participants alike, or not to be done. And again, obviously, this technique cannot be done without a sufficient number of participants. It is strictly a technique for a group context.

In contrast, a limits structure for an illusion of sexual omnipotence can be carried out with just the therapist and patient. In this case, too, the patient is instructed to lie supine with arms at the side. The purpose and meaning of the technique must be explained and agreed to by the patient. The therapist then provides resistance to the patient's pelvic movements by placing her or his hands on the hip bones and pressing down. The patient is asked to breathe deeply, through the mouth, and make vocal sounds on the exhalation while thrusting forward with the pelvis against the therapist's resistance. In this way the patient usually confronts her or his omnipotent illusion and can experience containment of that energy.

The limits structure for use with the illusion of sexual omnipotence involves voluntary movements of the pelvis. The orgastic reflex, however, involves involuntary pelvic movement. This involuntary reflex action can actually be avoided by the clinging to voluntary movements. There are techniques for approaching the orgastic reflex. One is pelvic thrusting, the harder form of the undulated breathing technique described in the previous chapter as a soft technique. For this harder and more advanced version the patient is invited to breathe deeply with vocal sounds on the exhalation and to thrust forcefully. So with each exhalation there is a thrust and a vocalization. The therapist coaches the patient to proceed with increasing force and speed and to "allow the body to take over," "to let whatever wants to happen, happen." This can lead to an orgastic reflex if the patient has dissolved the major part of her or his armor. As in the case of the soft version of this technique, the hard technique can be used lying or standing, the latter being more difficult.

Another hard technique for working toward the orgastic reflex involves relaxation and breathing. The patient is invited to lie supine and do the undulating breathing referred to above and explained in the chapter on soft technique. The added element which moves this into the realm of hard technique is that the therapist instructs the patient to hold the breath out as long as possible at the end of the exhalation. The therapist coaches the patient to let the inhalation come involuntarily and "allow the whole body to spasm as it wants to." This is a very advanced technique and is appropriate only with patients who are veterans of psychotherapeutic body work.

A final hard technique which encourages the orgastic reflex involves a specialized stress posture which focuses the muscular stress on the abdominals. The patient, starting in a supine position with knees bent and feet on the floor, is instructed to perform half a sit-up and hold that position as long as possible while breathing deeply and vocalizing on the exhalation. The vibrations are encouraged. The patient can relax into the starting position and allow the vibrations and spasms to continue into an orgastic reflex.

10. Expressive Technique

Expressive techniques in psychotherapy are focused on the action ▶ interaction ▶ satisfaction half of the contact episode. This is, of course, the expressive portion of contact. But, as discussed in an earlier chapter, because of the feedback loops in the contact/withdrawal cycle the opening up of the expression half may enhance and amplify the awareness portion (want ▶ arousal ▶ emotion). The expressive work involves movement of energy into the musculoskeletal system for processing. In this work support is given to the patient's acting on what he or she is organismically experiencing as growthful or natural, rather than self-interrupting and continuing the old pattern of avoidance. The patient is invited and encouraged to act in spite of the voice of the toxic introject, to act in the face of the catastrophic expectation.

Apropos of this encouragement of the patient's acting in spite of the threat of the toxic introject is a lesson offered in *The Teachings of Don Juan: A Yaqui Way of Knowledge* (Castaneda, 1968). Don Juan is instructing his apprentice, Carlos Castaneda, in the "enemies" which stand in the way of one's briefly experiencing being a "man of knowledge." The enemies are fear, clarity, power, and old age, and in each case Don Juan reveals what the apprentice must do to defeat that enemy in her or his path. To defeat fear, reveals Don Juan, one must feel it fully and then *act in spite of it*. This is the essence of disempowering the toxic introject. Hear the voice of the toxic introject, recognize its threat of catastrophe if one disobeys its injunction, feel the anxiety fully and then *act in spite of it*. By doing what the toxic introject forbids, and finding that no catastrophe ensues, one defeats the enemy of growth and aliveness. Meeting the enemy face to face on the battleground of action with persistence offers almost certain success *qua* growth.

The essence of the expressive techniques is taking action, concrete musculoskeletal movement. The action to be growthful, however, must carry symbolic meaning. So, the expressive technique, in order to be growth-producing, must meet two criteria. First, it must involve concrete (i.e., body) action. Second, that action must be the symbolic expression of the breaking of the injunction of the toxic introject. The symbolic meaning is, then, that of disobedience, negating the toxic or bionegative injunction. The toxic introject says "no" to life and the symbolic action of expression is the patient's saying "no" to that "no." A decision can be made on the verbal symbolic level not to obey an introjected toxic message, but it is the giving of life to the decision through the concrete body expression which makes the decision real. The body-action-symbol is what transforms, allows the patient to move beyond the deadness prescribed by toxic messages.

Much of the psychotherapeutic expressive work is verbal, of course. The use of the verbal aspect of expression has been presented well in the existing literature. I especially recommend to the reader the Gestalt therapy literature containing transcriptions of actual work. The following deserve careful study: Naranjo's *The Techniques of Gestalt Therapy* (1980), and Perls' *Gestalt Therapy Verbatim* (1969), *The Gestalt Approach and Eye Witness to Therapy* (1973), and *Legacy from Fritz* (1975). From these transcribed examples one can gain a feel for the Gestalt approach and appreciate the beauty and power of this way of working. The focus of the present chapter is the manifestation of such work on the plane of physical (body) expression.

When one has interrupted a contact/withdrawal cycle, there is "unfinished business," a tension remaining from the Gestalt not yet complete. When there is self-interruption, there is some body part which has not been put to full use. There are an arm and fist which have not hit, a jaw that has not bitten, tear glands which have not secreted, a throat which has not screamed, a belly which has not chuckled, a pelvis which has not thrust. So, the patient in self-interrupting has in a sense not only deleted a behavior but has been as if missing a body part. The expressive work allows the completion of the behavioral Gestalt and at the same time involves the reowning of the "missing" body part. For instance, the patient who retroflects his anger by clenching his fists (retroflected action) as he talks about his boss may be invited to pound on a cushion (concrete action) while letting the cushion represent his boss (symbolic interaction). The concrete body behavior then carries the symbolic meaning of expressing his anger directly to the appropriate (symbolized) target. He may thus break the rule of his introjected voice which demands "Do not show anger!" His aroused anger has then been allowed expression, and if given sufficient expression the behavioral Gestalt, i.e., the contact/withdrawal cycle has been completed. And in so doing, he has reowned his fists, no longer behaving as if he had not fists by which he can express anger.

This brief and much simplified example brings up for me an important point for clarification in expressive work. Expressive work may be practice for literally doing out in the world what one does symbolically in therapy, or it may not. Primitive expressions must be opened up to disempower the toxic introject, and this means extreme and dramatic symbolic behaviors. But those same extreme and dramatic behaviors would ultimately not serve the patient *in most cases* if literally carried out in the world. So the patient may be invited to punch and pound the boss to death, symbolically. It is important in such a situation to make clear to the patient that this work is symbolic and is neither practice for nor permission for literally doing this. When the patient understands the importance of symbolic acting out with spontaneous concrete action and distinguishes that from practice for literal acting out in the world, the therapeutic expressive work becomes much easier and freer. This is a learning of the difference between blocks and inhibition on the one hand and moral restraint on the other. In some cases the expressive work in the therapy session is indeed rehearsal for literal action out in the world.

As I see it, the forte of the Gestalt approach is the experiment. "Experiment" and "experience" stem from the same root, *experiri* — "to try." And "experience" means the actual living through, the having of personal and direct impressions. "Experiment" means an operation undertaken to discover some effect. And hence, the Gestalt experiment. The therapist can track the patient during their interaction, following until the patient reaches an impasse, a point of self-interruption in a contact/withdrawal cycle. When the self-interruption involves the action ►interaction ►satisfaction sequence directly then a Gestalt experiment involving body expression is in order. (I suggest that the reader review Figure 7 "Levels of the Therapy Task" in Chapter 4.) For the remainder of the present chapter I will use the term "experiment" to refer to the Gestalt experiment involving body expression work.

The experiment may be brief and simple or it may be highly and complexly developed into a major piece of work. This decision, made jointly by the therapist and the patient depends on the degree of impasse which the patient is experiencing, how much work is going to be done at this time, and what Zinker (1977) has termed "grading the work in terms of experienced difficulty for the client." In other words, the therapist and patient may decide to deal with a major or minor impasse (i.e., block or inhibition, respectively), and may want to do a little or a lot of work depending on time constraints, other issues in the person's life, and so on. Grading the experiment involves finding a level at which the client can work successfully. The idea is to let the experiment be the "next step," taking the patient beyond where he or she customarily stops. Too small a step wastes time, and too large a step may result in the patient's balking and not moving beyond the old and familiar. In this latter case, the attempted step may call forth greater anxiety than can be counterbalanced by the patient's self-support and the therapist's support taken together.

For an excellent exploration of the experiment I recommend *Creative Process in Gestalt Therapy* by Joseph Zinker (1977), Chapter 6.

One useful expressive technique which can be used without necessarily creating an elaborate experiment is that of *repetition*. The idea here is to invite the patient to repeat a spontaneous body expression over and over. This technique implies an inhibited expression, of course, not a completely blocked expression. But when an expression is allowed, but not with great frequency, the invitation for repetition can facilitate its disinhibition.

Another such technique is *exaggeration and development*. This means to take an expression which appears in diminished form and invite the patient to exaggerate that expression allowing it to develop into full-blown form. Again, as in repetition, exaggeration and development support a movement toward disinhibition.

A further expressive technique is *identification and action*. The essence of this technique is a translation of words into action. A thought, memory, idea, or image is identified and then expressed through body action. So, that which was experienced on the verbal-symbolic level gets translated into aliveness through the body.

These three techniques — repetition, exaggeration and development, and identification and action — are presented by Naranjo (1980) as procedures for the intensification of action. The focus here is on the patient's expanded expression.

In terms of the patient's experience of satisfaction following her or his action ►interaction sequence, there is a procedure emphasized by Pesso (1969, 1973) known as "accommodation." Accommodation is provided in order to facilitate satisfaction, to make the symbolic interaction more "real" (not literal, but "real"). It provides sensory feedback to the patient which validates the action ►interaction taken. In one-to-one work the therapist can accommodate, whereas in a group I find the procedure is smoother to have another group member accommodate the patient. The way this is done is to ask the patient what he or she would want to see and hear in response to her or his expression. The accommodator then agrees to do and sound the way the patient has requested. So, for example, the patient may want the accommodator to cry out and fall down as if hit when the patient hits a cushion. In this manner the patient has visual and auditory feedback of the effects of her or his expression. The action is concrete, the interaction symbolic, and the sensory feedback concrete, making the experience more real than without accommodation. Accommodation can be too real, or too intense for patients sometimes. The purpose, again, is to facilitate satisfaction. To this end, the experience of satisfaction following body expression, there are three levels of validation which can be used depending upon the intensity and "realness" required by the patient. The first level is *no accommodation*. The patient simply goes through the sequence of concrete action and symbolic interaction. The second level is to invite the patient to fantasize the desired impact of her or his expression on the target person. I label this *fantasy accommodation*. The third and most "real" level is *outside accommodation* or *role-play accommodation* where another person role-plays the target person, providing visual and/or auditory feedback. Outside accommodation, as implied by the above, is certainly not always required for satisfaction. I find that I use fantasy accommodation most often, reserving the role-play accommodation for those special, highly dramatic experiments. A final word about accommodation: It is, itself, a fine art. Good accommodation requires precise timing and appropriate magnitude of sounds and movements. In terms of timing, the accommodation requested must follow by a fraction of a second the patient's expression. For example, a cry of pain must come just after the cushion is kicked. If it precedes the kick, or if there is a delay between the kick and the cry, reality is lost and the drama quickly becomes comic. So, too, with movement accommodations such as falling or rolling in pain. Appropriateness and magnitude of movements and sounds are even more demanding. Overdone sound and movement usually are ludicrous, whereas underdone accommodation is just not validating. With some very basic Thespian skill, a good accommodation can be created. At times, the therapist may suggest sounds or actions for the accommodator to try and then see if the patient finds them validating.

I see the cornerstones of Gestalt therapy as being the I-Thou relationship and the principle of the "here-and-now." The I-Thou relationship has been discussed earlier and will be viewed again in a later chapter on ethics. As for the "here-and-now" principle, this is perhaps the most often misunderstood aspect of the Gestalt approach. It does *not* mean that material from one's past or anticipations or plans for one's future are not important. It does *not* mean that one must deal only with the current events of one's life in therapy. What is does mean is that what is personally growthful is experience, and experience takes place in one's present time and space. One's existence can be conceived in terms of extension along three dimensions — spatial, temporal, and conscious. So a person is located in space, time, and consciousness or awareness. *Growth or actualization of the self takes place in one's here-and-now existence under conditions of heightened awareness.* Thoughts, memories, plans, fantasies all can convey one out of the here-and-now in terms of the mental plane, but those events of thinking, remembering, planning, and fantasizing all occur in the here-and-now in terms of the body plane. Body experience is always right here and right now. One's power, one's "response-ability" for personal growth (autoplastic change) and for impacting others (alloplastic change) is a here-and-now function. I can never eat tomorrow's breakfast today, nor go back and change last night's menu. But I can bring my remembered history into the here-and-now, experiencing my present body/self and proceed to complete the emotionally unfinished business. And I can bring my plans or fantasies of my future into the here-and-now, experiencing my present body/self as a guide in altering my planning. I am remembering a beautiful pronouncement made by a Shaolin Priest several years ago on the television program "Kung-Fu": "To dwell in one's past is to rob the present, but to ignore one's past is to rob the future."

Perls learned from Reich that remembrances in order to be curative, or as is our perspective now, growthful, requires that the remembrances be accompanied by the appropriate affect. This is the basis for the Gestalt dictum of working in the here-and-now. So it is not sufficient that a patient remember the traumatic times, but those remembrances must involve the feelings which were felt at those times. With the feelings present, for psychological purposes the patient is reliving the trauma. But now, in the therapeutic setting, we have the possibility of processing the feelings, of allowing the natural process of the contact/withdrawal cycle to take place, thus disempowering the toxic introject and completing a piece of unfinished emotional business from the past.

All of the Gestalt techniques can be seen as ways of furthering the here-and-now experience, of expanding one's awareness of her or his embodied self in the moment. The techniques can be grouped under two categories, *concentration* and *presentification* (Smith, 1975). Concentration techniques are those which enhance awareness through making present experience more vivid. They involve the "opening up to" and the "staying with" one's contact with the world, while decreasing one's mode of distraction. (See Naranjo, 1980 for a full discussion of techniques.) Presentification refers to the bringing of the past or the future into the experienced present (Naranjo, 1970). In practice, of course, it is almost always the patient's conflicted past which is brought into the here-and-now for emotional processing.

Presentification involves making a past or fantasy happening now and actual by reliving—or "living"—that happening. The "living" comes through an enacting of the scenes with the appropriate words and body actions and interactions. As Perls (1973, p. 65) stated, "It is insufficient merely to recall a past incident, one has to *psychodramatically* return to it." In describing presentification Naranjo (1970, p. 53) had this to say: "This may take the form of an inward attempt to identify with or relive past events or, most often, a reenacting of the scenes with gestural and postural participation as well as verbal exchanges, as in psychodrama."

For Perls (1970, p. 14), "Now = experience = awareness = reality."

The most elaborate and complete form of expressive technique or Gestalt experiment consists of creating a psychodrama in which the patient is invited to go beyond where he or she is accustomed to stopping in the contact/withdrawal cycle. The therapist's task is to identify the point of patient self-interruption and to create an appropriate scenario in which the patient can psychodramatically act through the block or inhibition to an organismically natural completion. To design such psychodrama calls forth the therapist's creativity and imagination. Zinker (1977) has elaborated the steps of this creative endeavor to consist of the following. First is the laying of the groundwork, essentially a developing of rapport and a hearing of the patient's strands of communication until a unifying theme emerges. Second is the negotiation of consensus or arriving at agreement with the patient as to participation in the experiment. Third is grading of difficulty level. Fourth is the surfacing of the patient's awareness. Fifth is locating of the patient's energy or finding where in her or his body the patient is energized and where he or she is deadened. Focusing awareness and energy in the development of a theme is the sixth step. Next, or seventh, is the generation of self-support. Eighth is choosing the content for the experiment. Ninth is the enactment of that experiment. Tenth, and finally is the debriefing which may include asking the patient what he or she has learned, thus inviting a cognitive framing of the completed work.

A critical factor in expressive work is the experience of satisfaction. Patients often tend to set up their own psychodrama in a way that symbolically repeats again and again the historical unfinished business, thus leaving them frustrated and stuck. The therapist needs to be alert to this propensity, this repetition compulsion, and design the experiment in such a way that the patient completes the unfinished business. Many experiments may be done before the unfinished business is complete, but each experiment may be a unit of completion. The goal is to set up a situation which symbolically brings the patient face to face with her or his self-interruption, but which offers an opportunity to go on with new behavior to a validating, satisfying expression of feeling.

For the most part I prefer using empty chairs or cushions to symbolize the various people in the patient's drama, even in the group setting. This gives the patient more license for experimenting with expressions, both verbal and nonverbal, without concern for the safety of actual people present. This also prevents the complication of stirring reactions from role-playing figures which then can obfuscate the purpose of the psychodrama. Remember, I am dealing here with technique of expression at the level of symbolic acting through blocks and inhibitions. I am not wanting to deal with the techniques or uses of literal encounter here.

A major clue to look for in setting up an experiment is the location of energy in the body. What part or parts of the body appear energized? Once that clue is found, a situation can be arranged centered around the use of the energized body part for expression (action ► interaction). The patient may be aware of the symbolic meaning even before the expression, or he or she may express and in the course of that concrete action and interaction, the symbolic meaning may emerge. This is the dynamic of the contact/withdrawal cycle wherein a step in the flow may enhance steps which are upstream. In this case, the action ► interaction sequence leads to an increase in the awareness half of the cycle. The guideline I am presenting here is, *Go where the patient's energy is.*

Sometimes things are not so simple and there is not a musculoskeletal region which is energized, even when the patient tells her or his story. In such a situation there are four options which one can exercise in the service of proceeding to action. First, look for body areas which seem deadened. An area may be energized, unenergized, or deenergized. A deenergized area may be indentifiable by its conspicuous lack of energy — pale, cool skin, immobility, or stiffness. In this case the patient may be invited to act with the deenergized area. This guideline is: *Go where the patient's energy is forbidden.* The second option is for use when the energy is in the belly. Sometimes the patient shunts the energy out of the muscles which are available for action and into the belly, resulting in nausea. Invite the patient to tighten the belly as much as possible for a few moments and then relax suddenly and see where the energy goes. Almost always two or three of these tension and release sequences will energize the patient's body in a place which implies some particular action. (I learned this procedure from Pesso.) The third option is to invite the patient to fantasize being energized and see where the energy appears. This option can be used when in the course of working the patient develops a headache. He or she can then be asked to imagine that overcharge of energy moving out of the head and into the body. The energized area can then be the focus of action. The fourth option is to attend to raising the patient's energy level by use of one of the breathing techniques which have been discussed in previous chapters.

The technique by which Gestalt therapy often is identified is the "empty chair" technique. The empty chair is used as a locus for the fantasized target of the patient's expression. The expression may be a monologue wherein the patient stays in her or his chair and expresses to the target in the empty chair, or it may be a dialogue in which the patient switches back and forth between the two chairs also giving voice to the target person or thing. The latter procedure is in the service of the patient's reowning that which he or she has projected, as well as being a way of enlivening the experience. The dialogue often builds the emotional level as the patient shuttles between the two roles. So, as the patient in role as the target speaks the hurtful, frightening, or disgusting, the patient can hear and react to what was actually just heard.

The empty chair technique follows from a procedural rule of Gestalt therapy identified by Levitsky and Perls (1970) as "no gossiping." Gossiping is defined as "talking about" instead of "talking to." The latter of course, tends to prevent the avoidance of feelings. In the present context I am talking about full body expression, not just verbal expression. And so, as I have indicated, in doing this work I often substitute a cushion or folded Japanese mattress for the empty chair. This makes a safe target for the patient to hit, kick, throw out of the room, bite, pat, hug, or whatever.

Some final words about the empty chair technique have to do with a common error. That error is to stop too soon in the dialogue. The dialogue and expression are most useful when continued until the patient shows clear signs of satisfaction and is therefore ready for a natural withdrawal.

Earlier, in Chapter 4, I stated that an altered state of consciousness (ASC) often ensues when the patient is working at the level of enacted fantasy. I want to elaborate on the ASC here, quoting from an earlier article (Smith, 1975, p. 38–40):

"Both concentration and presentification, when profound, involve an ASC. Turning first to concentration, Polster (1970) as mentioned earlier, has called attention to the parallels between hypnosis and profound concentration. Another clue is offered by London (1967) in his review of methods of hypnotic induction. One of the features which he finds present in most induction methods is concentration. Through concentration one focuses strongly on some stimulus, be it internal or external, and concomitantly decreases the usual superficial scan of the environment. This is very clearly an instance of qualitatively changing the usual sensory input, which may then lead to an ASC. Considerable research in support of this notion has shown that there is a range of exteroceptive input which is necessary in order to maintain an anchoring in the concensually defined reality. Deviations above or below this range result in a fading of concensual reality or, in other words, the establishment of an ASC.

"Turning to presentification, we see a situation in which the patient behaves as if a past event, dream, or fantasy is now real and present. Clearly, the intense involvement with the dramatization of such non-conconsensual reality requires a decreased involvement with the usual consensual reality, again lessening the anchoring in the usual state of consciousness.

"I think this shows that Gestalt concentration and Gestalt presentification provide a sufficient condition for the establishment of an ASC. A second issue is the established ASC. Anyone who has experienced and observed intense Gestalt work will recognize the presence of an ASC in this work. During intense concentration or presentification there are combinations of the following features of ASCs.

"Alterations in thinking—Archaic modes of thought or primary process thinking in which the patient is reexperiencing his childhood thought patterns, may occur. Sometimes there is a dramatic recovery of forgotten material.

"Disturbed time sense—A happening of a few minutes may seem like hours. It is not uncommon in Gestalt groups for patients to be concerned about having taken up an inordinate amount of time in their working.

"Loss of control—A sense that one cannot stop the process until the process is complete. I have heard patients say after working that they did not plan to go so far, but once they started they just couldn't stop until it was over.

"Changes in emotional expression—Perhaps the most dramatic and therefore obvious occurrence which is sometimes present in Gestalt work is the rapid access to intense affect. Sometimes within minutes from starting to work, the patient explodes into grief, joy, or anger.

"Body image change—Patients doing a dialogue often report the real feeling of being split into two people or only a part of themselves. The parts are subjectively real. Another frequent experience is of a distortion of body size or proportions.

"Perceptual distortions—Things may look different, senses may be temporarily more or less acute. There may be quasi-hallucinations, such as a patient reporting after an empty-chair dialogue that he could 'really' see his father in the chair.

"Change in meaning or significance—Seeing of new relationships, finding of new perspectives is frequent.

"Sense of the ineffable—One of the few appropriate uses of the exclamation, 'Wow!' is just after doing heavy Gestalt work. Often the patient doesn't want to talk afterward, but just wants to 'sit with it.' Observers are sometimes very skeptical about what they have seen. In a recent workshop which I co-led, an observer reacted with anger to some Gestalt work he had just seen, and accused us, only partly in jest, of having rehearsed the whole performance the night before.

"Feelings of rejuvenation—Almost always, upon completion of Gestalt work, there is a feeling of comfort, relief, hope, and well-being.

"Hypersuggestibility—Once committed and into Gestalt work, patients are often very ready to try out rather uncritically whatever the therapist suggests. In addition, the patient is often highly receptive to parent-like injunctions from the therapist.

"The Gestalt techniques are aimed at the creation of a here-and-now experience which often is subjectively real and consensually unreal. For this subjective experience to be profoundly real requires, by definition, a state other than the normal state of consciousness. This condition is what Deikman (1969) has termed the 'reality-transfer,' when thoughts and images become real. My hypothesis is that the effectiveness of the Gestalt technique is related to the degree of realness of the subjective experience which ensues, or in other words the depth of the altered state of consciousness produced. But more importantly, the Gestalt therapist does not assume the role of the change agent, as does the charismatic style of hypnotherapist. Rather, he is a guide or facilitator in an I-Thou encounter, and the patient is responsible for both his own being and becoming."

To relate this material to some of the literature on ASCs, I offer the following, also from my 1975 article (Smith, 1975, p. 36-37):

"The term 'altered state of consciousness,' or ASC, implies a change from a normal or usual state of consciousness. Ths usual state of consciousness can be seen as that state in which one spends the major part of one's waking time, and which for that person, generally has an adaptive value in his environment. In an ASC one experiences a qualitative shift in his usual pattern of mental functioning.

"In his thorough discussion of altered states of consciousness, Ludwig (1969) offers a more complete definition, saying that ASCs are 'any mental states, induced by various physiological, psychological, or pharmacological maneuvers or agents, which can be recognized subjectively by the individual himself (or by an objective observer of the individual) as representing a sufficient deviation in subjective experience or psychological functioning from certain general norms for that individual during alert, waking consciousness' (p. 9-19).

"Ludwig goes on to expand his phrase, 'sufficient deviation in subjective experience,' by saying that 'it may be represented by a greater preoccupation than usual with internal sensations or mental processes, changes in the formal characteristics of thought, and impairment of reality testing to various degress' (p. 10). ASCs may be produced, according to Ludwig, by a wide variety of agents or maneuvers which interfere with the normal level of sensory or proprioceptive input, the normal motor output, the normal emotional tone, or the normal flow and organization of cognitive processes. Although the specific conditions under which ASCs are produced are quite varied, Ludwig lists a number of similar features which to some degree tend to characterize most ASCs. These features consist of alterations in thinking, disturbed time sense, loss of control, change in emotional expression, change in body image, perceptual distortions, changes in meaning or significance, a sense of the ineffable, feelings of rejuvenation, and hypersuggestibility."

Part IV
Personal and Ethical Considerations

Part IV contains the most explicitly philosophical material in this book. It addresses issues of values, containing clear statements of biases and judgments as to what is good.

Chapter 11 is on ethical issues involved in the conducting of a body-oriented psychotherapy. I make the point that these ethics are not in general any different from those of other types of psychotherapy, but that working with the body does present some specific applications of the general ethical principles which are important to recognize. In addition, some of the specific applications of the general ethical principles are peculiar to work with the body.

In Chapter 12, the final chapter of *The Body in Psychotherapy*, I explore personal energy dynamics and define aspects of the person who is relatively free from characterological blocks to full aliveness. I discuss what it means to "live" one's body. This chapter includes an expansion upon material presented earlier in the book, looking at some of the implications of that material for living and for life-styles. Finally, I extend the topic of personal energy dynamics into the realm of the interpersonal, speculating on interactional styles and their relationship to character style.

11. The Ethics of
Body-Oriented Psychotherapy

One of the terms used in defining ethics is "duties." So, in this chapter I will state some of the duties which I see as good and as appropriate for the body-oriented psychotherapist. The ethics for a body-oriented psychotherapist are not different in any general sense from those of other psychotherapists. There are, however, some ethical considerations which have an application specific to working with the body.

The first ethical duty which I see is what I term the "ego-syntonic imperative." By this term I mean that for one to function optimally in the therapeutic role it is essential that he or she relate to the patient only in ways that are congruent with who that therapist is. Techniques, as I have emphasized, are given life and meaning through the person of the therapist. It is imperative, then, that the therapist only interact with the patient through techniques which are consistent with the therapist's person. To use ego-dystonic techniques is to be mechanical and inauthentic. So, if a therapist feels like herself or himself in using a technique, if that technique seems to flow out of her or him, then it is an appropriate technique to keep in one's repertoire. Another facet of the ego-syntonic imperative is that the patient must work in the therapist's way, a way which allows the therapist to keep her or his integrity. John Warkentin called my attention to this point in a supervisory seminar several years ago. The basic idea is "I am who I am, and work how I work." If the patient wants some other kind of work, something which I don't do, then it is better not to see that patient. As Barry Stevens (1970, p. 7) put it, "When the wrong man uses the right means, the right means work in the wrong way."

When a sensitive and skillful body-oriented therapist offers a workshop or seminar demonstrating that style of work there are sometimes other therapist's patients present who are attracted to the body-oriented work. The patients may be attracted to the body work itself, experiencing some resonance and seeing that work as valuable for them. Or, another possibility, which can be operating with or without the first, is that the patient may form an almost instant and strong positive transference with the workshop or seminar leader, seeing her or him as very powerful or even magical. These patients may then want to become patients of the workship or seminar leader. The ethical duty is to be respectful of the already existing therapeutic relationship. In its bald form the ethical duty is to not steal another therapist's patients. This means to not agree to see another therapist's patients without that therapist's explicit agreement and consent, or unless the patient has first made a clear and clean termination with the first therapist. And the latter must be done without encouragement or help from the workshop or seminar leader. What feels ethically clear to me is as follows. First, for the workshops in which I have administrative control, I have printed on the application form a statement that I require all applicants who are currently in therapy to apply only with their therapist's knowledge and agreement to their participation. In the case of sponsored workshops I usually do not have the convenience of this procedure. Second, I never suggest that a participant follow up the workshop with work with me. Third, I never criticize the procedures of other therapists which participants may ask me about. Fourth, if a participant asks to see me I always inquire as to whether or not he or she is currently in therapy. If the answer is yes, I always suggest that he or she take the issue up with her or his therapist. On occasion I have been contacted by someone who is in therapy with someone else and who wants to see me in addition. If this has not been discussed and agreed upon by the therapist, I ask the person to take up the issue with her or his therapist. I have in this way worked with people who have concurrently been in therapy with someone else. In order for this to work, I have made it clear that the other therapist is the primary therapist and I am in the secondary role as consultant. Additionally, it is essential that there are explicit open lines of communication between the other therapist and me. In this manner the enterprise has been successful even when the other therapist has been very different from me in theoretical and procedural approach. I have done this, for instance, while the patient was currently in psychoanalysis. The ethical point is not to take advantage of the appeal of body work so as to be disrespectful of other therapists or therapeutic alliances.

In discussing expressive body work I mentioned that the expression may be a rehearsal for a literal expression out in the world, or it may be a primitive expression for symbolic processing in the therapy session. In the latter case, where the task is unblocking or disinhibiting a primitive level of expression, it is incumbent upon the therapist to clarify that the expressive work is not a permission for nor a rehearsal for carrying out that behavior in the literal world. The distinction must be made between the freedom which comes from opening up primitive channels of concrete expression which allow symbolic processing of previously blocked energy, and the responsibility of choosing appropriate literal processing in the social world.

A rather obvious ethical duty, but one I still want to mention is that of not using the power of body techniques as a way of aggrandizing one's ego. As has been written and often quoted with variations in wording, the therapist's function is to facilitate the growth of the patient, not to demonstrate how powerful he or she can be. This means to judge what intervention, if any, is in the patient's best interest at any given moment and to respond to that judgment. That often means to shun the temptation of the flashy or dramatic intervention. That temptation is perhaps greatest when there are witnesses to the work, such as in the workshop or seminar setting.

Closely related to the previous ethical point is one concerning enjoyment of the patient. Again, as stated above, the ethically guided task of the therapist is to facilitate the patient's growth, thus being with the patient in whatever manner serves that end and preserves integrity in the therapist. That means to shun the temptation to play with or have fun with the patient when that is not at that moment in the patient's best interest, when the playing would be serving an avoidance. The patient is not here for the therapist's entertainment. When therapy is done well, however, the therapist may appreciate and enjoy the patient in the context of good therapy process. Joking, playing, frolicking certainly have a place in therapy, as ways of growthful being, but not as avoidances of less pleasant work for the therapist or patient. After all, the patient is paying a fee.

Related to this is something John Warkentin shared in a supervision session. He said that therapy doesn't work when the therapist touches with erotic intent. That is not ethically guided work when the therapist touches in order to get turned on. The reason for touching must be nonerotic, nonseductive. Again, the patient is not here for the therapist's entertainment, erotic or otherwise. The therapist's touch must be respectful of the patient's therapeutic need.

Mentioned early in the present volume (Chapter 1) is what Buber termed the "I-Thou" relationship. The definition of the psychotherapy relationship in terms of the I and the Thou is fundamental. Especially in body-oriented psychotherapy it is easy to avoid the human involvement which may threaten to touch on the therapist's own pains and fears. The avoidance is made easy by mechanical application of body techniques. Doing these things to the patient is not likely to lead to any growth, and is making the patient an object to be manipulated, forced, or fixed. Buber's term "I-It" stands for this kind of *person to object* relationship. I see body techniques as ways of relating, *person to person*. Through skillful and compassionately guided techniques, the person of the therapist is revealed and the person of the patient acknowledged. The ethical point I see is for the therapist to be honest with the patient whether his orientation is I-Thou or not. My bias is for psychotherapy to be in the I-Thou context where personhood is the core of the process. In this process both patient and therapist undergo transformation. Body techniques are ways for the patient and therapist to relate.

Inevitably transference occurs in the therapy situation. When the patient has unresolved issues with her or his parents from the distant past, in some way these issues will appear in the therapy relationship. The workshop and seminar model of training tends to give little attention to working with the transference. In part this is because the transference may not manifest in any observable way until a therapist-patient relationship has existed for some period of time longer than is typical in workshops. In an ongoing therapy relationship, however, the transference feelings will be present and must be dealt with if the therapy is to be successful. Important to remember is that in a body-oriented approach to therapy the same transference phenomena occur as in a strictly talking therapy, but often occur sooner and sometimes more powerfully or dramatically. As Lowen (1971, p. XIII) has written, "In bioenergetic therapy, the physical contact brings both transference and counter-transference more sharply into focus." So, with physical contact between patient and therapist, the patient may feel love, sexual arousal, caring for the therapist, hurt, anger, resentment, and so forth in ways which are not genuinely with the therapist. These positive and negative transference feelings are highly important to recognize as such and to be processed appropriately.

In the above quote Lowen also mentions counter-transference. The touching which the therapist does tends to bring her or his counter-transference feelings quickly to the fore. These feelings, positive or negative, are important for the therapist to recognize for what they are and to deal with appropriately. This is a prime place where the therapist's own therapy is essential. This need for personal therapy continues and needs to be attended to from time to time throughout the therapist's career.

This mentioning of transference and counter-transference and its likely acceleration through body work brings me to the point of distinguishing between psychotherapy which involves body work and other body work. By nonpsychotherapy body work I include Structural Integration (Rolfing), Alexander Technique, Feldenkrais work, massage, Traeger work, Astin Patterning, Tai Ch'i Chuan, Yoga, Aikido, creative movement, and so forth. I know from my own experience that Feldenkrais work, massage, Tai Chi'i Chuan, Hatha Yoga, Kundalini Yoga, and Aikido are all valuable ways of personal growth. What I have heard and read about the other ways mentioned above leads me to believe that they, too, are of great value. As ways of growth all of these systems are valuable, either by themselves or as adjuncts to psychotherapy. They are not effective alternatives to psychotherapy, however. What these methods can do is greatly enhance body awareness, increase the options of aliveness in the body, and change old body habits which are dysfunctional. What they do not do is provide directly for the symbolic processing of previously blocked or inhibited emotion. *It is this emotional energy processing which is at the core of body-oriented psychotherapy.* Another way of conceptualizing this distinction is to say that the body systems facilitate growth where there is not a high degree of conflict, where the growth urge is not greatly blocked or inhibited by the presence of a toxic introject. Where toxic introjects are present the body systems are rendered relatively ineffective in and of themselves. They may be useful in getting the person to the point of bumping into a toxic introject, but they do not have the methodology or the relationship context for deep psychological work (Yoga and martial arts when taught as complete systems for living and in the Master-Apprentice model may be an exception.) The teacher of these methods is not trained to recognize or deal with transference and counter-transference issues. The ethical duty of one who calls herself or himself a psychotherapist is, as I see it, to deal with transference and counter-transference appropriately and to focus on the processing of previously blocked or inhibited emotional energy. So the ethical duty is different for the body-oriented psychotherapist from that of the practitioner of nonpsychotherapy ways of working with the body.

The body-oriented psychotherapist knows the possible and probable happenings which result from her or his techniques better than the patient does. So, I see it as the ethical duty of the therapist to work with certain cautions. One caveat has to do with invasion of the patient's private emotional life. Before getting into the application of any body intervention early in therapy it is appropriate to have the patient explicitly agree, having been informed of the possibility of strong emotional response to the proceedings. Otherwise, the new patient may implicitly agree to a procedure without knowing to what he or she is agreeing. The guideline here is informed consent. As therapy gets further along, the patient is informed by her or his history with the therapist. In other words, after working together for some time the patient is sophisticated with respect to the probable results of her or his therapist's techniques and knows what he or she is getting into when he or she agrees to try an experiment. Still, in this case, and obviously in the case of the new or a naive patient, it is the therapist's responsibility to grade the intervention to a level which the therapist predicts that the patient can benefit from rather than feel invaded.

A closely related caveat concerns the patient's going farther than he or she has support for and then getting a backlash. What this means is that the patient can, by the use of body interventions, open up and take steps in a previously blocked or inhibited contact/withdrawal cycle before the toxic introject has been sufficiently disempowered. The result, then, is that within a few hours after the therapy work the toxic introject comes forward with a vengeance, leaving the patient regretful of the work done and feeling affirmed in her or his catastrophic expectation. This situation can also be viewed bioenergetically as an overcharging without sufficient grounding. So again, the ethical duty of the therapist is to grade the level of the body work appropriately. The duty to the patient is to facilitate, as much as possible, steps which the patient can build on, one by one. The therapy process does involve progressive steps interspersed with retrogressive steps as Jung (1966) and others have made clear, but the big backlash caused by a forced giant step when a more moderate step would be solid gain is not in the patient's interest.

In all of this the therapist will not be perfect. What he or she can do is to keep impeccability as a guide, to be and do the best he or she can, moment by moment. The task is to do what one does as a therapist as well as one can. That is all. The task is not to make anything happen and the task is not to be exhibitionistic. In *Back to One*, Kopp (1977) in his elegant style emphasizes the importance of "concentrating one-pointedly on the basic work" rather than getting attached to the patient's "progress" or to one's ego-bound evaluations of one's performance. Kopp (1977, p. 6) recognizes a basic ethic in the therapeutic art when he states succinctly, "I run the therapy. They run their lives." Two people are involved, each with a sphere of responsibility. This means that what the patient does with her or his life is not an accurate index of whether or not I have done my work.

I want to close this discussion of ethics with a quote from Barry Stevens (1970, p. 231): "It is more important (to me) (now) to bring someone to life than to be moral."

12. Personal Energy Dynamics

"Life is a contact sport." Think about this. This is what the present chapter explores.

In Chapter 4 during my discussion of the levels of the task of psychotherapy I identified the first level as the facilitation of a richness and meaningfulness in the patient's living. This is a statement of a value position, a bias which I intend to expand upon herein.

I value aliveness. I see that which enhances aliveness as good and that which deadens as bad. Remember, aliveness is characterized by expansion into the "world" and relaxed contraction into the self. This is the rhythm of life. Deadness involves anxious contraction against expansion. Aliveness evolves. First comes an organismic vibration as one experiences an urge, a wanting. The vibrating organism may pulsate, reach a state of expansion to meet the want and a relaxed contraction following an experience of satisfaction. Then comes the graceful flow or streaming in the world, where the energy streamings within the body system are paralleled by the streamings of the organism in the larger system, the organism-in-the-world. (I acknowledge Keleman for calling my attention to vibration, pulsation, and streaming.)

Unfortunately, many people are phobic about life and therefore interpret anxiety as a signal to stop what they are doing or are about to do. Anxiety is a sign of blocked excitement, as shown earlier in this book, but is so often taken as a signal to shut down. The rule for growth, that is, expanded living, is to follow excitement rather than shrink. Going with excitement rather than anxiously contracting is the essence of living passionately. In life, anxiety is a perverse traveling companion (Smith, 1979).

The above implies a relationship between being and becoming to which I want to draw attention. Being, or good living, is served by spontaneous expression of emotions. Becoming, or growth is through emotional expression where it has previously not been allowed. So, growth or becoming is an amplification and deepening of being. To life, more aliveness is added.

The urge for experience is part of being alive. Experience comes from expanding into the world, from going out beyond what is familiar and known. Through experience one can become more. In discussing this facet of expansion Naranjo (1980) states that one intuitively seeks depth or fullness of awareness. When this is not experienced, more and more environmental stimulation may be sought. So, a craving for more takes the place of the natural need for depth. As I see it, when deep experience arouses anxiety, one can take flight into high stimulation. To avoid depth, keep busy, keep distracted, keep highly stimulated.

I have said that both being (good living) and becoming (growth) have bases in emotional expression. Expression of emotion requires an embodied self. Aliveness, therefore, calls for the "body-as-subject." Dublin (1981) suggests that the "disregarded body" or "body-as-object" is a mark of pathology. In contrast, the "lived body" is the experienced body and is tied to the lived moment (Dublin, 1972). The body-as-object means alienation from one's body and a diminished aliveness.

The "lived body" is the body of life, the "disregarded body" the body deadened. One who lives her or his body is organismically oriented, experiencing the self holistically rather than the self as a mental entity which "has" a body. Such a person feels the whole range of emotions deeply and expresses them spontaneously and fully, uses body sensations as input for cognitive and perceptual processes, has a high level of body awareness, experiences the locus of self in the body, experiences high levels of sensual and sexual pleasure, and takes care of the body, using it fully, but neither damaging it through misuse nor allowing it to deteriorate through disuse. The "lived body" is an alive body. The equating of the living of the body and an organismic/holistic experiencing of self is given scientific validation by a host of studies reviewed by Aikin (1979). In summary, Aikin (1979, p. 12) states his opinion that "empirical evidence supports the conclusion that motor activity is more than merely related to psychological activities in some parallel fashion, but emotion, perception and thinking literally *are* neuromuscular and other bodily activity."

As I look about I see many people who tend to value mind primarily or value body primarily rather than to value the organismic perspective which I equate with the "lived body." Interestingly, in both cases there tends to be an objectification of the body. The head oriented people tend to focus their growth and expansion in intellectual realms. So, such people prefer work which involves thinking, as they like rational process, planning, and cognitive understanding of things. These propensities tend to allow them to delay gratifications. In school settings they prefer to hang out in the class room, laboratory, and computer center. The head oriented person tends to be, in a sense, abstract and academic. The body oriented people, on the other hand, tend to focus their growth and expansion efforts on their physical being. They prefer, then, work which involves physical activity, the doing of things. So, they may well, in their action orientation, tend to be impulsive or at least prefer not to delay gratification. Rather than "figure out" they would tend to "try out." In school settings they prefer to hang out in the shop, the gym, or on the field or court. The body oriented person is, in a sense, concrete and practical. But, as I said, both relate to the body as an object. The head oriented person "has" a body which is downplayed and responded to mostly when it complains with aches or pains. At worst the body is ignored or even denigrated, probably through disuse. The body oriented person, too, "has" a body. It may be worked on and developed, but not "lived." At worst the body is damaged through misuse. I am writing here about two orientations which can be observed. My descriptions are simplified by focusing on the extremes. To caricature these extremes I offer the images of the ivory tower professor, abstract to the point of being disembodied, and the professional athlete, concrete to the point of being mindless. These are the extremes of fragmentation and imbalance of the person. Less extreme is fragmentation with balance. Herein, many people think of and experience themselves as "having" a mind and "having" a body, but in this dualism they strive for a balance and value their parts equally. The position which I am valuing most highly is one which is the step beyond balanced dualism, the organismic position. That is the position of "living the body."

In discussing body scripting in an earlier chapter I distinguished the use, disuse and misuse ("ab-use") of the body. The "lived body" is a body used. While neither disused or abused, the body truly lived is lived with excitement, enthusiasm, and passion. Growth into deeper and fuller being means to expand and assimilate, the assimilation taking place during the relaxation into contraction into the self. And, gradually the edge of the self where growth takes place is extended. I remember the Polsters talking, in a seminar, about growth being the expansion of the "I boundary" to include more and more of what is experienced. The extension of this growing edge is necessary for growth. There are three attitudes which one can take concerning that growing edge. First is the *phobic attitude*. Those who assume the phobic attitude retreat in anxiety from their growing ege, afraid of pain, embarrassment, or the catastrophe of the "too muchness" threatened by their toxic introjects. This phobic attitude defines the timid and the shy, the spectators of life. Second is the *impulsive attitude* of the fool. The fool, apparently ignoring real dangers and actual limits, forces through the growing edge. Such pushing and forcing of the growing edge inevitably results in injury, some degree of self-destruction. The fool is living out a toxic script as surely as the timid and the shy. The third attitude toward the growing edge is one of *respect and excitement*. Respect for the limits and the actual dangers of forcing, and excitement about the expansive possibilities make this attitude the one which allows most growth. The person with this attitude tends to be relatively free from toxic scripting, either by virtue of not having received a highly toxic script or by having gotten rid of such a script through some profound growth experience. This third attitude assumes a true "living" of the body. So, this creative participant in life "lives" the body or uses it. The fool suffers from the consequences of chronic abuse of the body. And the timid and the shy shrink into body disuse, with its pathological sequela. The choice is to participate in life creatively ("live" the body), to shrink from life (disuse the body), or to be the careless fool burned out or broken down (misuse the body).

To be alive is to take reasonable risks. In taking reasonable risks there will sometimes be expansion far enough or frequent enough to exceed the growing edge and result in organismic injury. Surely a body totally unscared reflects a life not fully lived. I believe that honest errors of judgment can occur when one is attempting to go beyond previous limits. One of the differences between the alive person seeking growth and the fool may lie in the preparation for the expansion. The growth-oriented person is disciplined. That means that he or she assesses readiness to expand, and if the best judgment is that he or she is not ready, then he or she waits. Discipline manifests as delay, planning, training, setting up the right conditions, whatever preparation is judged necessary to maximize the growthfulness of the experience. So, the fool may try a dangerous expansion on impulse, the growth-oriented person attends to timing, to the issue of preparation and readiness.

In the *Ultimate Athlete* George Leonard (1975) makes a convincing case for the organismically growthful possibilities of sports. He wrote of the transformational aspects of sports, in terms of human boundaries crossed, perceptions gained, and previous limits transcended. At the same time, he noted that sports share the common element of risk of injury or even death. Despite the risks, sports grow in popularity and the growth of dangerous sports he sees as truly phenomenal. Leonard accounts for this in part by saying that sports provide an arena for taking such risks without breaking the law. This urge for taking such risks may be in the service of balancing the societal pattern of trying to eliminate risk in many aspects of life. Leonard (1975) labeled this pattern the "insurance mentality."

Sol Roy Rosenthal has conducted research on "risk exercise sports (RE)," which he contrasts with "nonrisk exercise sports (non-RE)." He has found that the results on an individual from expending the same amount of energy on an RE sport and a non-RE sport are different. An example: running tends to leave one tired, skiing tends to leave one exhilarated. The enjoyment of many non-RE sports is related to competition, whereas the RE sports often are taken part in for their exhilerating effects. Rosenthal claims evidence that regular participation in RE sports increases "creativity," "productivity," and "efficiency" and "appreciably improves" one's sex life. The exhilerating effects of RE sports is created by the tension between high skill and calculated risk (Leonard, 1975).

In thinking about what Leonard and Rosenthal have said, it seems likely to me that the fully alive person will play some sport. The way he or she will play will not be to win, *per se*, or accomplish a record, *per se*, but will tend more to be playing for the experience of greater aliveness. The sport will be an arena for growth of self through expanded experiencing.

Sports are a way of exploring the limits. They involve the body in explorations of movement and the relationship between movement and time. Hanna (1980, p. x) has called attention to the fact that the living body is a moving body. Or, more precisely, he writes that life exists "as the organized movements of an individual body." He refers to the "quick" and the "dead," seeing autonomous movement as the prime trait by which we distinguish the two. Hanna makes a case that a diminished capacity for movement corresponds to a diminished aliveness. In his teaching, Hanna has found that most adults have little ability to sense the movements of their own bodies. The result, of course, is a diminished ability to move and control their bodies. The usual situation is for the person to reach adulthood with only a minimal development of the sensorimotor system, and then to steadily lose the abilities of body sensing and efficient body movement as he or she ages. This impaired development of sensorimotor and proprioceptive-somesthetic faculties is seen by Hanna as the major health problem of contemporary society. (I will return to the discussion of disease and health as they relate to the style of one's living a few pages hence.)

So, the "lived body" is a body moved. Sports offer the possibility of exploring, with awareness, the parameters of movement — strength, flexibility, coordination, endurance, timing. Why increase flexibility far beyond average with Hatha Yoga? Why increase strength far beyond average with weight training? Because these expand the realm of possibility, open more options for behavior, and because they offer greater breadth and depth of living.

Aliveness can be experienced profoundly, thus spiritually. Spiritual meaning can emerge from "lived body" awareness. Alan Watts has written that no matter how many philosophies one studies, how many spiritual exercises one practices, how many scriptures one searches, and how many spiritual teachers one consults, in the end one returns to the surprising fact of eating, sleeping, feeling, breathing, moving about, the surprising fact of being alive. This, Watts wrote, this surprising fact of being alive is the "supreme experience of religion" (Adam, 1976, p. 3). So it is that many writers have seen deadness as the origin of all other sins. The marvel and the mystery is to be alive.

The value called forth is life lived abundantly. This means *here* and this means *now* and this means *with awareness*. To live an abundant life requires that one not shrink or pull away, but that one embrace the world with passion and delight. By living abundantly, by embracing each new day with passion and delight one evolves. This evolution is the cosmic dance. The important thing is to live fully where you are, now. Then you will evolve. This lesson in the importance of experiencing fully each stage of life, each life circumstance is well portrayed by Hesse (1951) in *Siddhartha*.

Urges, those movements of desire from deep within are life being born. To respond is to say "Yes" to life, and to tighten the muscles so as to suppress the urge is to say "No" to life and join the parade of the dead. I am not talking about the impulsive actions which a body without benefit of mind makes, but the respectful action taken by an integrated organism in response to the deep stirrings within. Two lines from Blake's *The Marriage of Heaven and Hell* can instruct, if not inspire:

> He who desires but acts not, breeds pestilence.
> Sooner murder an infant in its cradle than nurse unacted desires.

I mentioned in an earlier chapter two levels of awareness, the awareness of wants or needs which naturally *leads to* action and interaction, and awareness which *comes from* action and interaction. I labeled these Level I and Level II awareness, respectively. Level II awareness comes from the experience of satisfaction or nonsatisfaction following an action►interaction sequence. Wisdom accrues with this second level of awareness. But the shy and the timid are deficient in this wisdom because of their tendency toward nonaction and noninteraction. Afraid of "too much" aliveness or afraid of making mistakes, the shy and the timid stay contracted. Again, Blake in *The Marriage of Heaven and Hell* may be of encouragement:

> No bird soars too high, if he soars on his own wings.
> If the fool would persist in his folly he would become wise.
> The road of excess leads to the palace of wisdom.

From the "lived body" perspective sex is more than a genital itch to be scratched every so often. "Sexual" is another word to describe and expand upon the "lived body." "Sexual" is a way of being and a way of responding to the world. It means coming together with passion.

To be sexual means to kiss the ground and embrace the trees, to roll on the grass and to smell deeply of the flowers. It means to feel excited when looking at a mountain peak and turned on when the breeze encircles the skin and tosses the hair. Such, by God and thank God, is passion.

To be sexual in the less encompassing sense means to relate to other people with this same passion. In its narrow sense, to be sexual means to relate to someone genitally. To be a fully sexual person involves all three of these levels of sexuality.

Turning to the genital sense of sexuality, I note that Reich, Lowen, and Perls, as well as many who have studied with them equate being alive and being sexual. As Lowen (1980, p. 19) states, "To be sexual is to be alive, and to be alive is to be sexual." The reduction of sexual feeling amounts to a psychological castration, as Lowen sees it. I mentioned in an earlier chapter that when one blocks a contact/withdrawal cycle short of action, the person is behaving as if he or she were without the body part which would be used if that action were allowed. So, not to be sexual is not only an incomplete behavioral Gestalt, but it is also an incomplete body Gestalt. Lowen (1980) believes that sexuality is the "key to being," and that the pelvis is the keystone bone in the body arch. If the pelvic muscles are armored, then the pelvis has reduced motility, thus upsetting the balance and harmony of the entire body.

If a person is not sexual in the "lived body" sense, and allows sex to be limited to the genitals, then that person will not be sexually fulfilled. There may be acts of sex, but not making love. The unfulfillment may lead to the seeking of more and more variety and greater and greater stimulation. The result is promiscuity and perversion, unless guilt holds those in check. This is the point Reich made when he wrote of secondary drives developing when primary (natural) drives are blocked. The secondary drives are harsh and a perversion of the natural primary drives.

I have already covered in earlier chapters Reich's theory of the sex-economic regulation of life energy and the role of orgasm in the maintenance of organismic well-being. Eva Reich once told me that her father used to say that if a person went for three months without an orgasm that person would get crazy.

Lowen (1980) has made the point that what is most feared in sex, and therefore what is most suppressed is explosiveness. It is this bursting forth, this high energy sexual explosion which is feared. Reich termed this "orgasm anxiety." By controlling sex, Lowen (1980) believes, one controls life. And to control sex, allowing sensuality but suppressing the orgastic explosion, is to flatten one's life. Lowen concludes that to harness the human animal to the economic machine the person must be "broken." He points out that man has known for a long time that wild animals can be made working animals by castrating them. The creative person is a sexual person, but the "productive" person is one whose wild animal sexuality has been tamed. Lowen (1980, p. 227) quotes Erich Fromm as making a similar point in his writing that the reason for vilifying sex is in order to break the human will.

When one "lives" her or his body, there will be a positive regard or caring for the body. The body is identified with and included in the personal pronoun "I." This body identification implies a certain life styling. When people live their bodies they will conduct their lives in such a manner tnat their bodies will be well used and abuse will be minimal.

One's character makeup will call for a style of life which has built in whatever misuse or disuse of body necessary to fulfill the destiny of that character. The life style chosen results in the evolving of the body structure to a condition which bespeaks the underlying character. In summary: character ►life style ►body structure. For example, the oral character out of her or his low energy and lack of robustness will tend to shy away from vigorous physical activity and seek safety and comfort. The result of this *disuse* of the body is a soft body with underdeveloped musculature. In addition, the undernourishment which is found in the orally repressed character (in its extreme, anorexia) or the overeating in the orally unsatisfied character (in its extreme, bulimia) constitute an *abuse* of the body. (Note that orally unsatisfied people tend to overeat of foods which can be sucked on, such as candy, or soft foods, such as pastries and other starchy foods, which don't require much oral aggressiveness to be eaten. They overeat of things which are soft, rich, or sweet, the very things which often have a high concentration of calories and relative lack of protein, vitamins, and minerals.) So through this disuse and abuse, the oral character, thin or fat, maintains a soft body with all of the vulnerabilities which attend.

So life style includes patterns of activity (exercise and rest), eating (nutrition), and environment (level of toxins – visual, auditory, chemical). In *Human Life Styling*, McCamy and Presley (1975) make a cogent case that every major degenerative disease is predictable and preventable during its early years of development. They refer to the major correlational factors of health (that which is normal, that is, symptom free) versus disease (that which is average, that is, symptoms increasing in number and severity with age) as the "Four Horsemen of Health." These "Four Horsemen" are exercise, stress reduction, nutrition, and environment. Their very readable book is dedicated to the idea of changing one's life style in order to live an optimal level of health.

Many other writers have addressed this topic of personal responsibility for wellness or disease based on chronic patterns of life style. McQuade and Aikman (1979), for instance, state that over 99 percent of Western people are born healthy but suffer disabilities or premature death

Figure 27. Characterological Tendencies Toward
            Disuse and Misuse of the Body

	Disuse	*Misuse (Abuse)*
Schizoid	Alienated from body. Undercharged hands, feet, face, genitals. Poor coordination of arms and of legs. Avoid sports-games, especially those involving interpersonal interaction.	Ignore body signals of needs. Ignore danger signals (extreme is catatonia).
Oral	Tired. Low energy. Shallow breathing. Avoid strenuous physical activity.	Overeating (extreme is bulimia) or undereating (extreme is anorexia).
Psychopath	Constriction or spasticity of diaphragm leads to diminished feelings.	Override body signals of needs or dangers in order to feel in control and maintain the "cool" image.
Masochist	Avoids joyous activity. Reduced aggression. Awkwardness of movement.	Compression of the body. Pressured, overburdened. Overwork. Push to the point of injury.
Rigid Female	Tension in neck and jaw (stiff with pride), chest and abdomen (protection of the heart), and pelvis (diminished connection of love and sex).	Overlook details of the body and its well-being. Ignorance of technical knowledge of the body and its well-being. Override discomfort to maintain the sexy or seductive image (e.g., wear high heels in spite of a pained lower back).
Rigid Male	Stiff with pride (limited flexibility of body). No time for recreational body activity (exercise, sports, games).	Overwork. Overextend. Inadequate rest and sleep.

because of "personal misbehavior" and toxic environmental conditions. Again, they declare prevention to be the solution. They provide a personal health profile for the evaluation of the risk of degenerative disease based on one's style of living.

A very thorough exploration of stress, the relationship between stress and disease, and the control of stress is offered by Pelletier (1977) in his *Mind as Healer, Mind as Slayer.* Cancer, hypertension, arteriosclerosis, rheumatoid arthritis, migraine, and respiratory disease are examined as stress disorders and prevention is explored in terms of shifts in life style which reduce the level of chronic stress.

A well "lived body" ("well" in both senses) is more than a body free from symptoms of disease. Ida Rolf (1962, p. 12) has emphasized that without muscular balance, one is not truly integrated. In her words, "It seems possible then, to consider muscular balance with its accompanying physical grace, beauty and coordination, with its greater psychological ease and emotional security, as an important hallmark of personal integration." With normal muscular balance or integration movement is performed with a minimum of energy expenditure, motion can be initiated in any direction with ease and speed, minimum preliminary adjustment of the body is required for initiating movement, internal organs are supported well without crowding, and there is a minimum of wear on the body parts. When these criteria are met, the organism will be healthier, having better stamina, more energy, and the ability to move quickly and gracefully (Schutz, 1967).

An extension of the topic of personal energy dynamics is interpersonal dynamics. The issues of interpersonal energy dynamics have to do with what happens when two or more persons, each with her or his characterological energy style, interact. Interacting can be viewed as a process of energy exchange. In terms of the amount of life energy available for interaction, the character types are arranged in ascending order from the schizoid character with the least to the rigid character with the most. Corresponding to the amount of life energy available for interaction, there is a level of energy which is comfortable for each character type to interact with.

Let us look at each of the basic character types in terms of their interactional styles. The schizoid character out of his fear of people and lack of a sense of having a place in the world of people will tend to avoid closeness and be disposed toward withdrawal. He or she will not make solid contact and so leaves the other person often feeling distanced, either by the schizoid's not fully being present or by her or his strange or even inappropriate way of partially contacting.

Out of their emptiness oral characters often invite others to prop them up and nourish them, leaving the other feeling drained and tired.

Figure 28.   Characterological Interactional Energy Styles

	Positive	*Negative*
Schizoid	Will not be invasive. Will not be demanding.	Will not make full contact. Will not get close.
Oral	Will be warm and cuddly. Will have access to child- like qualities, softness.	Will be infantile/depen- dent/draining. Will be pouty/disap- pointed/depressed when not satisfied. Will not reach out and ask.
Psychopath	Will lead. Will be charming. Will be interesting/excit- ing.	Will take over and take control. Will not be loyal. Will not trust or be vul- nerable.
Masochist	Will work hard for an- other. Will put up with a lot.	Will be negative/dis- couraging. Will be complaining/ whining. Will not give what others want. Will be stubborn.
Rigid Female (Hysteric)	Will get fairly close. Will be energetic/ener- gizing. Will be playful/fun.	Will be seductive. Will be unfocused/ impulsive/chaotic. Will be emotionally labile. Will not be deep/serious/ cognitively astute.
Rigid Male	Will get fairly close. Will be energetic/ener- gizing. Will problem solve/be cognitively astute. Will take action/be strong.	Will not relate on emo- tional level. Will be obsessive/com- pulsive/overly focused/ overwork. Will be inflexible/un- yielding.

So, in close relationships the oral character is dependent and infantile. In less close relationships they may appear very self-sufficient, as a result of their still living out the role of precocious child. They will tend not to have much energy to put back into a relationship.

The psychopaths can be close to those who need them, those over whom they can feel in control. They have a higher energy level than the orals, but use that energy in the service of being one-up in their relationships.

The masochists can be close in a submissive way. The tend to be negativistic and to bring others down. Being in a basically resistive stance, the masochist tends not to give others what they want. There is a fairly high level of energy present, but it is highly bound.

Rigid characters tend to have a high level of energy and tend to be able to form fairly close relationships. These people may energize those around them, but if contact is maintained too long, rigid characters can wear other people out.

Figure 28 summarizes the positive and negative tendencies of each character type's interactional energy style.

Moving away from the characterological perspective for now, I want to examine some patterns of interactional energy dynamics. When two people interact openly both are affected. We speak of two people impacting each other, or influencing each other. This happens in a context of openness, wherein there is an energy exchange. Two energy fields interact and both are transformed. The opposite, too, is possible. Two people can spend time together, even large amounts of time, and neither is impacted much. In this case there has not been much energy exchanged. Instead of openness there has been insularity. To insulate is the opposite of being open. The former prevents energy exchange, the latter allows the coming together of the energy fields. Both of these are necessary for richness in living, openness to take in positive energy such as support, protection, and nourishment, and insularity to keep out the opposite, negative energy.

I conceive of four modes of *energetic interaction*. Two are *open modes* and two are *insular modes*. (One can be most insular by not interacting at all.)

The open modes of energy interaction are *receiving* and *synergizing*, with the first being simple and the second more complex. The receiving mode involves openness to taking energy in from another. This is what is involved when one feels nourished, supported or protected by another. The receiving mode has been used when one feels better after having been with another.

In the synergistic mode there is an openness to receiving as well, but with the addition of one's own energy. The result is that the two energy systems merge and both people are affected. The result is more than the sum of the first person's energy and the second person's energy. Each person receives from the interaction as the back and forth energy exchange builds. Through the synergistic mode of interaction both

Figure 29. **MODES OF INTERACTIONAL
ENERGY DYNAMICS**

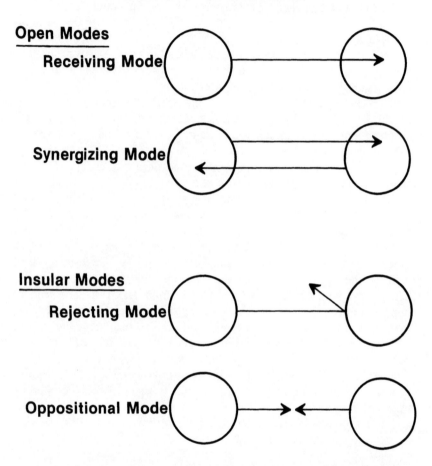

Open Modes

Receiving Mode

Synergizing Mode

Insular Modes

Rejecting Mode

Oppositional Mode

persons receive. Both persons join into the process and the mutuality of the process makes for a building of the effects of both energy fields.

Rejecting energy sent is the simple form of the insular mode of interpersonal energy dynamics. Just as the receiving mode is functional when the energy is positive (nourishing, supportive, protective), the rejecting mode is appropriate when the energy is toxic (nonnourishing, critical, attacking).

The *oppositional* mode of insularity involves not just the shutting out of energy, but the use of energy to stop the other energy field. The oppositional mode does not allow the other energy field to continue, but aggressively attacks it.

The functional pattern is to use the receiving and synergistic modes when positive energy is involved. It is appropriate to be open to positive energy. Furthermore, it is functional to use the rejecting mode or oppositional mode when toxic energy is being presented to one. It is life supportive to accept or magnify that which is itself biopositive, and to reject, or in extreme cases oppose that which is bionegative. Conversely, it is life negating to reject or oppose that which is biopositive or to be open to that which is bionegative. In the case of the rejecting mode, I find one of the Polsters (1973) insights relevant. They have pointed out that the territory between where one says "no" and the point at which one ultimately wants to say "no" is a zone of waste. Relating this idea to the interactional modes, there may be energy which would be beneficial up to a point, but beyond that would be detrimental. For instance, someone may approach with affectionate and erotic energy. I may be clear that I don't want to have sex with her, that to do so would not be in my best interest. But to say "no" at too great a distance from the act of sex would be to rob both of us of something which might be mutually nurturant. We might both enjoy talking, dancing, or holding hands. For me to assume the rejecting mode at too great a distance from being sexual would constitute a waste.

Toxic introjects demand pathological patterns of interpersonal interaction. So, the person with active toxic introjects may tend to be open to bionegative energy, assuming a receptive mode of interaction or even synergistically joining into the building of negative energy. An example of the latter would be to provoke the other's anger towards one. Or the person with active toxic introjects may tend to be insular towards biopositive energy, either assuming a rejecting mode of interaction or even opposing the biopositive energy.

The chronic assumption of the oppositional mode of interaction towards biopositive energy constitutes a symptom of what Reich (1949, 1974) wrote about as the "emotional plague." This term carries no defamatory connotation, according to Reich (1949), and does not refer to any conscious malice. Rather, a person is a victim of the plague to the extent that her or his natural, self-regulatory life manifestations have been suppressed. So, to the extent that one does not live her or his body, does not embody organismic aliveness, he or she is manifesting some degree of the emotional plague. In terms of the contact/withdrawal cycle, the emotional plague can be recognized by the preference for patterns of self-interruption over patterns of organismic satisfaction.

Out of the fear of one's own organismic aliveness, the plagued individual is threatened by aliveness in others. So, the plagued individual won't endure free and natural expressions of life either in herself or himself or in others. Baker (1967) has informed us that to the extent that someone tries to tear down others or control their lives, he or she is functioning as a plagued character. He goes on to give examples of plagued behavior: cruelty, criminality, hurtful gossip, and resentment of others' good fortune.

Much of the discussion of the emotional plague is focused on the level of political activity. As such, Baker (1967) has identified the plague character as one of the three "socio-political character types." The most thoroughgoing discussion of emotional plague and political institutionalization is Reich's (1974) book written sometime between 1943 and 1946, *Listen Little Man!* I refer the reader to these sources if interested. The political arena is beyond the scope of my intentions here.

The emotional plague does not actually define any additional character type, but is a description of an interpersonal dynamic which can occur in the context of any pregenital character. As I have defined it above, emotional plague is a term which refers to a chronic assumption of the oppositional mode of interaction with the life energy in others. What this means is that anyone with pregenital character dynamics operating may be threatened by the aliveness of another person, and in response may interact in an oppositional mode, trying to stifle such free and natural functioning in the other. Emotional plague behavior involves discouraging or stopping other people's aliveness.

With muscular armoring (retroflected action) comes the perversion of the organismic expressions. As Reich (1949) and Baker (1967) have stated, when expression passes through muscular armor, the natural and spontaneous quality of the primary drive is converted into the unnatural, hard quality of a secondary drive. And so we have love expressed pornographically, fear expressed as paranoia, anger expressed cruelly, coldly, and sadistically, happiness packaged and consumed as a commodity, and grief expressed as bitterness and pessimism. As these perverted, secondary drives become the style of one's expression, the other person, in order not to suffer must assume a rejecting mode of interaction. Too often, such perverse expressions are accepted or even interacted with synergistically. These perverse expressions are oppositional to natural, biopositive expressions.

I have not read in the literature any discussion of characterological styles of manifestation of emotional plague in interpersonal interactions. It seems to me that would be useful, and so I am suggesting a style of oppositional mode of interaction for each of the primary character types. Full, rich aliveness requires mutuality in relating. Every*body* needs some*body* sometime, and the cycles repeat with some considerable frequency. So, to live with richness and meaning requires interrelating in transpersonal ways, ways of interdependence. This give and take transcends the myopia of selfishness and allows us to give when full, take when empty, and share the resources which you and I bring to our relationship. A common quality, however, of all pregenital character types is myopic selfishness of vision. Remember, pregenital character structures limit, each in its respective way, the amount of energy available for contact. In addition, the respective patterns of armoring lead to perversions of the natural expressions of emotion, these secondary or perverted urges being toxic not only for the self, but to all of those with whom one so interacts.

More specifically, then, how is each character type likely to manifest in oppositional interactional form, that is, as emotionally plagued behavior? The schizoid has a passive style of emotional plague behavior. Since the schizoid structure involves a fear of interpersonal contact, the schizoid tends not to be very available. Not only is the schizoid not very available out of her or his cautiousness, but the schizoid usually has not developed very smooth or endearing ways of relating so that he or she may come across as socially maladroit or even incompetent. This latter quality refers not just to the superficial layer of manners, etiquette, and protocol, but to a deeper layer at which the schizoid may not understand or be able to empathize with what the other is experiencing. In extreme, this social behavior will be bizarre. So, both from her or his fearfulness of contact and lack of deep relational skills, the schizoid tends not to provide very strongly of nourishing, protective, or supportive contact. The schizoid passively opposes strong interaction and contact.

The oral character also has a passive style of emotional plague behavior. This differs from the schizoid's passivity in that the oral tends towards a passive-pouting style. First, the oral may feel too tired to respond to the needs of others. The chronic low energy of the oral means a weakness of sustained contact and thus a weakness of nourishment, protection, or support for the other. In addition, the oral is needy and tends to cling. This can drain the other, and the depression of the disappointed oral character can become intolerable to those who feel the demand of that passive stance. By their clinging and demand for attention oral characters passively oppose others' independence and moving on with their own lives.

With the psychopathic character we find an active style of plague behavior. Whether the seducer or the bully, the psychopath is focused on controlling others. This means that compassion for the other, interest in the growth or welfare of the other is secondary, if not altogether ignored. The psychopath tends, then, to be uncaring, unfeeling, and disloyal. Taking advantage of others and setting others up for a con-game are only logical ploys in the service of staying in control. An interesting behavior which I have witnessed on several occasions is the psychopath's encouraging someone beyond her or his limits and into predicaments of embarrassment or danger. To casual observation such behavior may appear as support to the other's growth or aliveness, when in fact it is the very antithesis of protection and limit-setting, two of the hallmarks of nonplague behavior. So, the psychopath actively opposes others' rising, growing, developing, by controlling and to the end of being in control.

With the masochistic character we find again, a passive emotional plague style. More specifically, it tends to be a passive-agressive style. So, central to the masochist's character is the resistant "I won't," that this influences her or his response to others' wants. Often, then, the masochist is unwilling to give the other whatever it is that he or she wants, instead taking a stubborn position of withholding support, nurturance, or protection. Rather than responding to the wants of others the masochist often discourages and pulls them down with a pervasive negativity. The masochist takes the stance, when in doubt, say "No." On the surface this negativity may appear to be caution and the setting of limits, in the interest of the other person. But on closer examination this behavior is revealed as a pervasive negativism, pessimism, even bitterness focused on the discouragement of the aliveness of the other person which the masochist herself or himself so painfully lacks. The masochist passively opposes joy, freedom, spontaneity — aliveness.

An active style of emotional plague behavior is once again met in the rigid character structures. First, the rigid female or hysteric. She, with her high energy and interpersonal orientation often is exciting, "turning people on." But she promises by this behavior more than she follows through with; she offers a lot and delivers little, leaving the other person feeling empty after a while. Her emotions tend to be shallow, although quickly accessed, so with time she is revealed as ingenuine to a degree. The chaos of her life, brought about by her emotional liability, her disinclination towards careful or deep thought, and her tendency to use denial as a way of dealing with the unpleasant, make her a difficult partner. The upshot of this is that genuine support, protection, and nourishment do not flow from the hysteric with any abundance. The hysteric actively opposes deep feelings and deep or careful thought.

Turning to her male counterparts, the compulsive character and the phallic-narcissistic character, we find an emotional plague behavior based on the subordination of personhood to the attainment of technical goals. There is a mechanical, inflexible quality to the rigid male. He may be hard and competitive, in the extreme, cold and ruthless in getting his goal met. Feelings are seen as inconvenient, at best, or a sign of weakness to be overcome and kept under control, at worst. This disparagement of the emotional aspect of personhood leaves the rigid male limited in his emotional sensitivity and availability. His emotional plague behavior consists of the active opposition of feelings.

The healthy alternative, what we can term the evolved person, the person of high consciousness, the actualized person, the genital character, or the person who organismically "lives" her or his body, is not bound to any great degree by the characterological fetters discussed above. Such a person exhibits minimally or not at all the emotional plague behaviors. Conversely, such a person can enjoy and even delight in the aliveness, growth, evolution of others. (Figure 30 summarizes the characterological styles of emotional plague behavior.)

Turning now to the parameters of energy, I have found a fruitful model in the Semantic Differential (Osgood, Suci, and Tannenbaum, 1957). Osgood and his colleagues developed the Semantic Differential through factor analytic methods as a way to measure connotative meaning. They found three consistent orthogonal factors of meaning: evaluation, potency, and activity. I have found it helpful to think of the life energy in terms of those three parameters. Energy evaluated is emotion. In terms of the contact/withdrawal model, energy is experienced at the stage of arousal. To be aroused is to be excited, to be energized. When the energy is differentiated into an emotion, that energy has been evaluated. Thus, the energy becomes identified along the dimensions of love — hate, happy — sad, trusting — fearful, and so on.

The second parameter of energy is potency. This pertains to the dimension of weak — strong, or simply low potency — high potency. Any energy, regardless of how it is evaluated as emotion has this dimension.

Activity is the third parameter of energy. It pertains to the dimension of latent — manifest. Energy, evaluated as emotion, at any moment can be totally contained or latent, or it can be totally manifest, being lived out. Oftentimes it falls somewhere between the two extremes of this dimension. In terms of the contact/withdrawal model, the activity dimension relates to the extent of action ►interaction sequences.

Thinking in terms of these three parameters of energy is often useful in describing or understanding interpersonal energy dynamics. Contact, or interaction, is fueled by the aroused energy in response to an organismic want. The three parameters of energy call attention to what emotion is felt (evaluative dimension), how strongly it is felt (potency dimension), and to what extent that emotion lived out through action and interaction (activity dimension). The avoidant self-interruption in the contact/withdrawal cycle maintains latency of an emotion over a period of time, which is organismically disrespectful. So, latent energy is at the core of the incomplete Gestalt, or in Gestalt language, the "unfinished business."

In relationships there is a tendency for variability of energy over time. This variability may affect any one or a combination of the three energy parameters. One example which I witness in my practice is a

Figure 30.   Characterological Styles of
                    Oppositional Interaction
                    (Characterological Styles of
                    Emotional Plague Behavior)

Schizoid   Passive opposition to contact with others.
                    Weak, cautious contact means limited nourishment,
                    support, protection, and limits offered. May not recog-
                    nize or understand needs in others.

Oral   Passive/pouty opposition to others' independence.
                    Low energy means weakness of sustained contact and
                    thus a weakness of nourishment, support, protection,
                    and limits offered. Clinging, demandingness, disap-
                    pointedness and depression can drain others.

Psychopath   Active opposition to others' rising in order to be in con-
                    trol. Compassion for others, interest in growth or
                    welfare of others is subordinated to being in control
                    of them. Hence, uncaring, unfeeling, disloyal taking
                    advantage of others.

Masochist   Passive-aggressive opposition to others' joy, freedom,
                    spontaneity. Stubborn withholding of nourishment,
                    support, protection, limits. Negativity, pessimism,
                    bitterness, discourage others' aliveness.

Rigid Female   Active opposition to deep feelings and deep thought.
                    Creates chaos through emotional lability and shallow-
                    ness, and use of denial rather than coping. Turns
                    people on to her and then fades rather than delivering
                    nourishment, support, protection, and limits.

Rigid Male   Active opposition to feelings.
(Compulsive   Personhood subordinated to attainment of goals.
and Phallic-   Feelings denigrated leaving him emotionally insen-
Narcissistic)   sitive and unavailable.

change in the evaluative factor from love to hate without a change in the
potency factor. The result is that a person moves from loving someone to
hating that person with an equal potency. If activity remains high, then
we have a situation of uproar and potential danger. I believe that the most
dramatic shifts in relationships occur when there is a change in the evaluative factor. Changes in the other two factors can be surprising, but tend
not to be shocking or dramatic. I invite the reader to think about some

examples of her or his own relationships and how they have evolved over time along each of the energy parameters.

An interesting arena for speculation is the affect of energies on interpersonal attraction. Reich (Baker, 1967) purported to find that individuals have different rates of orgonotic pulsation which are not related to respiratory rates or heart rates. The rate may vary from day to day, depending on emotional changes and atmospheric conditions, but stays within a range characteristic of that person. Baker (1967) suggests that harmonious rates may be experienced as attraction and disharmonious rates as repulsion. So, is there a field reaction between people based on the harmonics or dischords between rates of orgonotic pulsations?

In addition to rate of orgonotic pulsation, there is the question of energy level. Baker (1967) states that when people of dissimilar energy levels attempt to relate sexually there is an interference of satisfaction. I speculate that more broadly speaking when two people of greatly dissimilar energy levels try to relate there will be frustration and a degree of dissatisfaction. To the degree that the two organismic energy systems are dissimilar, there will be a corresponding experience of separation. Consider the statements "You are too much," and "You are not enough for me." My guess is that the people who enjoy each other the most, over time, are people with similar levels of energy and similar rates of energy pulsation.

References

Chapter 1

Baker, E. *Man in the Trap*. New York: Macmillan, 1967.

Bates, W. *The Bates Method for Better Eyesight without Glasses*. New York: Pyramid, 1976 (1940, 1943).

Beisser, A. "The Paradoxical Theory of Change." In: Fagan, J., and Shepherd, I. (eds.) *Gestalt Therapy Now*. Palo Alto: Science and Behavior Books, 1970.

Emerson, P., and Smith, E. "Contributions of Gestalt Psychology to Gestalt Therapy." *The Counseling Psychologist*, 1974, 4, 4, 8–12.

Fierman, L. (ed.) *Effective Psychotherapy: The Contribution of Hellmuth Kaiser*. New York: Free Press, 1965.

Freud, S. *The Ego and the Id*. New York: Norton, 1960.

_____. *Jokes and Their Relation to the Unconscious*. New York: Norton, 1960.

_____. "The Moses of Michelangelo" (1914). In: Rieff, P. (ed.) *Character and Culture*. New York: Collier Books, 1963.

Kelley, C. *Education in Feeling and Purpose*. Santa Monica, Cal.: Radix Institute, 1974.

_____. *Orgonomy, Bioenergetics, and Radix: The Reichian Movement Today*. Ojai, Cal.: Radix Institute, 1978.

Levitsky, A. and Perls, F. "The Rules and Games of Gestalt Therapy." In: Fagan, J. and Shepherd, I. (eds.) *Gestalt Therapy Now*. Palo Alto: Science and Behavior Books, 1970.

Lowen, A. "The Body in Personality Theory: Wilhelm Reich and Alexander Lowen." In: Burton, A. (ed.) *Operational Theories of Personality*. New York: Brunner/Mazel, 1974.

_____. *Bioenergetics*. New York: Penguin, 1975.

_____. *The Language of the Body*. New York: Collier Books, 1971.

_____. Lowen, A. *The Language of the Body*. New York: Collier Books, 1971.

_____, and Lowen, L. *The Way to Vibrant Health*. New York: Harper & Row, 1977.

Mann, W. *Orgone, Reich, and Eros*. New York: Simon & Schuster, 1973.

_____, and Hoffman, E. *The Man Who Dreamed of Tomorrow: A Conceptual Biography of Wilhelm Reich*. Los Angeles: Tarcher, 1980.

Naranjo, C. "Present-Centeredness: Technique, Prescription, and Ideal." In: Fagan, J., and Shepherd, I. (eds.), *Gestalt Therapy Now*. Palo Alto: Science and Behavior Books, 1970.

Perls, F. *Ego, Hunger, and Aggression.* New York: Vintage, 1969. (a)

———. *The Gestalt Approach and Eye Witness to Therapy.* Palo Alto: Science and Behavior Books, 1973.

———. *Gestalt Therapy Verbatim.* Moab, Utah: Real People Press, 1969. (b)

———, Hefferline, R., and Goodman, P. *Gestalt Therapy: Excitement and Growth in the Human Personality.* New York: Dell, 1951.

Pesso, A. *Experience in Action.* New York: New York University Press, 1973.

———. *Movement in Psychotherapy.* New York: New York University Press, 1969.

Raknes, O. *Wilhelm Reich and Orgonomy.* Baltimore: Penguin Books, 1971.

Reich, W. *Character Analysis.* New York: Noonday Press, 1949.

———. *The Function of the Orgasm.* New York: Orgone Institute Press, 1942.

Shapiro, D. *Neurotic Styles.* New York: Basic Books, 1965.

Smith, E. "The Role of Early Reichian Theory in the Development of Gestalt Therapy." *Psychotherapy: Theory, Research and Practice,* 1975, 12, 3, 268–272.

———. "The Roots of Gestalt Therapy." In: Smith, E. (ed.) *The Growing Edge of Gestalt Therapy.* New York: Brunner/Mazel, 1976.

Chapter 2

Mann, W. and Hoffman, E. *The Man Who Dreamed of Tomorrow: A Conceptual Biography of Wilhelm Reich.* Los Angeles: J.P. Tarcher, 1980.

Reich, W. *The Function of the Orgasm.* New York: Simon and Schuster, 1973.

Saeger, L. "The Historical Development of Bioenergetic Concepts: A Foundation for the Emerging Technology of Psychophysiological Therapeutics." In: Cassius, J. (ed.) *Horizons in Bioenergetics.* Memphis: Promethean Publications, 1980.

Smith, E. "The Psychobiology of "Yes" and "No." In: Fagen, J. *Therapeutic Kinesiology,* in preparation.

———. "Seven Decision Points." *Voices,* 1979, 15, 3, 45–50.

Chapter 3

Baker, E. *Man in the Trap.* New York: Macmillan, 1967.

Enright, J. "An Introduction to Gestalt Techniques." In: Fagan, J. and Shepherd, I. (eds.) *Gestalt Therapy Now.* Palo Alto: Science and Behavior Books, 1970.

Hamilton, E. *Mythology.* New York: Mentor, 1942.

Keyes, K. *Handbook to Higher Consciousness.* Berkeley: Living Love Center, 1972.

Perls, F. *Ego, Hunger and Aggression.* New York: Vintage Books, 1969.

———. *The Gestalt Approach and Eye Witness to Therapy.* Palo Alto: Science and Behavior Books, 1973.

_____, Hefferline, R., and Goodman, P. *Gestalt Therapy*. New York: Dell, 1951.

Polster, E., and Polser, M. *Gestalt Therapy Integrated*. New York: Brunner/Mazel, 1973.

Reich, W. *The Cancer Biopathy*. New York: Farrar, Straus and Giroux, 1973b.

_____. *The Function of the Orgasm*. New York: Simon and Schuster, 1973a.

Saeger, L. "The Historical Development of Bioenergetic Concepts: A Foundation for the Emerging Technology of Psychophysiological Therapeutics." In: Cassius, J. (ed.) *Horizons in Bioenergetics*. Memphis: Promethean Publications, 1980.

Smith, E. "Seven Decision Points." *Voices*, 1979, *15*, 3, 45–50.

Zinker, J. *Creative Process in Gestalt Therapy*. New York: Brunner/Mazel, 1977.

Chapter 4

Naranjo, C. "Present-Centeredness: Technique, Prescription, and Ideal." In: Fagan, J. and Shepherd, I. (eds.) *Gestalt Therapy Now*. Palo Alto: Science and Behavior Books, 1970.

Perls, F. *The Gestalt Approach and Eye Witness to Therapy*. Palo Alto: Science and Behavior Books, 1973.

_____. *Gestalt Therapy Verbatim*. Moab, Utah: Real People Press, 1969.

Reich, W. *Character Analysis*. New York: Noonday Press, 1949.

_____. *The Function of the Orgasm*. New York: Simon and Schuster, 1973.

Smith, E. "Altered States of Consciousness in Gestalt Therapy " *Journal of Contemporary Psychotherapy*, 1975, 7, 1, 35–40.

_____. "The Impasse Phenomenon: A Gestalt Therapy Experience Involving an Altered State of Consciousness." *The Gestalt Journal*, 1978, 1, 1, 88–93.

Chapter 5

Allport, G. *Personality: A Psychological Interpretation*. New York: Holt, 1937.

Birdwhistell, R. *Introduction to Kinesics: An Annotation System for Analysis of Body Motion and Gesture*. Louisville: University of Louisville, 1952.

_____. *Kinesics and Context*. Philadelphia: University of Pennsylvania Press, 1970.

Blazer, J. "The Language of Legs." *Playboy*, June 1969, *16*: 4.

_____. Blazer, J. "Leg Position and Psychological Characteristics in Women." *Psychology*, 1966, *3*: 5–12.

Braatoy, T. *Fundamentals of Psychoanalytic Technique*. New York: John Wiley and Sons, 1954.

Brooks, C. *Sensory Awareness*. New York: Viking Press, 1974.

Corliss, R. and Rabe, P. *Psychotherapy from the Center*. Scranton: International Textbook Co., 1969.

Critchley, M. *The Language of Gesture*. 1939.

Darwin, C. *The Expression of the Emotions in Man and Animals*. New York: Appleton, 1898.

Deutsch, F. "Analysis of Postural Behavior." *Psychoanalytic Quarterly*, 1952, *21*: 196–214.

Dittman, A. "The Relationship Between Body Movements and Moods in Interviews." *Journal of Consulting Psychology*, 1962, *26*: 480.

Duncan, S. "Nonverbal Communication." *Psychological Bulletin*, 1969, *12*: 118–137.

Efron, D. *Gesture and Environment*. 1941.

Ekman, P., and Friesan, W. "Nonverbal Behavior in Psychotherapy Research." In: Shilen, J. (ed.), *Research in Psychotherapy, Volume III*. Washington: American Psychological Association, 1968.

Fast, J. *Body Language*. New York: M. Evans and Co., 1970.

Feldenkrais, M. *Body and Mature Behavior*. New York: International Universities Press, 1949.

Feldman, S. *Mannerisms of Speech and Gestures in Everyday Life*. New York: International Universities Press, 1959.

Fenichel, O. *The Psychoanalytic Theory of Neurosis*. New York: Norton, 1945.

Fierman, L. (ed.) *Effective Psychotherapy: The Contribution of Helmuth Kaiser*. New York: Free Press, 1965.

Fossey, D. "Making Friends with Mountain Gorillas." *National Geographic*, 1970, *137*(1): 48–67.

Fretz, B. "Postural Movements in a Counseling Dyad." *Journal of Counseling Psychology*, 1966, *13*: 335–343.

Fromm-Reichmann, F. *Principles of Intensive Psychotherapy*. Chicago: University of Chicago Press, 1950.

Geller, J. *Manual for Categorizing Movements of the Hands and Arms*. (unpublished manuscript, Yale University, 1968).

Griffith, R. "Anthropodology: Man a-foot." In: Baeyer, V. and Griffith, R. (eds.) *Condito Humano*. New York: Springer-Verlag, 1966.

Hall, E. *The Silent Language*. New York: Fawcett World Library, 1959.

————. "A System for the Notation of Proxemic Behavior." *American Anthropologist*, 1963, *65*: 1003–1026.

————, and Hall, M. "The Sounds of Silence." *Playboy* June 1971, *18*: 6.

Harper, R. Wiens, A. and Matarazzo, J. *Nonverbal Communication: The State of the Art*. New York: Wiley, 1978.

Jacobson, E. *Anxiety and Tension Control*. Philadelphia: Lippincott, 1964.

————. *Progressive Relaxation*. Chicago: University of Chicago Press, 1938.

James, W. "A Study of the Expression of Bodily Posture." *Journal of Genetic Psychology*, 1932, *7*: 405–437.

Jourard, S. *The Transparent Self*. New York: D. Van Nostrand, 1964.

Krout, M.H. "Autistic Gestures, an Experimental Study in Symbolic Movement." *Psychology Monograph*, 1935, *46*.

_____. "A Preliminary Note on Some Obscure Symbolic Muscular Responses of Diagnostic Value in the Study of Normal Subjects." *American Journal of Psychology*, 1931, *11*: 29–71.

_____. "The Social and Physiological Significance of Gestures (a differential analysis)." *Journal of Genetic Psychology*, 1935, *47*.

Levitsky, A. and Perls, F. "The Rules and Games of Gestalt Therapy." In: Fagan, J. and Shepherd, I. (eds.) *Gestalt Therapy Now*. Palo Alto: Science and Behavior Books, 1970.

Levitt, E. "The Relationship Between Abilities to Express Emotional Meanings Vocally and Facially." In: J. Davitz (ed.) *The Communication of Emotional Meaning*. New York: McGraw-Hill, 1964.

Lewis, H. and Streitfield, H. *Growth Games*. New York: Harcourt, Brace, Jovanovich, 1970.

McNatt, V. *Nonverbal Communication: A Study of Satir Typology, Interpersonal Attraction, and Self-Esteem*. Doctoral dissertation, Georgia State University, 1973.

Mahl. G. "Some Clinical Observations on Nonverbal Behavior in Interviews." *The Journal of Nervous and Mental Diseases*, 1967, *144*: 492–505.

_____. "Nonverbal Anticipation of Verbalization." Paper presented on symposium: "New Approaches to the Study of Facial Expression and Body Movement." Annual meeting, American Psychological Association, 1966.

. Maranon, G. "The Psychology of Gesture." *Journal of Nervous and Mental Diseases*, 1950, *112*: 469–497.

Mehrabian, A. "Communication without Words." *Psychology Today*, 1968a, *2*(4): 52–55.

_____. "Relationship of Attitude to Seated Posture, Orientation, and Distance." *Journal of Personality and Social Psychology*, 1968b, *10*: 26–30.

_____. "A Semantic Space for Nonverbal Behavior." *Journal of Consulting and Clinical Psychology*, 1970, *35*: 248–257.

_____, and Ferris, S. "Inference of Attitudes from Nonverbal Communication in Two Channels." *Journal of Consulting Psychology* 1967, *31*: 248–252.

Morris, D. *Manwatching*. New York: Abrams, 1977.

Needles, W. "Gesticulation and Speech." *International Journal of Psychoanalysis*, 1959, *40*: 291–292.

Osgood, C., Suci, G. and Tannenbaum, P. *The Measurement of Meaning*. Urbana: University of Illinois Press, 1957.

Otto, H. and Mann, J. *Ways of Growth*. New York: Grossman, 1968.

Parkinson, C. "What Does It Mean When You Gesture?" *Picture*, May 24, 1970, 25.

Paulk, D. "Kinesic Effects on Perceived Attributes of Attraction." Master's thesis, Georgia State University, 1973.

Penn, J. "Talk to Your Baby in Body Language." *My Baby Magazine*, 1971, *29*(5): 4.

Perls, F. *Ego, Hunger, and Aggression*. New York: Vintage Books, 1969.

_____, Hefferline, R., and Goodman, P. *Gestalt Therapy*. New York: Julian Press, 1951.

Peterson, S. *A Catalog of the Ways People Grow*. New York: Ballantine Books, 1971.

Reich, W. *Character Analysis*. New York: Noonday Press, 1949.

Reusch, J. "General Theory of Communication in Psychiatry." In:

Arieti, S. (ed.) *American Handbook of Psychiatry.* New York: Basic Books, 1959.

_____, and Kees, W. *Nonverbal Communication.* Berkeley: University of California Press, 1956.

Rosenfeld, H. "Instrumental Affiliative Functions of Facial and Gestural Expressions." *Journal of Personality and Social Psychology,* 1966, *4*: 65–72.

Scheflen, A. "Communication and Regulation in Psychotherapy." *Psychiatry,* 1963, *26*: 126–136.

_____. "Communication Systems Such as Psychotherapy." In: Masserman, J. (ed.), *Current Psychiatric Therapies, Volume V.* New York: Grune and Stratton, 1965.

_____. "The Significance of Posture in Communication Systems." *Psychiatry,* 1964, *27*: 316–331.

Schlosser, P. "Liking as a Function of Physical Attractiveness, Kinesic Behavior, and Affiliative Tendency." Doctoral dissertation, Georgia State University, 1977.

Schutz, W. *Joy.* New York: Grove, 1967.

_____. *Here Comes Everybody.* New York: Harper and Row, 1971.

Shapiro, D. *Neurotic Styles.* New York: Basic Books, 1965.

Shapiro, J. "Agreement Between Channels of Communication in Interviews." *Journal of Consulting Psychology,* 1966, *30*: 535–538.

Shatan, C. "Unconscious Motor Behavior, Kinesthetic Awareness and Psychotherapy." *American Journal of Psychotherapy,* 1963, *17*: 17–30.

Smith, E. "Postural and Gestural Communication of *A* and *B* "Therapist Types" During Dyadic Interviews." *Journal of Consulting and Clinical Psychology,* 1972, *39*(1): 29–36.

Voices, 1970, *6*, Special Issue.

Watzlawick, P., Beavin, J. and Jackson, D. *Pragmatics of Human Communication: A Study of Interactional Patterns, Pathologies, and Paradoxes.* New York: Norton, 1967.

Weiss, P. "The Social Character of Gestures." *Philosophical Review,* 1943, *52*: 182–186.

Chapter 6

Baker, E. *Man in the Trap.* New York: Collier Books, 1967.

Dychtwald, K. *Body-Mind.* New York: Jove, 1978.

Hall, C. and Lindzey, G. *Theories of Personality* (second edition). New York: John Wiley, 1970.

Horney, K. *Our Inner Conflicts.* New York: Norton, 1945.

Keleman, S. "The Foundations of Emotional Biology." *The Journal of Somatic Experience,* 1981, 4, 1, 8–21.

_____. *The Human Ground: Sexuality, Self and Survival.* Palo Alto: Science and Behavior Books, 1975.

_____. *Somatic Reality.* Berkeley: Center Press, 1979.

Kretschmer, E. *Physique and Character.* New York: Harcourt, 1925.

Kurtz, R. *Training Manual: Ron Kurtz Method of Body Centered Psychotherapy.* Putnam, Ct.: Hakomi Institute, 1981.

_____, and Prestera, H. *The Body Reveals.* New York: Harper and Row, 1976.

Lowen, A. *Bioenergetics.* New York: Penguin, 1975.

_____. "A Hierarchy in Characterology." *Energy and Character*, 1974, 5, 3, 3-6.

_____. *The Language of the Body*. New York: Collier Books, 1971. (Originally published as *Physical Dynamics of Character Structure*, 1958).

Reich, W. *Character Analysis*. New York: Noonday Press, 1949.

Shapiro, D. *Neurotic Styles*. New York: Basic Books, 1965.

Sheldon, W., Dupertuis, C., and McDermott, E. *Atlas of Men*. New York: Harper, 1954.

_____, Hartl, E., and McDermott, E. *Varieties of Delinquent Youth*. New York: Harper, 1949.

_____, Lewis, N., and Tenney, A. "Psychotic Patterns and Physical Constitution." In Siva Sankar, D. (ed.) *Schizophrenia: Current Concepts and Research*. New York: PJD Publications, 1969.

_____, and Stevens, S.S. *The Varieties of Temperament*. New York: Harper, 1942.

_____, Stevens, S.S. and Tucker, W. *The Varieties of Human Physique*. New York: Harper, 1940.

Wohlman, B. *Contemporary Theories and Systems in Psychology*. New York: Harper, 1960.

Chapter 7

Butler, G. "Hypothesis of Excessive Meridian Energy." *American Journal of Acupuncture*, 1974, 2, 210-211.

Dychtwald, K. *Body-Mind*. New York: Jove Publications, 1978.

Lowen, A. and Lowen, L. *The Way to Vibrant Health*. New York: Harper and Row, 1977.

Pesso, A. *Movement in Psychotherapy*. New York: New York University Press, 1969.

Chapter 8

Baker, E. *Man in the Trap*. New York: Macmillan, 1967.

Berdach, E., and Bakan, P. "Body Position and the Free Recall of Early Memories." *Psychotherapy: Theory, Research, and Practice*, 1967, 4, 3, 101-102.

Kroth, J. "The Analytic Couch and Response to Free Association." *Psychotherapy: Theory, Research, and Practice*, 1970, 7, 4, 206-208.

Lowen, A. "Breathing, Movement, and Feeling." New York: Institute for Bioenergetic Analysis, 1965.

Perls, F. *Ego, Hunger, and Aggression*. New York: Vintage, 1969.

_____, Hefferline, R. and Goodman, P. *Gestalt Therapy: Excitement and Growth in the Human Personality*. New York: Dell, 1951.

Reich, W. *The Function of the Orgasm*. New York: Simon and Schuster, 1973.

Satchidananda, Swami. *Integral Yoga Hatha*. New York: Holt, Rinehart and Winston, 1970.

Steen, E. and Montagu, A. *Anatomy and Physiology*. New York: Barnes and Noble, 1959.

Walther, D. *Applied Kinesiology*. Pueblo, CO: Systems, DC, 1976.

Chapter 9

Baker, E. *Man in the Trap*. New York: Macmillan, 1967.

Konia, C. "Orgone Therapy: A Case Presentation." *Psychotherapy: Theory, Research and Practice*, 1975, 12, 2, 192–197.

Lowen, A. *Bioenergetics*. New York: Penguin, 1975.

————, and Lowen L. *The Way to Vibrant Health*. New York: Harper and Row, 1977.

Pesso, A. *Experience in Action*. New York: New York University Press, 1973.

Chapter 10

Castaneda, C. *The Teachings of Don Juan: A Yaqui Way of Knowledge*. New York: Ballantine, 1968.

Deikman, A. "Deautomatization and the Mystic Experience." In Tart, C. (ed.) *Altered States of Consciousness*. New York: John Wiley, 1969.

Levitsky, A. and Perls, F. "The Rules and Games of Gestalt Therapy." In Fagan, J. and Shepherd, I. (eds.) *Gestalt Therapy Now*. Palo Alto: Science and Behavior Books, 1970.

London, P. "The Induction of Hypnosis." In Gordon, J. (ed.) *Handbook of Clinical and Experimental Hypnosis*. New York: Macmillan, 1967.

Ludwig, A. "Altered States of Consciousness." In Tart, C. (ed.) *Altered States of Consciousness*. New York: John Wiley, 1969.

Naranjo, C. "Present-Centeredness: Technique, Prescription and Ideal." In Fagan, J., and Shepherd, I. (eds.) *Gestalt Therapy Now*. Palo Alto: Science and Behavior Books, 1970.

————. "The Techniques of Gestalt Therapy." Highland, N.Y.: The Center for Gestalt Development, 1980.

Perls, F. "Four Lectures." In Fagan, J., and Shepherd, I. (eds.) *Gestalt Therapy Now*. Palo Alto: Science and Behavior Books, 1970.

————. *The Gestalt Approach and Eye Witness to Therapy*. Palo Alto: Science and Behavior Books, 1973.

————. *Gestalt Therapy Verbatim*. New York: Bantam, 1969.

————. *Legacy from Fritz*. Palo Alto: Science and Behavior Books, 1975.

Pesso, A. *Experience in Action*. New York: New York University Press, 1973.

————. *Movement in Psychotherapy*. New York: New York University Press, 1969.

Polster, E. "Sensory Functioning in Psychotherapy." In Fagan, J. and Shepherd, I. (eds.) *Gestalt Therapy Now*. Palo Alto: Science and Behavior Books, 1970.

Smith, E. "Altered States of Consciousness in Gestalt Therapy." *Journal of Contemporary Psychotherapy*, 1975, 7, 1, 35–40.

Zinker, J. *Cretive Process in Gestalt Therapy*. New York: Brunner/Mazel, 1977.

Chapter 11

Jung, C. *The Practice of Psychotherapy.* Princeton, N.J.: Princeton University Press, 1966.
Kopp, S. *Back to One.* Palo Alto: Science and Behavior Books, 1977.
Lowen, A. *The Language of the Body.* New York: Collier, 1971.
Stevens, B. *Don't Push the River.* Moab, Utah: Real People Press, 1970.

Chapter 12

Adam, Michael. *Wandering in Eden.* New York: Alfred A. Knopf, 1976.
Aikin, P. "The Participation of Neuromuscular Activity in Perception, Emotion and Thinking." *The Journal of Biological Experience*, 1979, 1, 2, 12-32.
Baker, E. *Man in the Trap.* New York: Collier, 1967.
Dublin, J. "A Bio-Existential Therapy." *Psychotherapy: Theory, Research and Practice*, 1981, 18, 1, 3-10.
_____. "Language as Expression of Upright Man: Toward a Phenomenology of Language and the Lived Body." *Journal of Phenomenological Psychology*, 1972, 2, 2, 141-160.
Hanna, Thomas. *The Body of Life.* New York: Alfred A. Knopf, 1980.
Hesse, Hermann, *Siddhartha.* New York: New Directions, 1951.
Leonard, George. *The Ultimate Athlete.* New York: Viking Press, 1975.
Lowen, A. *Fear of Life.* New York: Collier, 1980.
McCamy, J., and Presley, J. *Human Life Styling.* New York: Harper Colophon Books, 1975.
McQuade, W., and Aikman, A. *The Longevity Factor.* New York: Simon and Schuster, 1979.
Naranjo, C. *The Techniques of Gestalt Therapy.* Highland, N.Y.: *The Gestalt Journal*, 1980.
Osgood, C., Suci, G., and Tannenbaum, P. *The Measurement of Meaning.* Urbana: University of Illinois Press, 1957.
Pelletier, K. *Mind as Healer, Mind as Slayer.* New York: Delta, 1977.
Polster, E. and Polster, M. *Gestalt Therapy Integrated.* New York: Brunner/Mazel, 1973.
Reich, W. *Character Analysis.* New York: Noonday Press, 1949.
_____. *Listen, Little Man!* New York: Farrar, Straus and Giroux, 1974.
Rolf, I. "Structural Integration." *Systematics*, 1963, 1, 1, 3-20.
Schutz, W. *Joy.* New York: Grove, 1967.
Smith, E. "Anxiety—the Perverse Traveling Companion." *Voices*, 1979, 15, 1, 27-29.

Index